WHERE ENGLISH GIRLS A[...] FOR DR[...]

La Discotheque

ON GIRL IN
—CLACTON, N

They were suffering fr[...]
m of a cold, wet weekend[...]
. High tide was at m[...]
them was just the wro[...]
with nothing to do the[...]
and hoping something we[...]
Hamett said that at the[...]
night he had to close the[...]
s hotel bars for fear of g[...]
and starting brawls. Th[...]
not comparable with[...]
boys of a few years ago[...]
ude, obscene and totally[...]

insulted passers-by, he[...]
middle of the road to sto[...]
on to cars and da[...]
property. Th[...]
and he h[...]

CLUB

nn
th Circular)

    Mbrs. 4/6

D
    Mbrs. 5/6

AWKINS
    Mbrs. 7/6

AME
CE TICKETS ARE
E CLUB at 6/6d.
    Mbrs. 4/6

LEAVES
    Mbrs. 4/6

ORNER
    Mbrs. 5,6

ARTISTE
Y GUY
& the SOUL AGENTS
    Mbrs. 4/6

ER DAVIES
    Mbrs. 4/6

MARQUEE

90, WARDOUR STREET, L[...]

Every Saturday afternoon, 2.30-5.30 p.m [...]

"THE MA[...]
TURD[...]

op of the Pops
duced by Gu[...]
Pers

    : 3/6

Modern Jaz
DICK MO,
TONY KIN
nce with [...]
NNY HO,
é José Car
RK LEE[...]
reet Run[...]
ACTION
porting
ers' Tick[...]
er 28th

ing:
ILKIE
HAR[...]
d and [...]
ER B[...]
INES

CLUB | **NOVEMBER NEWSLETTE**

UR STREET, LONDON W.1. (GER 8923)

DUDLEY MOORE | NEW MAR[...]
RETURNS | **RECORD C**

by John C. Gee

Great News for all jazz fans this
month with the return of that brilliant pianist and satirist **Dudley
Moore** to the Marquee after a long
absence. Dudley was, of course, one
of the original members of "Beyond
he Fringe" which made theatrical
story in London and on Broadway.

Dudley Moore returns then on
unday, November 15th in compa-
y with his old boss, **Johnny Dank-
orth** and his Orchestra. Johnny's
aturday night date on October 17th
as such a tremendous success that
returns to another Saturday
ssion on November 21st in com-
y with the Joe Harriott Quintet.

After several weeks of
the opening session of the
Record Club will take
Sunday November 15th
Doors open 2.45 p.m. Gue:
Buck Clayton, Mark Murp
phrey Lyttelton and it
Freddie Hubbard, the you
rican trumpet player. T
ber Jazz Record Releases
be reviewed. Admission wi
follows: Marquee Members
Guests — 4/-. Refreshmen
also be available.

ctober 11th with **Ruby Braff**,
ught forth just about everybody
oon rehearsal even the Rolling
y Lyttelton's Wednesday night
nth with star musicians drop-
elton Band ... **Don Rendell**,
eard at the Club on a recent
with his own Quintet featuring
urday, November 7th ... The
astic that only personal callers
ickers of the **Manfred Mann**
worth Orchestra ... Joe Har-
rom the new Noel Coward
ease ... **Annie Ross, Terry**
st three of the many perso-
er at the Marquee ... Ame-
ersonal appearances at the

MEMBERSHIP

Membership is on a quar
basis and the subscription is
5/- till the end of Decem
1964. Application Forms may
obtained from the Secreta
Marquee Club either in writi
or on personal application. T
Marquee is open nightly fre
7.30 to 11.00 p.m. and admissi
prices, unless otherwise stated
are as follows:
  Mon. Thur.:
    Members: 5/-, Guests: 7/6
  Tue., Wed., Fri.:
    Members: 5/-, Guests: 6/-
  Sat., Sun.:
    Members: 6/-, Guests: 7/6
  Sun. (Jazz 625)
    Invitation to Members Only.

VENING WITH THE BLUES"
er 26th 1964 — 7.30 — 11.30 p.m.
HUBERT SUMLIN
"LONG JOH[...]

Th[...]

Sunday, September 7, 1969   **7d.**

No. 4577

AND TIME TO GIVE A WARNING TO EVERY PARENT...

Can YOUR kid buy this?

YOUR KID may pick up a
magazine in a discotheque
or record shop.

It will look way-out,
switched-on and hippy.

And it will contain pre-
cise details of sexual practices that make Fanny Hill
seem as depraved as
Goldilocks.

It is in such journals that
advertisements of the three-
in-a-bed type appear.

That's the sort of literary
freedom that the so-called "underground"
magazines, Oz and It, are getting.

Now another hippy journal,
called SUCK, is about to be
launched. Available under plain
cover from Amsterdam. Just
what it will contain is not
certain.

Bearded **Jim Haynes**, who
runs London's hippy centre, the
Arts Lab in Drury Lane, where
the magazine will be sold, said:
" If you think that pictures of
people making love is pornography you're wrong. Pictures
of bombs dropping on people is
pornography. Love is beautiful."

It is. But not the way Oz
and It portray it. I hope that
the new journal does not follow
their example.

Filth can be swept under the
carpet out of sight. But then
[...] to get rid of it.

LEFT: The
kind of ad-
vertisement
that Oz has
... "increase
your plea-
sure."

**Hippies
gape as**
HELL'S
ANGELS
menace
ArtsLab
in drug,
orgy,
police,
rape,
loot,
gon[...]
ba[...]

RIGHT:
The kind
of front
page that
Oz has
... a
kinky
embrace.

Richard Neville, proprietor
and editor of Oz, estimates they
sell about 30,000.

Both
can u[...]
politic[...]
with three   a zany

HIGH SIXTIES

HIGH SIXTIES

THE SUMMERS OF RIOT & LOVE

ROGER HUTCHINSON

MAINSTREAM
PUBLISHING

First published in Great Britain in 1992 by
MAINSTREAM PUBLISHING COMPANY (EDINBURGH) LTD
7 Albany Street
Edinburgh EH1 3UG

ISBN 1 85158 437 4

A catalogue record for this book is available from the British Library

Typeset in Garamond by CentraCet, Cambridge
Printed in Great Britain by Mackays of Chatham, Chatham

To Caroline

Contents

Sure, she knew folks who had no problem at all with the past. A lot of it they just didn't remember. Many told her, one way and another, that it was enough for them to get by in real time without diverting precious energy to what, face it, was fifteen or twenty years dead and gone. But for Frenesi the past was on her case forever, the zombie at her back, the enemy no one wanted to see, a mouth wide and dark as the grave.

THOMAS PYNCHON, *Vineland*

PREFACE

On the morning of New Year's Day, 1972, I received at my flat in south Yorkshire a telegram from Felix Dennis, one of the defendants at the *Oz* trial of the previous summer, which asked if I would like to go to London and help edit that magazine. I reported for duty within 48 hours. *Oz* had effectively lost the remainder of its triumvirate, Richard Neville and Jim Anderson, both wearied by the trial and its aftermath, concerned at the failure of the newssheet *Ink* which they had launched in 1971 with much optimism and publicity and which had lurched from one crisis to the next, and both despairing of the generation which *Oz* had entertained and represented on both sides of the globe for most of the 1960s. Despite Felix's determination to keep alive a publication which, after all, paid his and several other people's wages, *Oz* would be published only sporadically until its death two years later, and in the summer of 1972 I accepted an offer to move across London and edit its stablemate, *International Times*.

Richard and Jim had, of course, been right. The time had already run out for *Oz*, and it was rapidly running out for *IT*. People such as myself had arrived (with, I think, comparatively few illusions) in the dogdays of the era which had spawned and supported those magazines. Sales of upwards of 40,000 copies (and in the case of the post-trial issue of *Oz*, upwards of 100,000) had diminished to between 15,000 and 30,000 an issue, and the glass was falling. They were supported by no publishing group, bulwarked by no set of shareholders, financed by no interested bank. A change of their editorial direction could be accomplished only within the strictest of limits and with the unnerving danger of losing the residual readership resident in inner-city squats or lost civilisations in the mountains of the Celtic west. They were fated to die with the youthful fashion which had shaped them and, just a few years later, it became obvious that that was the most fitting end.

There was nothing for it, then, but to poke the ashes and wander curiously about the rubble; and to take so much enjoyment out of the remnants of the 1960s that the thought hardly occurred: what must it have been like, back in the early Sixties? There were clues in plenty. I moved into the west London flat of a dignitary of the pioneering days, a man whose name was Howard Parker but who was known (misleadingly to some, for he had an intense hatred of heroin and all narcotic drugs) everywhere as 'H': a minor legend of the music business who had been Jimi Hendrix's road manager and confidante, who had a deep regard for John Lennon, Frank Zappa and—at the time of our cohabitation—the primal scream therapies of Arthur Janov; whose preferred way of starting the day was to play, very loud, the Alice Cooper single 'School's Out' while cake-walking across the floor in his underpants miming on an electric guitar, his waist-length blond hair flying behind; and whose preferred way of ending it was to cruise around London in a flat-topped sedan, looking (usually with success) for action and hanging u-eys wherever necessary. If 'H' was any kind of a pointer, and he obviously was, some interesting things had happened in the south of England while I was a teenager in the north.

'H' died in 1973, in an implausibly mundane boating accident in the Dodecanese, and the most dependable of guides was gone. A good part of the rest of my time in London was, I now suppose, spent trying to work out what it was that had formed characters like 'H', memorable people who, when they went, left nothing behind them other than a few paragraphs in rock'n'roll histories, some amplifiers from recording studios and a *Times Atlas of the World* (which I still possess). It was not possible to do so properly then, with the bailiffs knocking and the printers foreclosing on half-a-decade's worth of debt, while the acid visions were not entirely faded and many still clung, even in the metropolitan streets, to the notion that young people, by growing their hair, wearing bright clothes and dancing to a fiercer beat, would change the very nature of the race. Twenty years on, with a bit of spare time and an encouraging publisher, it seemed like a better time to engage with those influences and to attempt an exploratory essay.

I did not set out deliberately to do so, but I have written a book which is as much about London at a certain time as it is about anything else. That will not please a good many of my friends, but I cannot make an apology for it. Only there, it seemed to me then and it seems still to me now, did the fantasy truly flourish. Only there were sufficient numbers gathered in sufficient strobe-lit venues to make it apparent to anybody with a single eye that, when the planets were in the appropriate alignment, anything was possible—even, hilarious as it now seems, the repossession of the world.

ROGER HUTCHINSON
SKYE, 1992

LETTER

Dear Mainstream,

How smart of you to get Roger to write *High Sixties*. It's the best book yet on the period: friendly, fair, wise and thorough. He's one veteran who managed to hang on to his brains and memories, with a viewpoint shaped by the period but not glued to it. Time-lapse gives the book context and the painstaking detail its richness—Roger reveals more about life in the underground than any of us knew at the time (if only we had).

More than the music, the movies or my acid flashbacks; this book evokes summers-of-love-London like it was yesterday, and makes me want to do it all over again. Hell, why not?

All the best

Richard Neville
Australia

CHAPTER ONE

SIGNALS

What way we made in 1945 and in the following years depended largely on our age, for right at that point, at the point of the dropping of the bombs on Hiroshima and Nagasaki, the generations became divided in a very crucial way.

JEFF NUTTALL, *Bomb Culture*

The 1950s were the last Imperial decade. Just 20 years earlier the British Empire had reached its geographical limit: the colonial offices in Whitehall had continued to accumulate one small territory after another, doggedly piling high an in-tray of responsibility and stored future troubles while, outside their windows, the mother country slid reluctantly down the international scale of comparative military and industrial power. By the 1950s most of those territories, small and large, had found their own colour on the map, but Britain still looked towards their shining skies. The 1950s was the last decade when it was possible, when it was credible, for the country to be governed in one week by a Prime Minister who had ridden in a cavalry charge at Omdurman, and in the next by a man who would lead his people and their conscripted army almost unilaterally, against the wishes of the United States of America, the United Nations, and most of their western allies, into a war to protect colonial assets in a sovereign Muslim state. In future, those allies' consent would be required. For all of their protestations to the contrary, for all of their smug talk about taking a long time to anger, for all of their piously expressed desire to live—like retired gangsters—forgetful of old enmities and in harmony with the world, the British proved in the 1950s that they were an interfering, warlike people, and that they enjoyed being so.

The 1950s were a decade of flaccid self-satisfaction at home and idiotic pretence abroad. While two wars were being fought by British troops, in South-East Asia and on the banks of the Suez

Canal, while British atomic bomb tests shuddered the Monte Bello Islands in the soft underbelly of the planet, those left at home, seabound on the windswept edge of Europe, were disturbed hardly at all. It was only as a public failure that the Suez adventure rocked their complacency; their lonely furrow wavered slightly and was straightened again by the sacrifice of the Queen's chief minister. For them, it was an unportentous decade of holiday camps and blooming hedgerows, steady jobs and subterranean urban vices, terrible tinkling pop tunes, family cars, transistorised radios and new television sets. Impossible as it seemed at the time, life could never travel for long on the cosy gauge of the 1950s.

But, while they lasted, those years recreated a fantastic image of Great Britain. Tanned servants of the Crown returning to London on annual furlough from Kenya or the Turks and Caicos Islands throughout the 1950s may have found no less and few more causes of annoyance in the old country than at any time since the previous century. There was, it is true, some incomprehensible lower-middle-class ranting at the Royal Court Theatre, rather than a decent show; there were more blacks on the streets and manning the running boards of London's buses; there were strange noises issuing from the Expresso Bars, and the occasional sighting of young proletarians queerly clothed in Edwardian suits ... but there was a new Elizabeth on the throne and a terrace of Tories in Downing Street; there were Britons astride Mount Everest, and Britons busting the four-minute mile. Four-power nation conferences involved the USA, the Soviet Union, France and, of course, Great Britain—a country which might not yet be sending up Sputniks, but whose aviators had just completed the first non-stop flight over Antarctica (1600 miles in 10 hours 57 minutes). At Lords, England could still beat the West Indies by an innings and 36 runs (M. C. Cowdrey, c Walcott b Sobers, 152 runs); and at the Old Bailey women could be sent to the gallows for shooting a chap. And, all in all, the lot of a District Commissioner was still, in most of the right places, an enviable lot.

The 1960s were to take the 1950s and their steady, logical antecedents, their certainties and responsibilities, their values and their assumptions, and shake them until their eyeballs bubbled. That may be all, but that was done. Those oak-smoked politics and that suety culture were to be scorched as if by acid and a different country was to emerge, shakily, from the fracas. If war it was, it was in Britain largely a war of violent words and images, most hysterically and inaccurately fired by the descendant, threatened class. Our District Commissioner who might have found, in 1955, nothing more disturbing in town than Peter Hall's production of *Waiting for Godot*, would little more than ten years later be writing to the newspapers to insist that, as a matter of some urgency, half of the young men of the country be pressed into military service to combat the relentless subversions of the other half. Britain, in that short time, became a foreign country to him. It so comprehensively rejected all that was dear and familiar in his past that he knew, at sundown, that return was impossible.

He bickered and ranted. His age group rebelled against their young. His magistrates insulted and imprisoned them, his police-men harassed and arrested them, his publican friends barred them from their premises and his journalist peers wrote lies about them. It was oddly paranoid behaviour, even by those who had woken to discover that an Empire had slipped away in the night. His chosen authors—Charteris, Fleming, even, at the end, dear old P. G. Wodehouse—deviated crazily from the plots of their novels to include bitter tirades at the children of the nation: at loud-mouthed students and their unwashed sluts; at jungle music, vacant long-hairs, evil, dope-inspired conspiracies; at all the vile, contagious habits of their own offspring. Towards the end of his paean for the mythic delights of the 1950s in the winsome series of novelettes collectively titled *The Darling Buds of May*, H. E. Bates discovered that he had unwittingly stumbled into the early 1960s and was therefore obliged to introduce a menace more sinister by far than the Comintern or the officers of the Inland Revenue: a small group of long-haired young men and women who, armed with air rifles and a vicious vocabulary, visited a state of terror and siege upon Bates's community of placid goodwill. Bates's message was plain. Demons had grown within the holy womb of Britain: demons, practising inter-uterine cannibalism.

The era was thereby elevated as much by reaction as by its own activities. And they did not forget, those politicians who dripped egg-yolk on university steps, those bilious newspaper columnists, and those unforgiving policemen who were obliged to truncheon unarmed demonstrators in the tumult of Grosvenor Square. They would not easily forget what happened between the Chatterley trial and the shearing of the editors of *Oz*, between the rumble of those south-bound scooters and the bonfire of bewigged scarecrows outside the Central Criminal Courts. With an unremitting flow of dark references, by calling up the ghosts of permissiveness and rebellion to answer for our contemporary faults, they have invested those ten or eleven years with a wild importance when most other people—most, indeed, of the rebels and debauchees—had been happy to assume that nothing happened other than a small social earthquake. Not many died.

In fact, established, adult society broadcast its own distress signals of change and decay as the 1950s turned into the 1960s. They were not all strong signals, and one or two have had retrospectively attributed to them a flattering degree of influence on subsequent events, but they were signals, of a kind.

In October 1959 the Edwardian stylist Harold Macmillan, who had inherited his worried Conservative Party from Sir Anthony Eden after the shame of Suez, won a remarkable General Election victory. He collected a post-war record of 49.4 per cent of the vote (bettering Labour's previous high of 48.8 per cent in the 1951 election which they *lost* due to the imbalance of the constituency system) and went to the Queen with a neatly rounded overall majority in the House of Commons of exactly 100 MPs.

Three months later Macmillan celebrated by taking a turn around that most intractable of the colonised continents, Africa. It was a tour *de force*. Macmillan was possibly the only prime minister of recent times who made a virtue out of appearing older than he was. That foible, that technique, would work against him dramatically within three years, as the 1960s gathered momentum, but in Africa in the January and February of 1960 this affable rogue played the harmless, well-intentioned old buffer to the point, and almost past the point, of caricature, and his performance swept the board so thoroughly that he was safely back home in England before it was realised by his erstwhile hosts that they had been on the receiving end of one of the three memorable political speeches of the 1960s.

Having braved the equatorial waters of the Gold Coast in a traditionally manned longboat and dressed in a leopard skin while being inducted as a Bantu tribal chief, having played the old man delighting in the liberated antics of his grandchildren from Accra to the Veldt, Macmillan wound up on 3 February 1960 addressing the South African parliament in Cape Town. Clothed in a suit at last, and with one eye on the calendar, he told Prime Minister Dr Hendrik Verwoerd and the assembled representatives of the apartheid state that their days were numbered.

'The most striking of all impressions I have formed since I left London a month ago,' drawled the arch-patrician, 'is of the strength of this African national consciousness. In different places it may take different forms, but is happening everywhere. The wind of change is blowing through the continent. Whether we like it or not this growth of national consciousness is a political fact ... It is our earnest desire to give South Africa our support and encouragement, but ... there are some aspects of your policies which make it impossible for us to do this without being false to our own deep convictions about the political destinies of free men, to which in our own territories we are trying to give effect.'

As Macmillan sat down, an extraordinary thing happened. Whether or not the Boers had experienced a previously unsuspected difficulty in understanding the English language; whether or not they were unused to the labyrinthine clauses and gentle tones of an experienced British politician trying to make an unpopular point; whether or not they heard and understood what they chose to, and whether all that banging on about 'national consciousness', 'earnest desire' and 'support and encouragement' sank in without its acidulous qualifications, may never be known. But as Macmillan sat down, the two houses of the South African parliament rose to their feet and cheered.

Then he went home, to newspapers trumpeting the words 'Wind of Change'. Almost exactly a month later Hendrik Verwoerd, presumably having studied the text of Macmillan's speech, compared the British prime minister's attitude towards black Africans with Neville Chamberlain's appeasement of Hitler. And a fortnight later, on 21 March 1960, as if to clarify to the world the position of South Africa's rulers on the vexed question of white supremacy, South African policemen murdered 69 unarmed black demonstrators at Sharpeville. Three weeks after *that*, Verwoerd himself was hospitalised by a failed assassination attempt. Thanks in no small part to a prime minister who was soon to be swept away himself by the rip-tide of the changing times, South Africa had been established as a seminal issue of the 1960s.

Most unusually for a pragmatic Conservative, Macmillan had been seen to suggest that Britain, stripped of the power which devolves from real economic and political strength, could move its barricades to a different hillside and there occupy the moral high ground. These contour lines became important to the 1960s, although not many Conservative leaders made the same mistake again. But then, in what remained of that decade, not many Conservative leaders were given the chance.

Eight months after Harold Macmillan's timely flight from Cape Town, the city of London, which had distinguished itself by staging several epochal dramas in the late 1950s, hosted another great theatrical first. The trial of Penguin Books Limited at the Old Bailey between 20 October and 2 November 1960, under the Obscene Publications Act for attempting to bring out a cheap (3s 6d), unexpurgated paperback edition of D. H. Lawrence's last novel, *Lady Chatterley's Lover*, is popularly identified as the event which swung open the heavy gates at the entrance to the fairy grotto of the rest of the 1960s. It was certainly a performance of its time and place and, unlike Macmillan's deliberately conceived Catechism to the Boers, it occurred almost organically. The trial of a British publisher for publishing a novel by one of Britain's leading twentieth-century writers could have taken place nowhere else in the western world but Britain—and not only because almost no other country in the western world had bothered to ban the book in the first place.

Effectively, the Chatterley trial was an enormous error by the police and the Director of Public Prosecutions. They were prosecuting under a new Act which had been specifically designed to protect 'serious literature' from such harassment (and the bill's political sponsor, Roy Jenkins MP, would stand up in court and attempt to say just that). They had selected an author whom nobody could attempt to describe as a common pornographer (William Burroughs' *The Naked Lunch*, for example, or Nabokov's *Lolita* could more easily have been caricatured as pieces of worthless foreign sleaziness). And they had to convince an educated middle-class jury that they would be better off protected from such material (it was later discovered that nine of the twelve jurors had entered the courtroom already determined to acquit).

The error was possibly compounded—although the tone of the event was certainly heightened—by the selection of Mr Mervyn Griffith-Jones as prosecuting counsel. Here, at its very beginning, was a great figure of the 1960s: an upright product of public school, Oxford, and an earlier, happier age; a serious, high-minded figure who set his stall carefully, as the years rolled by, against the degeneracy of the century. More than any of his type, Griffith-Jones, a generally courteous, handsome man, who, in the words of one defence witness, 'really believed that he was arguing

on the side of the gods, of serious, *good* people', did so much to
encourage what he hoped to prevent. His famous lines are part of
history. His request of the jury to protect their fragile charges
('would you approve of your young sons, young daughters—
because girls can read as well as boys—reading this book? Is it a
book that you would have lying around in your own house? Is it
a book that you would even wish your wife or your servants to
read?') may have lost the Chatterley trial at its outset. His Old
Etonian sneer at the flat-vowelled, determined Richard Hoggart
('the question is quite a simple one to answer without another
lecture. You are not at *Leicester University* at the moment.')
certainly sold the pass. The Chatterley trial would not have been
the Chatterley trial without Mervyn Griffith-Jones. The early
1960s would not have been what they were without Mervyn
Griffith-Jones. Undaunted by Chatterley, he progressed in 1963
to prosecuting Stephen Ward ('a thoroughly filthy fellow' he told
that jury) for living off the immoral earnings of Christine Keeler
and Mandy Rice-Davies, and gained a conviction which can only
have been slightly less welcome because Ward was, by then,
comatose in hospital after taking an overdose of sleeping pills. He
died within hours of Mervyn's triumph. And in the following year
Griffith-Jones took his overdue revenge on works of English
literature which feature women who Do It, by successfully
prosecuting John Cleland's eighteenth-century romp, *Fanny Hill*.
The obscenity trials of *Last Exit to Brooklyn*, *The Little Red
Schoolbook*, *Oz* and *Nasty Tales* magazines came too late for
Mervyn Griffith-Jones, however. In 1967 he became a judge.
Sadly, he was on the bench during not one of those trials.

Trials in error, trials by outrage, failed and successful: they
could not have taken place without Jenkins's Act. As a backbench
Labour MP this young icon of liberalism steered through the 1959
Obscene Publications Act in an attempt to 'provide for the
protection of literature; and to strengthen the law concerning
pornography'. Jenkins intended to draw a line between exploitative, profitable (and prosecutionable) pornography, and art and
literature of (usually unprofitable) merit. In his defence, it may be
said that the line became baffling and blurred in the unpredicted
1960s. To his discredit it must be added that some curiously
illiberal prosecutions of printed matter took place during Jenkins'
spell as Home Secretary between 1965 and 1967.

But whatever Jenkins' intentions were in 1959, they were

certainly not that a D. H. Lawrence novel should be prosecuted 12 months later. No sooner had Penguin Books been charged than he wrote to *The Spectator* bleating that the police had assured him that such prosecutions would be put behind them in the bright new age of Jenkins's Act. Only under-counter photographs of people doing unspeakable things were, from then on, supposed to be hauled before the bar, along with their unappetising publishers. Jenkins was not to know—or was he?—that the difference to many policemen between Penguin Books and the unappetising pornographer was that Penguin Books did not give policemen money. This important distinction, which was apparent to most radical or even liberal publishers, to many journalists, and to anybody else with a sceptical eye on the times, did not become official public knowledge until 1977 when 12 of Soho's finest policemen were jailed for a total of 84 years for, according to the judge, 'an evil conspiracy which had turned the Obscene Publications Squad into a vast protection racket.' As the QC, Geoffrey Robertson, who as a junior counsel assisted John Mortimer in the *Oz* defence, puts it: 'The trials of *Lady Chatterley's Lover*, *Last Exit to Brooklyn* and the underground press appeared almost to have been calculated to divert public attention from police involvement in London's thriving pornographic marketplace.' Anybody other than a Queen's Counsel might replace the words 'appeared almost to have been' with 'were'.

And so Jenkins's Act was used, in October 1960, to prosecute that which Jenkins's Act had been designed to protect. The police laughed in the face of the intention of the law, and the office of the DPP—more, in its case, from doltishness than venality—went along with the police. In his opening address to the Chatterley jury defence counsel Gerald Gardiner attempted to point this out.

'Pornography,' he said, 'means literally the writings of prostitutes, but it is now used in a much more general sense, and you may think the best definition is "dirt for dirt's sake"—works which we have all seen and can see on bookstalls, not excepting our Sunday papers. That which is put in for the purpose of selling them has no art, no literature . . . And so we have this Act passed for two purposes. It is an Act, it says, to amend the law in relation to the publication of obscene matter, to provide for the protection of literature and to strengthen the law concerning pornography. So it is plain—is it not?—that its intention is to amend the law in two ways: first of all, by making it easier to prosecute real pornography and, secondly, to provide for the protection of literature ... to be obscene within the meaning of the Act, the book must, taken as a whole, tend to deprave and corrupt, which obviously involves a change of character leading the reader to do something wrong that he would not otherwise have done.'

Eight days later, on 28 October, Gardiner decided that the point might bear repeating. He called as a defence witness Mr Roy Jenkins MP and—aware that he was about to engineer a piece of legal subterfuge—told his junior counsel, Jeremy Hutchinson, to conduct the cross-examination.

'In the Obscene Publications Act,' said Hutchinson stealthily, 'I think you know that the Preamble amongst other things says, "To provide for the protection of literature". In your view,' Hutchinson asked Jenkins, 'is this book *Lady Chatterley's Lover* literature?'

Jenkins wasted no time.

'Yes, it most certainly is. Indeed, if I may add, it did not occur to me in the five years' work I did on the Bill—'

He got no further. 'I really don't think,' interposed Mr Justice Byrne instantly and, in law, correctly, 'we want to go into that.'

If the Not Guilty verdict which was delivered to Penguin Books Ltd on 2 November 1960 (a decision which enabled the company to increase their print-run of *Lady Chatterley's Lover* from a pre-trial 200,000 to 3,000,000 copies, all of which sold within three months, explaining Mr Justice Byrne's wry refusal to grant the defendants legal costs) was a harbinger of the 'permissive' 1960s—or even, as Mary Whitehouse among others came to see it, the single stroke which slashed the drawbridge rope and let the vandals thunder into civilised society—the trial itself, the pageant, was of a different age. The trial of *Lady Chatterley's Lover* said more about the times that were passing than the times which were about to begin. It was staged for the most part in a courtly manner, and had as much resemblance to, say, the trial of *Oz* magazine ten years later as did a medieval joust to the Battle of the Somme. The area of combat was understood and agreed upon in advance by prosecution and defence, like feudal barons negotiating the date, time, place and scale of their conflicts. Penguin Books knew that the police were waiting to prosecute their unexpurgated version of *Lady Chatterley's Lover* and so Sir Allen Lane, Penguin's founder and chairman, told his solicitors to invite the police to come round to Penguin and collect a dozen pre-publication voucher copies, rather than involve some poor bookseller on the Charing Cross Road. Detective Inspector Charles Monahan duly called in at High Holborn on 16 August 1960 (the official publication date was to have been 25 August), took away the books, and served the summons three days later. No doors were broken in, no filing cabinets ransacked, no violent threats were issued. Other, later victims of the police interpretation of Jenkins's Act would not be so lucky.

And no individual was charged. The 1959 Obscene Publications Act carried with it a maximum prison sentence of three years. It was agreed by all parties that no good cause would be advanced by having Sir Allen Lane sitting for a fortnight in the dock with *that* kind of sword dangling over his distinguished brow (from the prosecution's point of view, the jury would be less likely to convict if it meant jailing such an intelligent old gentleman; and from the defence's point of view . . . well, if the worst came to the worst, Sir Allen did not want to go to *prison*). So the abstract publishing company alone was charged, and throughout the trial of *Lady Chatterley's Lover* the dock stood empty. Richard Handyside would enjoy no such immunity when the law went for *The Little Red Schoolbook*; no such quaint, olde-worlde courtesy would be extended to the editors of *Oz*.

The Chatterley trial may have been what Penguin Books' Dieter Pevsner calls 'a battle between two eras', but it was a strangely schizophrenic battle: the lines were not yet properly drawn. And if the battle was won by the forces of enlightenment, as the liberal intelligentsia of the time liked to think, then the powers of darkness and reaction showed so few signs of acknowledging their defeat that it must be asked, where was the victory? What tangible results were logged, outside the bank account of Penguin Books? Because the prosecutions continued—not all under the Obscene Publications Act, but they continued—of Alexander Trocchi's *Cain's Book*, seized in 1964 in a police raid on a Sheffield bookshop, charged with and found guilty of obscenity because, according to the appeal judge, it advocated drug-taking. *Fanny Hill* was successfully prosecuted; a poetry anthology called *The Golden Convulvulus* was, in late 1965, ruled to be 'indecent'. Aubrey Beardsley prints were taken by police from a Regent Street bookshop. Twenty-one drawings by Jim Dine were lifted by uniformed officers from the Robert Fraser

Gallery. *Last Exit to Brooklyn* was prosecuted between 1966 and 1968. Compendium Books was relieved of half of its stock. Whenever it showed its head above the parapet, the emergent 'underground' press was in danger of being stunned by a summons.

The only conceivable good that the Chatterley trial and its Not Guilty verdict did for those later victims was to indicate that it was possible to fight and win such a prosecution. But it is arguable that many, if not all of them would have fought—and won, or lost—anyway. And too often they were insufferably burdened by the weighty defence mechanism which was pioneered by Penguin Books and which became the standard text for obscenity defendants: the formidable array of expert witnesses to the artistic, literary, social and even religious merit of the item under discussion.

As if it matters, there may have been a larding of pornography and obscenity in some of these productions. As if it matters . . . because it certainly did not matter to the police and to the prosecuting authorities. Throughout the 1960s cynical, profitable, fat-cat pornography prospered: it grew more rich and more daring and more confident as the decade progressed. While impecunious artists, struggling poets and avant-garde publications bowed before a blizzard of legal documents, the purveyors of undiluted, unpretentious tit, bum, cock, cunt and worse strolled on, mink-coated and obviously immune to prosecution under the Act which had promised to 'strengthen the law concerning pornography'. Their immunity may in part be explained by the fact that dirty books and films marketed by seedy, semi-criminal syndicates did not threaten the established order (they were, after all, traditionally part of the established order) in the same way that the brash, lascivious issue of a self-proclaimed counter-culture set out unashamedly to shake society. That was the preferred interpretation, for many years, of the counter-culturalists themselves. The truth may be more mundane. If one of the advantages of being a member of the Obscene Publications Squad in the 1960s and the first half of the 1970s was a welcome increment which was gained as the result of pretending that some pornographic books and films were either not available in Britain, or that, if they were, they and their manufacturers were impossible to trace, then those officers of the Obscene Publications Squad who wished to retain that increment were faced with a problem. In order to justify the continued existence of the Squad (and, thereby, the increment) they had to bring prosecutions under the Act which had gifted them their name. Apart from an occasional cosmetic raid the increment-payers were, by definition, out of court. That left only the principled liberal publishing houses, the backstreet artists, and the scruffy producers of mimeographed poetry magazines. These people also had the habit of pleading Not Guilty, which invariably resulted in noisy, much-publicised court proceedings, and a veneer of well-intentioned industry coated the members of the Obscene Publications Squad. To this extent the trial of Penguin Books in the October and November of 1960 was not so much as C. H. Rolph cleverly describes it, a trial of Lady Constance Chatterley for committing adultery with a lover who used four-letter words, as the trial of Sir Allen Lane for not paying graft. And as such, it most certainly was a harbinger of things to come.*

And, almost incidentally, it became a trial of the ideas of D. H. Lawrence—ideas which, if Lawrence had been a more accessible writer, might have led to him being recognised as a true shaman of the 1960s. His words and deeds were a counter-cultural model, even down to their thick dusting of unreconstructed sexism. His second novel, *The Rainbow*, had been declared to be obscene by Bow Street Magistrates' Court in 1915, and consequently banned. Lawrence grew to hate the machine age, particularly as evidenced in his native country, and he travelled the world in search of an alternative. 'Modern society is a mill that grinds life very small,' he wrote. 'The machine has got you, it is turning you round and round and feeding itself on your life . . . [We are] a poor blind, disconnected people with nothing but politics and Bank Holidays . . . mankind has got to get back to the rhythms of the Cosmos.'

---

* The use of the obscenity and indecency laws became a standard part of police ordnance when dealing with subversive publications well outside the Metropolitan area, of course. In 1971, while I was editing a cheerful little magazine called *Styng* in Yorkshire, I was visited by three members of the local constabulary and informed that an early issue of the magazine was to be charged on two counts of obscenity. Astonished, I rifled through the pages to locate the items in question. One of them was Jeff Nuttall's cartoon strip, revived in *Styng* after a long absence from the pages of *International Times*, retitled 'The Early Lobster', and drawn under the pseudonym Captain Blood because of Nuttall's concern for the feelings of the authorities at his place of work, Leeds Polytechnic. The putatively obscene frames featured a melting candle in a broad-brimmed hat which claimed to be 'experienced' and sang to itself 'All de noice goils love a . . .' I felt vaguely flattered that *Styng* should receive such attention. The policemen obviously felt that they were only doing their bit in helping to provincialise a popular drama which had been too long monopolised by London, and part of me agreed. We talked briefly, in suitably hostile and suspicious tones, and then they left me to warn the magazine's printer that he too was vulnerable to prosecution. He dropped us, and our unpaid bills.

Lady Chatterley's Lover was his last novel. It was instantly banned in both Britain and the United States of America, which came as no surprise to Lawrence, who published it privately in Italy in 1928, two years before his death. As much as it was an attempt to reclaim the language of shameless sex from the gutter, *Lady Chatterley's Lover* was Lawrence's revenge on his erstwhile persecutors ('How beastly the bourgeois is, especially the male of the species') as personified in Constance Chatterley's crippled, cuckolded, titled husband.

The bitterness that D. H. Lawrence felt towards him and his kind was not lost on his posthumous prosecutor, the Treasury Counsel Mervyn Griffith-Jones. At one time Lawrence considered calling the book *Tenderness*. This word was picked upon by Griffith-Jones in his closing speech. He was not to know, in November 1960, that he was confidently holding up to ridicule the kind of sentiment which would shortly be adopted as a desideratum by half of the youth of the developed world.

'What about tenderness?' Mervyn Griffith-Jones asked the Chatterley jury. 'Is that a theme which it is in the public good to read as expressed in this book? I will tell you how it is expressed in this book, in the words of the book itself: "Tenderness, really— cunt tenderness. Sex is really the closest touch of all. Cunt tenderness." That is the tenderness that this book is advocating through the mouth of one of its chief characters. And again may I quote from my note: "I believe in something"—this is Mellors [*the gamekeeper, Lady Chatterley's lover*] speaking—"I believe in being warm-hearted. I believe especially in being warm-hearted in love. I believe that if men could fuck with warm hearts and women took it warm-heartedly, everything would come all right." '

Griffith-Jones looked up. 'That is put before you as a theme which justifies this book for the public good, the theme advocating to the young of the country who are going to read this book: "Fuck warm-heartedly and everything will come all right." Does it justify it?'

'Yes,' hundreds of thousands of the young of the country would have chorused unreservedly, if read that extract and asked that question just a few short years later. 'Yes, it does. Wow.'

The Chatterley trial was about sex. So many of the paroxysms which trembled British society at the beginning of the 1960s were inspired by sex. The country—or, at least, the adult establishment of the country—seemed like some virtuous adventurer, returned home in late middle-age from hectic, far-flung parts and for the first time noticing aghast the stirrings inside his trousers. Sex, what was to be done about sex? Allow it? Ban it? Hide it? Put one's head back under the pillow and hope that it goes away?

In the early spring of 1963 the eighteen-months-old satirical magazine *Private Eye* devoted a two-page spread to a lampoon of Edward Gibbon's *Decline and Fall of the Roman Empire*, which it titled 'The last days of Macmilian'. The central illustration, by the brilliant young cartoonist Timothy Birdsall, showed the prime minister (in a toga) chortling on a couch, a grape in his left hand and his right resting on the buttocks of a naked young woman who was feeding him champagne. At 'Macmilian's' side senators (in togas and bowler hats) whispered to each other under Birdsall's explanatory caption: 'Horrid old pooves plotting'. At the back of the villa were 'models disporting themselves with famous names' in a swimming pool beneath a sign that read: 'Mixed Bathing. Per Wardua Ad Astor.'

The text surrounding Birdsall's frieze, which was written by Christopher Booker, read in part: '. . . while natural debauchery became the small talk of a capital long sated with public offerings of vice and harlotry of every description, among the clerks and eunuchs of the administration the old standards of the Republic had vanished altogether. Men proclaimed their love not for their wives, but for each other—and the strange loyalties thus formed, stretching up into some of the highest places in the land, allowed laxity, indulgence and even treason to flourish unchecked.

'At this time too, the Chief of the Praetorian Guard, Sextus Profano, came under widespread suspicion for his admission in the Senate that he had been acquainted with Christina, a beautiful girl known well to many of the great figures of society despite her lowly origins . . .'

'Sextus Profano' was John Profumo, the Secretary of State for War in Macmillan's government. 'Christina' was Christine Keeler, a part-time model who Profumo had first met by the swimming pool at Cliveden, the country home of Lord William Astor. Keeler, along with other young women, had been introduced to Cliveden by Dr Stephen Ward, a fashionable osteopath who leased from Astor a cottage in the grounds of Cliveden for a peppercorn rent. The 'horrid old pooves plotting', the 'strange loyalties . . . stretching up into some of the highest places in the land' were references to the case of William Vassall, a clerk at the

Admiralty who had been found guilty, in October 1962, of spying for the Soviet Union and imprisoned for 18 years. It emerged that Vassall was gay and had consequently been blackmailed. Prurient rumours about Vassall's superiors at the Admiralty swept the land, and became somehow confused in the public mind with the odd, cryptic connections being hinted at in the national press between the Minister for War, beautiful young women, and swimming pools at stately houses . . .

In fact there was no connection between the Vassall and the Profumo affairs, except that they were both to do with a nation's convoluted attitude towards sex, and that they conspired to paint the great and the good of the land with a liberal coat of hypocrisy. On 29 June 1960 Macmillan's Conservative majority in the House of Commons had rejected the recommendations of the Wolfenden Committee (which had been sitting since 1957) that homosexual intercourse between consenting adults should be decriminalised. Two months later *Lady Chatterley's Lover* was prosecuted on the grounds that it described adulterous sex. By 1963 it was beginning to look as if the security of the nation was, at least in part, in the hands of gay men (which of course, in the natural run of things, it was), and that senior members of the Cabinet, Peers of the Realm and even (it was once tangentially hinted) members of the Royal Family spent a good deal of their spare time fucking women who were not their wives (which of course, they did).

Viewed from the safe distance of thirty years the storyline of the Profumo affair is just a shade seamier than a Barbara Cartland novelette. Once again it is difficult to imagine any other European country of the time staging such a drama, to such traumatic effect. Indeed, ten years later in Britain (by which time the 1960s had run their therapeutic course) similar indiscretions in high places merely resulted in the early retirement of a couple of junior ministers. But in 1963 John Profumo's brief dalliance with a woman who swore that she never took a penny of his money, brought down an apparently indestructible prime minister and cost Macmillan's party that huge parliamentary majority which he had traipsed off to celebrate in Africa in the January of 1960.

It was an ordinary scandal, but it was revealed in nudges, winks and innuendo. The reticence of the press of the time to be in any way explicit about the peccadilloes of their rulers, of the friends of their proprietors, meant very little of that which journalists knew to be happening was actually reported to the nation. The resulting fretwork of hint and rumour was further complicated by a couple of minor court cases concerning Christine Keeler's friends and admirers, and—not least—by Mandy Rice-Davies' (another protégé of Stephen Ward, and for a while Keeler's friend) extraordinary taste in men. The teen-aged Mandy's connections with the ineffable slum landlord Peter Rachman and (after Rachman's death in France) the crooked insurance broker Dr Emil Savundra, more even than the revelation that Keeler had been seeing the British Minister for War and Captain Eugene Ivanov (a Russian military 'attaché') simultaneously, gave the whole tacky business a shivering sense of dank, bizarre, routine corruption in high places.

And the girls themselves did not help. Even when demurely dressed for the Old Bailey, the free-wheeling sexuality of Rice-Davies and Keeler told its own merry story. Not that it had to. Unlike John Profumo, Christine and Mandy were not particularly ashamed. When, after reeling off a string of her former partners from the dock, Mandy Rice-Davies dropped in the name of Lord William Astor, prosecuting counsel Mervyn Griffith-Jones (who was, this time, prosecuting Stephen Ward for procurement) hastily interjected that he was sure Miss Rice-Davies knew that Lord Astor had denied any personal impropriety. 'Well,' replied Mandy instantly and with a pretty giggle, 'he would say that, wouldn't he?' Oh, there were delights here, delights which only the imagination could plumb, delights which left the public rhapsodically reeling and the government gasping for air.

There were three victims of the Profumo affair. Stephen Ward was driven to suicide; John Profumo was toppled by a lie which stood in sharp comparison to Mandy Rice-Davies's engaging frankness; and Macmillan's government was felled by the recoil of his cultivated image. Ward took an overdose of sleeping pills before verdict was delivered in his Old Bailey trial, slipped into a coma, and died shortly after being found Guilty. His funeral in London was a quiet affair: not one single former friend or relative attended it.

Profumo, having made the mistake of telling the House of Commons that his brief relationship with Christine Keeler had been absolutely chaste, was disproved by later revelations and had no option other than to resign. He stopped just short of putting on a sackcloth, but wandered off to do what an apologetic press was later (ten years later) to describe glowingly as 'charity work in the

East End of London', a job which was to earn this Mother Theresa of Shoreditch a mention in the list of minor honours. Harold Macmillan gave the game away by appearing to be so out of touch with the decade which—in terms of post-colonial politics—he had kick-started in 1960, that he was incapable of selecting Ministers of War who were able to keep their trousers up when in the company of charming young women who also dated Russian spies. How was I to know? Macmillan appeared to ask. How could a chap like me tell if people are doing such dreadful things?

When the prime minister was asked in the House of Commons if he had not smelled a rat when presented with a copy of a letter from Profumo to Keeler which began 'Darling ...', he played the amiable old codger once too often. 'I do not live among young people much myself,' he protested, as if the word 'darling' was just another curious example of the hep terminology regularly employed by his Minister of War. 'I do not live among young people much myself ...' Nobody laughed fondly this time, nobody thought how quaint. Everybody shook his or her head in pitying wonderment, and began to think about employing a new prime minister.

And there were two beneficiaries of the Profumo affair (if we discount, as we probably should, Mandy Rice-Davies, who flew away to open a string of night-clubs called 'Mandy's' in Tel Aviv, and the doomed, oddly spectral figure of Lord Home of the Hirsel, who replaced Macmillan as leader of the Conservative Party and, for nine months, as prime minister of Great Britain). The circulation of the magazine *Private Eye* rose in the summer of 1963 from 35,000 to 80,000; and less than a year later Harold Wilson moved into Number 10 Downing Street. The morality tale of Profumo, Keeler, Ivanov and Ward was as manna to the postgraduate satirical magazine which had been launched in London in October 1961. It was not so much that *Private Eye* printed, or even knew, all of the sorry ins and outs; it was more that they gave the impression of knowing.* In the world of

---

* Following Birdsall and Booker's 'Last Days of Macmilian' fresco, Stephen Ward hurried along to the *Private Eye* offices to make a visit which has entered the magazine's inhouse folklore. 'I see you know everything,' he gasped to the interested staff. With great presence of mind Richard Ingrams and Willie Rushton nodded seriously, adding: 'Just refresh our memories ...' Ward poured out his tale of secret service harassment, desertion by former friends and patrons, and personal innocence. Unfortunately for Ward, he may as well have gone to the *Daily Express* for all the space that was subsequently afforded to his tale. In 1963 *Private Eye* saw itself almost entirely as a medium of satire. Irreverent as the magazine was, serious political exposure was outside its brief.

revelation by innuendo *Private Eye* was then, as ever since, king. Little more precise detail about the Profumo affair appeared in *Private Eye* than appeared anywhere else, but the scandal suited wonderfully their blend of sly hint and pastiche. Contained in these pages, somewhere between these lines, was surely to be found the truth. None the wiser? Well, surely *next* issue ... *Private Eye*'s fortnightly sales slumped again after the end of the Profumo affair, but the magazine had established a bridgehead. Almost alone, for a year or two, among the nervous post-colonial British press, *Private Eye* was not only unconcerned about rocking the boat: it saw rocking the boat as one of life's chief delights.

Harold Wilson had become leader of the Labour Party after the sudden death of Hugh Gaitskell in January 1963, and was establishing a new image both for himself and his party when the Profumo affair fell like a gift into his lap. Wilson had more sense than to muddy his own hands in these waters. He left the business of hounding Profumo (and, therefore, Ward) to one of his MPs, George Wigg. Wigg appeared on television, Wigg whispered to the press, Wigg chivvied the police and the security services into looking more closely at Stephen Ward's connections and at his sources of income, Wigg hectored in the House of Commons and Wigg called Lord Hailsham a 'lying humbug' when the latter tried to separate the fortunes of the Conservative Party from the affairs of John Profumo. Wilson sat back, watched the dazed Macmillan fumble with the new amorality, and accrued the benefits. The Profumo affair may not in itself have cost the Conservative Party the general election which followed it in October 1964, but it gave Harold Wilson the sharp contrast that he required between a dissolute old order and his own 'white heat of the technological revolution', pledged in the second memorable political speech of the 1960s. The Conservative Party's bizarre decision to replace Macmillan with an unelected Scottish earl who unfortunately joked that he was not very good at maths and had to add up with the help of matchsticks merely furthered Wilson's cause.

And there was probably a third, unwitting, beneficiary of the Profumo affair: it gave the 1960s a launching party. In this strange environment the uncertain decade was fledged: among court cases and anarchic magazines; where the famous, the young and the beautiful experimented with soft hallucinogenics bought from black men in noisy clubs; with the feeling that sex no longer *mattered* that much, as a vouchsafe of marriage or an item of exchange; in a western world whose elders had lost control of themselves, of their class, of their generation, of their *countries* . . .

These were merely signals, no more than that. The schoolboy flicking disappointedly through the first unexpurgated edition of *Lady Chatterley's Lover* to be published in Britain did not instantly conclude that his life must follow a path of free and shameless love. The Ted, or even the Mod, was likely to be quite unmoved by Harold Macmillan's injunction that fresh, destabilising breezes were sweeping the dark continent. The Rocker who may have been unexpectedly touched by the news of President Kennedy's assassination merely laughed, a few months earlier, at Profumo's mortification, Mandy's wit, Ward's death . . . for already, in these early years, young people had a culture of their own. It was sited at quite a distance from the Palace of Westminster, Cliveden and the Old Bailey, and weekly it was moving further from these places, further from these signals.

Signals they were, and roughly decoded they informed their younger recipients that the colonial world of their parents was lost forever, and that their parents were consequently rather confused about most things of any importance—such as war, peace, sex and religion. They led, in short, to the happy conclusion by the young that they did not particularly want to be like their parents. The young had jobs, money and mobility, and so for the first time in modern history they were able in many ways to divorce themselves from the adult world. They were able to create their own heroes and villains, fill the cultural vacuum with their own music, wear (and design) their own clothes. Eventually they would grope towards forming their own ideas about social, personal and political life, they would publish their own magazines and newspapers, organise their own festivals, push up their own spokespeople, theorists, comedians, polemicists, and politicians, display the same shared contempt for international boundaries, and talk, from San Francisco to Sydney, by way of Solihull, vivid dialects of the same language. The young did not take over, until they became old and strange themselves, but they made the 1960s: they painted its face and accelerated its heartbeat. To the detriment of almost every other group in society, the young and the beautiful picked up the 1960s and took the decade home as a toy.

CHAPTER TWO

WHEELS

The Mods were on one side. We, the Rockers, were on the other and no one else seemed to matter. The Mods were our automatic enemies and we were theirs. Why it came about, I don't know. It was the accepted system.

BUTTONS, A ROCKER

Great Britain would never be motorcycle country. That maze of antique highways and hedgerowed lanes, the graded speed limits which stuttered downwards every few hundred yards, the narrow metalled turnpikes, hump-backed bridges, traffic lights and zebra crossings—anyone with a decent set of wheels would hardly get out of second. There was the North Circular Road around London, there was the Ace Café, there were limited stretches of the old Roman highway, the A1, north of Highgate, and after November 1959 there was, in two-lane prefabricated splendour, the M1, Britain's first motorway, between the capital and York-shire. But these were no highways for bikers raised on *The Wild One* and rumours of the Gypsy Tour in Hollister, California, of rumbles in Monterey and Tijuana, of Labor Day Weekend riots, rape, assault, intimidated citizens and nervous sheriffs. These benign stretches of tarmacadam would never be Highway 69, the burn-up between Ealing and Richmond not quite the same as Oakland to Bakersfield. The South London Outlaws, the Black Fen, the Nightingale, the Ace Men and the Flying Horsemen would never, no matter how hard they tried, be Hell's Angels.

But some did try, on the stolen or second-hand last issue of the British motorcycle industry, on 500cc Triumph Speed Kings or 250 Francis Barnetts, growling outside the Busy Bee in Watford, making runs through the complacent suburbs, and fighting. Fight-ing each other, and fighting Mods. It was, for these persevering Rockers, an uphill struggle.

Few tried harder than Peter Welsh. Born in Islington in 1948, Welsh was burdened by his given name only until 1962 when, as a young biker, he decorated his leather jacket with extra studs, like an oil-stained parody of a Pearly King, and became known as Buttons. A stout, uncompromising character, Buttons was later (so much later—almost a decade later) to visit California as a guest of the San Francisco chapter of the Hell's Angels and to return to London equipped with both his red and his brown wings (the one signifying that the wearer had performed cunnilingus on a menstruating woman, the other that he had enjoyed buggery), with a canon of appetising stories, and with the sworn mission to establish a chapter of the Hell's Angels in England. But that, in 1962, was in Buttons' tea leaves. In 1962, Buttons was merely fighting Mods. It was not a role ever likely to attract Marlon Brando, but to Buttons and the Walthamstow Rockers in the early 1960s, fighting Mods was pie, just pie.

Buttons and the lads would routinely make their way down to Leyton Baths dance-hall, where a nervous segregation obtained. 'We covered the front near the stage and the Mods hung in the dark of the rear hall. There used to be a lot of closed fighting, sometimes with knives, and people would stumble out of the Baths cut and bleeding. I think,' Buttons reflected, looking back from a wiser age, 'this was possibly the main reason why the Baths were eventually closed. It was like a holy war. We were under no limitations other than what we imposed on ourselves. Nobody controlled us.'

On a Sunday evening in September 1965, Buttons' reputation as a scourge of young men in Chelsea boots caught up with him, and his Mod-fighting days were almost ended—not least because, by the time that Buttons was finally released from the various hospitals and borstals to which he was directed after the events of that autumn day, there were no more Mods about. They had metamorphosed in their millions, and disappeared as swiftly and as cleanly from the streets of the country as did the British motorcycle industry, leaving their erstwhile opponent scratching the ground of the East End of London like a ruffled mastodon. But on 26 September 1965, outside the Bonanza Amusement Arcade in Hackney, Buttons had no reason to suspect that the established order would take such a turn. There he stood, at ten o'clock in the evening, on the corner of Lamb Lane and Mare Street, by the park which is known as London Fields, when upwards of 30 Mods poured out of the nearby Regal Cinema and ran, scattering across the narrow east London road, towards him. There was only one response to *that*.

'We ran up Lamb Lane to the building yard and grabbed weapons. We grabbed our tools and by then the Mods were at the bottom of the street. We charged the crowd of Mods rather than wait. We'd learnt previously that waiting to get yourself kicked in worked out worse than if you went in first . . . As I ran into Mare Street there was this big fellow with a knife. He attacked Ritchie, who waited for the guy to lunge, let the knife slip by him and hammered the Mod on the neck with a pickaxe handle. The squishing sound coupled with the skin splitting was a nice effect. Another of our lads hit a Mod full force in the guts with a pickaxe handle. The Mod just stood there sort of dazed, looking bewildered and holding his stomach and walked away. I figured he was pilled up to the eyeballs. You don't just walk away from a blow like that . . . I was running full pelt after this one Mod when I noticed a fellow standing near the kerb. He was holding a single-barrelled gun with a hammer or bolt action, and he looked like he was trying to cock the gun or load it. I saw his face twisted up because he was having trouble with his shooter so I went for him with the iron bar raised in my right arm. I turned my body slightly to throw the bar at him.

'The gun went off, and from running more than fifty yards at full pelt I stopped like I'd just come up against a brick wall. I fell to my knees. I always remember the blood. It reeked and I felt sick.'

As a general rule, Mods did not enjoy hand-to-hand combat any more than they liked tooling around with the engines of their scooters. Both activities spoilt their clothes. Unwittingly, Buttons had run full-pelt into style with a cautionary twelve-bore. He was threatening with an iron bar the first genuinely widespread classless youth cult of the twentieth century. The Mods were the first of the young iconoclasts with a membership in every settlement in the land.

They had their vague antecedents, of course: both Mods and Rockers were likely to be the children of Teddy Boys, but until the arrival on the scene of the neatly structured Mod with his or her mobility, dress-sense, music, dance, drugs and (the begetter of them all) decent wage packet, the youth culture which has dominated Britain ever since could hardly be said to have been born. The Mod was a product of comparative affluence, of a level of youth employment which began to die almost with the last days of the decade and which, 20 years later, seemed a tinted dream. But in the early 1960s many teenagers were able to command an acceptable weekly wage of £10 to £15. Three singles (nobody bought LPs) could be had for a pound, it was two bob to get in at the Lyceum, sixpence or ninepence for an amphetamine ... a young hairdresser named Vidal Sassoon charged 25 shillings for a girl's Nancy Kwan cut, a ready-made Mohair suit came from 20 guineas, corduroy hipsters from two quid ... and for 20 pounds you could put a deposit on a Lambretta or a Vespa motor scooter.

Those scooters as much as any other item became the central image of Mod. Usually just 150cc, rarely more than 200 and often as little as 100, they were not bought for power.* They were bought for their price, and their low petrol consumption, for their customised style, for the fact that they could be kick-started and ridden with the minimum of fuss and dirt, and because, no matter how tiny their cubic capacity, they took their owners out of and away from the terraces and the suburbs, towards the sands, the spangled pier and the crashing sea. Less demonstrably, perhaps, than a biker loved his Norton, the Mod felt for his scooter. He felt warmth and gratitude. He would cluster it with headlights until its fragile front guards looked like the magnified eye of an insect, he flew pennants from it and bought it five different horns, he screwed chromium statuettes to it and decorated its perfunctory windscreen with smart transfers. He polished his scooter until it posed no threat to his hipsters and new crepe soles. He cared for it because, if it broke down on a run, the Mod would be presented with two demoralising alternatives: to fiddle about in its greasy interior, or to catch a bus. He cared for it, above all, because upon his scooter he could go anywhere and do anything. It was his wheels.

'Modernists' was the original name, taken from the Modern Jazz movement of the late 1950s and early 1960s, the music of

---

* The Vespa Super Sport, a 150cc model, proudly advertised its top speed as 65.3 m.p.h. The Lambretta range could be had for as little as £109 17s 6d, plus purchase tax, but the 150cc model, single-seat, went for £159 17s 6d (pillion extra). 'To country or coast,' the advertising copy read, 'easily, breezily, stylishly for less than a halfpenny a mile.' If the capacity and the speed of these machines seem puny, it may be worth recalling that these were the days before legislation compelled motor-cyclists to wear crash-helmets. Bareheaded, in an open-necked Fred Perry sports shirt, sitting upright on a pair of wheels the size of a bowler hat whch were held together only by a single metal tube—*anything* over 30 mph *seemed* fast.

Charlie Mingus and Dave Brubeck and the Modern Jazz Quartet, as opposed to that of Acker Bilk and Tin Pan Alley, and here is a hint as to where Mods did *not* come from. They owed little or nothing to beatniks and to the bearded habitués of folk clubs: they did not deceive themselves with serious intentions. Without doubt they were young and iconoclastic and before long it would be the Mods—more than even the marchers to Aldermaston, or the early experimenters with hashish, or (to Buttons' chagrin) the Walthamstow Rockers—who would attract the opprobrium of the law and the national press, who would inspire the violent insults from the magistrates' benches and who would receive the vengeful prison sentences which, across the Atlantic, were reserved for left-wing agitators and Hell's Angels. But Mods did not go looking for this trouble, and they were shocked and angered when it was delivered to them. They were not without a cause, but their cause was simply style, maximum enjoyment . . . *release*. That these things would come to be seen as being socially and politically subversive was, to the first young iconoclasts, strange indeed.

There was a story, much loved, repeated and embellished within the fledgling peace movement, of an incident in 1961 at a sit-down demonstration outside the Ministry of Defence. The 89-year-old Lord Bertrand Russell, the great philosopher and logician who, in his impish old age, became the lovable Nestor of the extra-parliamentary campaign against nuclear weapons, was walking away from the Ministry building having pinned a message of protest to its door. Silence and tension hung heavily about his short walk back to his squatting comrades, the dilemma of the police clearly evident over whether or not to arrest this venerable elf for obstructing the highway. (Almost anybody else would have been arrested, as Russell was on a later occasion.) Then a 'tousled youth' in jeans came dancing down the street, bawling ('in hoarse cockney'—very important, that hoarse cockney): 'Good ole Bertie!'

What relief from those three words! What vindication! Working-class youth, that shout declared, could not only identify the celebrities of the Committee of 100, it also supported their aims. 'Good ole Bertie!' in that rough young voice—it was enough, surely, to shake even Hugh Gaitskell's Labour Party from its dogged defence of the bomb. 'Good ole Bertie!' It made all the arrests and the humiliations, all the interminable meetings and marches in the rain seem suddenly worthwhile, because, if working-class youth was on one's side, who, eventually, could gainsay the cause? Had he not existed, that tousled youth would have had to be invented.

He was not invented, of course, but nor was he, in 1961, typical. His contemporaries, the broad mass of his contemporaries, were too involved in the politics of style, and in the developing culture of cool (to say nothing of deflecting the attentions of Buttons and his friends) to spend time holding CND banners aloft in the tedious drizzle.

The evolution of Modernist into Mod was a matter of music, clothes, stimulants, dance, ways of walking and ways of standing still. The last two were comparatively straightforward. They owed much to the pioneering slouch and stroll of David McCallum (not Robert Vaughn) in the television series *The Man From Uncle* (a far-sighted piece of futurism in which a United States secret agent—Vaughn—found himself collaborating with a Soviet spy— McCallum), and of Steve McQueen (again, emphatically *not* Robert Vaughn) in *The Magnificent Seven*. Insouciance was the desired effect, unhurried cool ... 'You'd have to look totally relaxed, but right; you put your leg against the wall, you'd put your hands in your Levis or your jacket pocket with your thumbs sticking out.'

These manners of stance and perambulation had a lot to do with complementing, or at least not spoiling the line of, the subject's clothes. Mods had an excellent dress-sense. They had the wit and the style not to look to America, but eastwards, to Europe, and largely to Italy. Italian shoes, jackets and suits were set off by broad dark glasses, a pastiche of cappuccino ('frothy coffee') in the Expresso bars, and the hegemonous haircut. The intricately trimmed and parted or blown-back coiffure which would be measured as short by all succeeding generations but which, by the barbershop standards of the late 1950s and early 1960s, was described as *long*, could not possibly have been sculptured by any old corner-shop trimmer. In order to service their demand, Mods consequently gave birth to the previously unthinkable in Britain, the High Street men's hairdresser. Later in the 1960s those institutions would be seriously threatened by the less fastidious tastes of the successors to Mod, but between 1962 and 1966 the sun shone and men's stylists made hay.

The musical taste of Mod has, in the intervening decades, been simplified and caricatured until, in the popular eye, it may often seem to be little more than the slashed and crashing chords, the furious lyrics of their major home-grown band: The Who. For a while, certainly, The Who were as Mod as a band could be. Pete Townshend and Roger Daltrey were 'faces': pacesetters of the scene. So, for that matter, were Rod Stewart and Steve Marriott (who even named their group after that peergroup plaudit, calling themselves the Small Faces); but Townshend, Daltrey, Entwhistle and Moon laid bare an unsuspected nerve in their stuttered, unambiguous request of their elders to 'f-f-f-f-fade away' in *My Generation*, the simple honesty of *Can't Explain*, and above all, perhaps . . .

> I can go anywhere (way I choose),
> I can live anyhow (win or lose),
> I can go anywhere for something new,
> Anywhere, anyhow, anyway I choose.
> I can do anything (right or wrong),
> I can talk anyhow (to get along).
> I don't care anyway, I never lose,
> Anyway, anyhow, anywhere I choose . . .

The Who had scene credibility. In Shepherds Bush, Watford and Wealdstone, at Railway Hotels and Trade Union Clubs their temporary residencies had attracted Mods by the hundred. They were taken over in 1964 by a diamond-sharp character, one Pete Meaden, a self-defined resident of 'the pulse of the city', a man whose goal, while he lived (and he died young, as such people must) was to be 'neat, sharp and cool, an all-white Soho negro of the night'. Meaden changed their name to The High Numbers and issued their first (failed) single *I'm The Face*.* But an incapacity for doing successful business goes arm in arm with dying young in the entrancing character of people like Pete Meaden, and his boys were shortly bought from him for a few hundred pounds by two Mods of more earthly qualities. Kit Lambert and Chris Stamp

---

* Nowhere was the early marriage of art school chic to Mod cool better celebrated than in the early posters advertising The High Numbers. Clean white artwork reversed out of solid black, with bold lower case sans-serif lettering down its right-hand side, accompanied by a bleached image of Roger Daltrey in profile, gave way as the band changed its name to the singular Who logo: six plain letters with one embellishment, an arrow which originally pointed upwards out of the 'o', and was then moved to extend the vertical thrust of the central 'h', a graphic representation of the group's one central image: Pete Townshend's windmilling right arm at its apex, before crashing down on a rudimentary chord.

changed the name back to The Who, put it about that Townshend spent £100 a week on clothes, told him and Daltrey to prepare their own material, sat back and banked the dosh. Townshend's art-school education did the rest. There, he had been the admiring pupil of one Gustav Metzger, who had published an 'auto-destructive manifesto' in 1959. Metzger described auto-destructive art events as 'monuments to Hiroshima, where the material is squirming, writhing, where heat-bursts puncture the material. Auto-destructive monuments,' wrote Metzger, 'contain the brutality, the over-extended power, the nausea and unpredictability of our social systems.' On stage one lonely night, in the swirling shadow of Daltrey, Townshend took auto-destruction to dine with rock and roll. Towards the end of a set he took his Fender by the neck and, with white, grimly set features, smashed it upon the stage, against the microphone stand, through the mesh of the massive, miaowing speakers . . . in such ways did the exeception prove the rule, and did peaceniks (for Gustav Metzger was also a member of the Committee of 100) influence the careless culture of discontented youth.

But who, before The Who, was there for Mod? Not, in their early days, the Rolling Stones, too scruffy by half, and besides they ripped off (or 'covered', as the music industry carefully described it) perfectly good Chuck Berry numbers such as 'Come On'; and certainly not those anodyne moppets from Liverpool with their Tin Pan Alley tunes, their 'I Belong to You's and 'I Wanna Hold Your Hand's, those ersatz reminders of the detested dross of the 1950s—'Gilly Gilly Ossenfeffer' with a rhythm guitar; 'I See The Moon' with a nasal northern drawl and a basin cut. For a year or two at least, there was nothing particularly new about the Beatles.

What did they find to dance to, in the musical trough of the early 1960s? What was there, after the cultivated idiosyncrasy of Modern Jazz? There was American, mostly black American, electric soul. There was rhythm and blues. There were Dionne Warwick and Little Eva, Otis Redding, John Lee Hooker and the Isley Brothers. There were 'Green Onions', 'Do The Dog', 'Let The Good Times Roll' and 'Parchment Farm'—in the original, always in the original, booming through the cellars and the clubs of the suburbs and the city like rolling thunder, lifting the thousands of pale, wide-eyed teenagers into set and steady dance routines, beating through the strobe-lit, endless night. And slowly, steadily, live acts emerged to meet the mood. There were the Yardbirds at the Crawdaddy Club in 1963 (standing in for the Rolling Stones, who had just gone off to support Bo Diddley on tour) with their young Mod guitarist, Eric Clapton. There was Alexis Korner at Beat City, John Mayall's Bluesbreakers at Klooks Kleek, the Animals at Tiles, and everybody, but everybody, at the Marquee.

The clubs were the muster stations of Mod. Within cavernous walls of bare, damp brick, the young dedicatees congregated—and not only at weekends. In the Greater London area, if nowhere else, there was a possible, attainable apogee of style; quite unreachable by most but, like another planet, always there. It would begin on Monday evening at the Scene Club, fit in a dance on the Tuesday, and then move on Wednesday to La Discotheque. On Thursday: back to the Scene, the Marquee, or the Lyceum. Friday evenings saw *Ready, Steady, Go!* on television ('The weekend starts here!'), followed by the Scene or La Discotheque. Saturday morning, continues Richard Barnes, a south London Mod of the time: 'shopping down Carnaby Street, then to Imhoff's or some obscure record shop in Hampstead or Brixton. Saturday night to the Flamingo and Allnighter. Leave the Allnighter at four in the morning and go to a Sunday morning street market such as Petticoat Lane or Brick Lane for breakfast and to browse among the record and clothes stalls. Sunday afternoon back to the Flamingo for the afternoon session. Sunday evening to the Crawdaddy club in Richmond, ending up for a cappuccino at L'Auberge coffee bar by Richmond Bridge until midnight.'

It was a punishing, impossible schedule, but it was the grail. The trick was to be *there*, to be *seen*, to surrender rarely—if at all—to sleep and to the sullen comforts of the family home. And, above all, the place to be seen was Soho, whose narrow boundaries embraced the majority of these vital venues. Soho, a sixpenny bus-ride from the most distant suburb, where the High Numbers could be heard and seen dancing the Block: Pete Townshend with studious application in dark glasses, Keith Moon aping to his side, Roger Daltrey cracking up with laughter. The Block . . . 'crouch down, arms slightly bent, palms facing floor. Place one foot very quickly in front of the other, twisting heel as it lands. Spin round on back of heels, improvising intricate footwork. Tommy Tucker's "High Heel Sneakers" is good . . .'; The Ska, The Dog, The Hitch Hike, The Shake ('Stand firmly with one foot forward, arms stretched out, swing from side to side, nod the head. Shake the body from the hips and occasionally jump to the left or right. The Isley Brothers' "Twist And Shout" is a good Shake record.'). You saw it at the Scene, and next week the nation saw it on *Ready, Steady, Go!* To miss a night could be to miss a lifetime. The known world had a centre, and it was to be found within a square mile of the junction of Wardour Street and Shaftesbury Avenue, London, West One. Sixpence to get there, two bob to get in, a shilling or so for soft drinks—oh, and another bob or two for the pills that got you through the night. Through the night—hell, that got you through the *week*.

Mod, at its edgy, chattering, careening best, could not have happened without the recreational use of amphetamines. The legend 'SPEED KILLS' was painted in enormous letters on one wall of the Marquee, and just inside the entrance to La Discotheque, and past the ticket office, surrounded by notices which advertised future attractions and regretted the absence of passouts after 3 a.m., was a poster which read: '*£50 Reward: The management will pay £50 to any person who can provide concrete evidence direct to the police that any member of the management of The Discotheque Club is responsible for the sale of purple hearts*—The Committee.'

In the first half of the 1960s Purple Hearts became the most celebrated of the drugs used by young people for non-medical purposes. They filled the headlines and energised the police. They were small, cheap and relatively mild. (A small handful would be swallowed without second thought by an experienced clubber and one Mod who collapsed outside the Flamingo in Wardour Street was discovered, after timely application of the stomach pump, to have taken 76 of the rosy triangular tablets. He survived.) And they did the job—the job being to keep awake and alert for up to (and occasionally beyond) 48 consecutive hours. They were manufactured by Smith Kline and French of Welwyn Garden City, marketed as Drinamyl, and commonly prescribed by doctors as an antidote to depression. They became a form of subterranean currency, as everyday a commodity as—almost literally—sixpenny pieces, and the arrival of the police at any nightclub in the land was for a year or two invariably greeted by the patter of hundreds and thousands of Purple Hearts hitting the concrete floor, like a faery round of applause.

Drinamyl fittingly took its nickname from the United States

decoration for those wounded in action. Fittingly, because it was probably the Second World War which broadcast the recreational use of drugs widely among the working classes of the western world. Amphetamines, which were not properly developed until the late 1920s, were introduced into the medical cornucopia in the 1930s, and were issued like ammunition to soldiers of both the Allied and the Axis forces between 1939 and 1945. After Hiroshima, the huge war-time stockpile of drugs became available on the world market, and in many industrial nations amphetamines of various strengths were freely dispensed, with or without prescriptions. Housewives were routinely gratified with tumblers-full of amphetamine and depressant barbiturates to help them combat their strange existence; President John F. Kennedy, in constant pain from back injuries and Addison's disease, swung through his truncated period in office with the assistance of a daily cocktail of cortisone, procaine (a synthetic preparation of cocaine), and amphetamine.

There were generous portions of both hypocrisy and naïvety in the response of the British press and government to the discovery that a good number of the young of the land were taking stimulants to help them dance all night—a fact which was cleverly pointed out by the Rolling Stones in their song 'Mother's Little Helper'—but neither of those failings was ever likely to make journalists and politicians pause for thought. Henry Brooke, the Home Secretary in Macmillan's government, paid an anonymous visit to Soho, professed himself to be deeply disturbed, proposed a maximum fine of £200 or six months' imprisonment for those caught in possession of Drinamyl without an enabling prescription, and persuaded Smith Kline and French to repackage their goods in a different colour and a different shape. There being no trade so finely adapted to the hiccuping demands of the free market, so responsive to its whims and little local difficulties as the trade in illegal drugs, the price of Purple Hearts jumped by between 50 per cent and 100 per cent (to between ninepence and a shilling) and a range of other, less notorious, stimulants were put on sale.

Blues, dexes (dexedrine), and Black Bombers fuelled a world of sinister romance, a world which the tabloid press could not be expected to ignore. 'EXPOSING THE DRUG MENACE—A SUNDAY MIRROR WARNING TO PARENTS', shouted that newspaper in the May of 1964. 'ONE NIGHT WE BOUGHT

1,000 PURPLE HEARTS'. The *Sunday Mirror*'s reporters had, in fact, paid £18, or about fourpence each, for the poteen of the stimulant business: 1,000 amphetamine sulphate tablets—a cheap and rough form of speed not particularly favoured by Mods. But no matter, the point was made. The young of the land had created and were patronising a black, alternative economy of such enormous potential that, with their continuing support and protection, it could only grow in size, sophistication and diversity.' Scornful of Henry Brooke and the *Sunday Mirror*, regardless of laws—new and old—which were brought into play to counter it, and dismissive of the medical and moral advice of adult society, the import, wholesale and retail trade in illegal drugs by young, white British males began its bullish ascent.

These, then, were the people who blew poor Buttons off his feet. These were the thousands who made tracks for Clacton, Brighton and Margate in the spring and summer of 1964 and 1965, and who, in doing so, generated in their elders the first of the mass hysterias of the 1960s. They were not all, of course, zipped on amphetamines (although most would like to *think* that they were), and they did not all have a scooter (or even a pillion seat). Not all of them preferred Bo Diddley and Mose Allison to the Rolling Stones (a good number of them, by the law of averages, must even have bought Beatles' singles) and most were not possessed of a pair of Zigoni shoes or a Mohair-and-tonic suit. Some, just possibly, may never even have been to La Discotheque or danced on *Ready, Steady, Go!* Mod was a broad church; there was room for most within its cool, appraising patronage. Room for most, excepting those regrettable few with oil-stained jeans and lank and matted hair, torn leathers, unwashed socks, and pretensions to owning a fast, expensive motorbike.

Here are two photographs, both taken in 1964. The first is of the beach at Margate in May. It measures 12 square inches, and it is not big enough. From outside of the frame Mods pour in; wearing parkas, dark glasses, and Fred Perrys done up at the neck. Once there, in centre-stage, they stand and look around, at the sky and at each other. Some light a cigarette, some laugh at a joke, and some watch approvingly as the hundreds beyond the camera's lens park scooters on the promenade and troop like a cup final crowd down the old stone steps to the sea. In the foreground sits an unexpectant family, a canvas windshield between them and the gathering storm, grandfather in flat cap, jumper and jacket, mother helping baby to build sandcastles. Who *are* all these teenagers? To whom do they belong?

The second is a much smaller print, of the Walthamstow Rockers. Buttons is there, wearing his buttons, beside an engaging youth in brothel creepers. A lad in an outsize cheese-cutter cap gazes nervously over their shoulders. In all, Buttons' Walthamstow Rockers number eleven and there is no evidence of a single motorbike between them. Great Britain would never be motorcycle country—Buttons and his friends stood not a chance; the Mods versus Rockers clashes of 1964 and 1965 mattered hardly at all. They were simply a sideshow on the edge of the main, unpublicised event: the first reckless collision between the young iconoclasts and three of the Four Estates of the Realm.

The press, the Lords Temporal, and the Commons were first jolted into reaction by occurrences at a small Essex holiday resort during the Easter weekend of 1964. Clacton-on-Sea stands 12 miles south-east of Colchester, overlooking the grey English Channel. In 1964 those who worked in Clacton (and that was by no means all of the adult population: the town was both a dormitory and a retirement residential zone) worked largely in the tourist trade and in light—extremely light—industry. Clacton would never gather the nerve to advertise itself as a fashionable resort, but it was handy enough, and therefore fashionable enough, to the residents of the East End of London. Throughout the 1950s, with their slow but steady consolidation of working-class wages, Clacton had become one of the seaside towns which expected regularly to benefit from day-trippers and holiday weekenders, from the sale of whelks and the hire of deckchairs, from the noisy lure of the arcades and the patter of the bingo-stalls, the vending of fish and chips and of cardboard cowboy hats.

And for those from the urban conurbations who owned a set of motorised wheels, Clacton had another advantage. It stood just a few miles from the A12, a stretch of highway which followed a smooth, straight course out of London, through Romford and Ilford, north of the Essex Marshes towards Lowestoft and the Anglian seaboard. The A12 was a flat and undemanding trail, and it made Clacton-on-Sea just two hours' ride from the outskirts of London for anybody in possession of a Lambretta LI 150.

Mods had visited Clacton before that Easter weekend of 1964, but never in such numbers. The town had a population of 30,000, and about a thousand sharply-dressed young people had congregated on the sands, the promenade and the pier by 29 March, Easter Sunday. They had chosen a bad weekend. It was wet, windy and cold—the coldest Easter Sunday, it was later revealed, since 1884. Hundreds of teenagers, many of whom had arrived on the previous day and spent a doleful, drugged and drunken night on the beach, zipped their parkas and toggled their duffle coats against the chilling wind, and huddled over formica-topped tables in the cafés and the pubs. Then, in the early afternoon, Clacton-on-Sea shut down for the day. The pubs and those of the cafés which had chosen to open so far in advance of the season proper emptied. At midday the tide was fully in, rendering even the beach unusable. A thousand Mods determined to make their own fun.

The pier was still open, but charging a shilling for entrance. Some boys jumped the turnstile. Others experimented with using the promenade helter-skelter from finishing-line through to start. One young man stole a sevenpenny ice-cream, in that he received it from the stall-keeper and, rather than hand over the cash, ran away. A small group tried to shake refreshments out of a soft drinks machine. Scuffles broke out, mostly unconvincing affairs between Mods themselves, but one or two Rockers who had unwisely eschewed their normal meet 30 miles down the Essex coast at Southend in favour of a jaunt to Clacton, were chased with more sound than fury through the nervous provincial streets. Those stallholders who were still open, quickly closed down or refused to serve anybody over the age of 14 and under the age of 25. A starting pistol was repeatedly fired into the air from the pillion seat of a scooter which puttered back and forth along the sea front. Some unaffiliated young bloods disgorged from their Ford Consuls and Cortinas and joined in the fun, one of them throwing a chisel—inaccurately—at a group of policemen. As the tide went out small bands of youths chased loudly up and down the damp sands, dismantling beach-huts as they passed. Deck chairs were thrown through the windows of some of the establishments which, it was rumoured, had failed to serve putative customers in Fred Perry sports shirts.

Nobody was hurt at Clacton-on-Sea over the Easter weekend of 1964, but on Sunday there were 60 policemen on duty in the town, and they made 97 arrests. On the following day, Easter Monday, reinforcements were brought in from the furthest reaches of the county of Essex, as far away as Harlow on the distant border with Hertfordshire. They had little to do. A group of two dozen Mods were refused breakfast in a café; they stood their ground, and the frightened proprietor called in the police. Two arrests were promptly and arbitrarily made, and equally promptly resisted. A helmet went flying, and the two young men were frogmarched out of the café. A group of about a hundred Mods, male and female, quickly assembled and followed the arresting officers and their victims down the street until two patrol cars arrived on the scene and another group of policemen disembarked from them and waded, truncheons held high, into the crowd of protesting teenagers. The two hungry Mods were shovelled into one of the cars and sped to Clacton police station, later to be discharged for the lack of evidence that they had committed any offence against the law of the land.

But that was more or less that. By late on Monday morning the majority of the thousand Mods, their clothes already wet and by then clearly in danger of being further damaged by the rough hands of the law, had pointed their multiple headlights south-west along the A12, towards Ilford and Romford, Barking, Woolwich and Richmond. Or they dug out their weekend return tickets, and caught the train. Of the hundred who had been arrested between Friday night and Monday morning, only 24 were eventually charged, and only two with crimes of violence. There was violence in Clacton-on-Sea that Easter weekend, but it was violence against property, and it amounted to £513 in repair bills to beach huts, deckchairs and plate-glass windows. Most of the 24 were charged with obstructing the police in the course of their duties, or with the use of 'threatening behaviour'. If Britain had, as the press coverage and parliamentary uproar was to suggest, unwittingly nurtured a generation of Visigoths, then they were Visigoths who, when it came to the finer points of loot, rape and arson, lacked conviction.

There was, however, not much news about at the end of March 1964. Civil war in Cyprus and a tidal wave in Alaska were proving to exercise a limited hold on the domestic audience. The sacking of Clacton landed upon newsdesks like a blessing. It became the leading front page story in every national newspaper in Britain (with the singular exception of the London *Times*, whose front page was filled with classified advertisements until 1966, and the headlines were heaven sent. Everybody knew of Marlon Brando's biker film, *The Wild One*, even if they only knew of its title; and everybody knew of Home Secretary Henry

Brooke's furtive visits to the young people's clubs of central London, and of his subsequent Drugs (Prevention of Misuse) Bill. '"WILD ONES" INVADE SEASIDE—97 ARRESTS' announced Easter Monday's *Daily Mirror*. Beside a photograph of a couple of confused youths talking to a policeman with a large Alsatian at his side, the *Mirror*'s report told of 'fighting, drinking, roaring, rampaging teenagers on scooters and motor-cycles . . . A desperate SOS went out from police at Clacton, Essex, as leather-jacketed youths and girls attacked people in the streets, turned over parked cars, broke into beach huts, smashed windows, and fought with rival gangs. Police reinforcements from other Essex towns raced to the shattered resort, where fearful residents had locked themselves indoors . . .'*

The *Mirror*'s reporter had not, of course, been in Clacton on that apocalyptic Sabbath. By Monday, however, the Essex coastline was thick with journalists. 'Last night,' Ann Leslie told readers of the *Daily Express*, 'Clacton was still flinching as violence fizzed and fizzled like a dying bonfire under the Easter Monday rain and a chill wind sweeping off a sulky sea . . . a whole town has come under mob rule . . . These young people, born into a society of free orange juice, glass school rooms, neat council homes, are brave enough to clatter down like locusts on Clacton . . . What are they trying to prove, these Mods, doll-like, meticulous, blasé . . . ?' And those purple hearts? 'There's no use saying I don't take them,' a boy called Lucky told the *Daily Herald*. 'Maybe you can see it. Everybody takes them now.'

Drugs, drink, and the dangerous use of motorised vehicles, whatever their causative links to classrooms with windows and the issuing of orange juice to infants, were never likely to be ignored by the two Houses of Parliament. On Tuesday, 31 March, Henry Brooke's Drugs Bill was published. In April, Frank Taylor MP demanded of the House of Commons: 'That this House in the light of the deplorable and continual increase in juvenile delinquency and in particular the recent regrettable events in Clacton, urges the Secretary of State for Home Department to give urgent

---

* The assistant editor of the *Daily Mirror* apparently admitted later that his newspaper's coverage of the events at Clacton had been 'a little over-reported'. For lyrical flights of fancy the *Mirror*'s reportage compared nicely with the Glasgow *Daily Record*, which told its readers that Mods were to be identified by their bell-bottom trousers, high boots, bowler- or top-hats and rolled-up umbrellas—uncannily like the street gangs in Anthony Burgess's novel about the tyranny of youth, *A Clockwork Orange*.

and serious consideration to the need for young hooligans to be given such financial and physical punishment as will provide an effective deterrent.'

Clearly, it was time once again for the birch. In the House of Lords the Earl of Arran focused his eccentric gaze on the Vespas and Lambrettas, tabling a motion which called for the raising of the minimum driving licence age from 16 to 19 'in view of the invasion of Clacton by young motor cyclists on Easter Sunday'. On 1 April, April Fool's Day, Arran was quoted in the London *Evening News* as saying: 'I am truly sorry for Clacton—a nice warm-hearted place. If some town had to cop it, I would have preferred Frinton. They are snooty at Frinton.'

After that Easter weekend of 1964, Mods found themselves indissolubly linked in the media and in the public fantasy to Rockers, a section of society which they generally despised and which most of them would sooner have simply ignored. Like any minority thirsty for recognition, Rockers contrarily blossomed in this shower of unexpected publicity, which seemed to reinforce their quaint view of themselves as a tightly-knit band of hard-bitten outlaws, slow to rouse but devastating in their anger. What could be more satisfying to a Rocker (or more demeaning to a Mod) than to be described on the front page of Britain's most popular daily newspaper as 'Wild Ones'? It was a prize not to be lightly cast aside, and for this, as much as any other reason, the scuffles and the shouting at south coast resorts, and the consequent delighted hubbub in the press, achieved a crazed dynamic throughout the spring and summer months of 1964 and 1965. When, two months after Clacton, the Whitsun holiday weekend of 1964 came around, the police, the media, the parliamentarians and the magistrates were ready. Everybody was ready.

Very few Mods returned to Essex that May. Instead, they travelled south, to Bournemouth, to Brighton and to Margate. The small assembly of Hampshire and Dorset youngsters which met beneath Georgian façades and frosty, respectable stares in Bournemouth were accused of causing £100-worth of damage to beach furniture, and 56 of them were arrested. But Brighton and Margate gained most notoriety that Whitsun weekend; Brighton because in that town there really were widespread running skirmishes between the more militant Mods and groups of Rockers; and Margate because of the unforgettable, wonderfully quotable comments and Rhadamanthine sentences which were delivered by Dr

George Simpson, the chairman of the local magistrates' court. By Whitsunday and Monday, Brighton was thronged by up to 3,000 Mods, crammed and jostling along the promenade and inside the overworked cafés. But there were a couple of hundred Rockers, jeering on the fringes of this mass event, this prototypical festival without music, this rally without speeches, gathering without a focus . . . Punches, kicks and deckchairs were thrown, and a small amount of blood—mostly greaser blood, the Mods congratulated themselves—was spilt. While the majority stood around and assessed the available talent, in different areas of the beach, two Mods received minor stab wounds. Their fellows, upon receipt of this information, might well have exacted a terrible price from the Rockers, had there been enough Rockers around to make themselves obvious. But, by the end of Sunday, 17 May, there was hardly a Rocker in sight at Brighton. One or two stragglers were beaten up on the sands before mounted police rode in and arrested a total of 76 people. At 7.30 p.m. on Whit Monday, in a curious precursor of tactics which were to be employed for the 'control' of football crowds, 300 policemen formed a cordon between the beach and Brighton railway station, and marched the remainder of the holiday-making Mods along this blue corridor to the London train. At Preston Park station, a mile and a half up the line, local police officers were detailed to allow no young person off the train unless he or she could provide incontrovertible proof of residence in the vicinity.

Brighton in May, 1964, was probably the biggest, the most eventful, and—by virtue of its several fights and its two stabbings—the most dangerous of all the celebrated Bank Holiday fracas of the mid-1960s. Margate, over the same weekend, attracted fewer people, made a voguishly disproportionate number of arrests (64), and suffered very little damage. But Margate achieved overnight fame because one of its magistrates articulated most successfully the fear and the loathing which middle England felt, from its guts to its throbbing temples, for this phenomenon of its own invention: its feckless, carefree, stoned and drunken post-imperial young.

George Simpson, a small, jowly man, had been a general practitioner of medicine in the Kent resort for 24 years when Margate was visited by a few hundred Mods and a couple of dozen Rockers at Whitsun, 1964. On the Sunday evening, having been made aware that he was to be a busy fellow in the magistrates' court on the following morning, Simpson and his wife wandered through Margate to assess the level of disruption. Mrs Simpson admitted to seeing nothing more than 'how tired the policemen looked ... the town was full of dirty grubby teenagers' (a peculiarity which, she considered, 'must not be allowed to happen again'), while at her side her husband was silently composing incendiary comments and considering the benefits of prison sentences in moulding the characters of the young.

On the morning of Whit Monday Dr Simpson was presented with his first case, a young Londoner who pleaded guilty to using 'threatening behaviour'—that catch-all charge used so often by the police after randomly hauling a specimen of the enemy from the security of his colleagues' company. George Simpson then delivered his first, and most celebrated, homily and sentence.

'It is not likely,' he told the young man, the crowded press box, and the rest of Great Britain, 'that the air of this town has ever been polluted by the hordes of hooligans, male and female, such as we have seen this weekend and of whom you are an example. These long-haired, mentally unstable, petty little hoodlums, these sawdust Caesars* who can only find courage like rats, in hunting in packs, came to Margate with the avowed intent of interfering with the life and property of its inhabitants. Insofar as the law gives us power, this court will not fail to use the prescribed penalties. It will, perhaps discourage you and others of your kidney who are infected with this vicious virus, that you will go to prison for three months.'

Even the policemen in the court whistled in surprise. And Dr Simpson had only just started. He was dealing with a 'general pattern of deliberate viciousness', he told reporters later, which had reached 'colossal national proportions'. If the rot was destined to be stopped by a little man in little Margate, by a Captain Mainwaring of the magistrates' courts, then so be it. George Simpson handed out prison sentences where possible, detention sentences to the under-aged, and fines of £50 to £75 (a month to two months' wages) when the spirit of leniency fell briefly upon him, accompanying each judgement with a pithy insult ('the dregs of these vermin ... this procession of miserable specimens') while

---

* Those two words, 'sawdust Caesars', dominated the headlines on the following day, and have become George Simpson's legacy to British social history. It is difficult to uncover the meaning of this curious expression. It is not, as many supposed at first, a quotation from great literature, and nor is it an antique folk-saying. It is only possible to assume that Dr Simpson, inspired solely by a fondness of alliteration, invented it.

girlfriends cried out from the gallery, and the national press, wide-eyed and excited, scribbled furiously to keep apace of the doctor's riotous imagination.

The hour had come, but not the man ... George Simpson, the Leonidas of the British bourgeoisie, with Margate his Thermopylae, became a hero for a day. His views upon most imaginable subjects were sought by the press, he was profiled and praised and prayed for, and then he slipped back into the obscurity from which he had, however briefly, hauled himself. Outside of Margate, George Simpson was never heard from again. Mods did not return to Margate, not only because of the welcome which waited for them there, but because they believed in switching regularly the venues of their Bank Holiday meets. George Simpson, as a consequence, was given no more opportunities to air his mixed metaphors and practise his dismal sarcasm. And his actions did not, of course, stop the arrests in other parts of the country. How could they have done so? A large proportion of the young people picked up by the police and charged with obstruction, or threatening behaviour, or loitering, had actually done *nothing*, other than turn up at the seaside in the middle of a national panic. They were the objects of exemplary arrests, carried out to pacify the citizenry and (more in hope than expectation) to deter their peers. They were arrested so that the Bournemouth police could not be accused of lagging behind those in Clacton, or Brighton behind Bournemouth, or Margate behind Brighton ... and most of the youngsters who pleaded guilty did so because they believed that the fines would be reasonably light in view of their lack of previous convictions, because they believed that a guilty plea would encourage the magistrates in their moderation, and, most importantly, because they recognised, correctly, that no matter what their plea and no matter how strongly argued and substantiated was their case, justice would not be done to them; they would be found guilty as charged.

In the dying months of his ministerial career, Home Secretary Brooke pushed a new Malicious Damage Bill through parliament. It received its third reading in the House of Commons on 2 July, and became law on 31 July. 'I hope that, with the help of the House, it will be in operation before the August Bank Holiday,' stated the Home Secretary. 'NEW MOVE TO STAMP OUT MOD VIOLENCE', applauded the headlines. The August Bank Holiday began on the following day, the first of the month. The

Home Office restrained itself from calling a state of emergency from Lands End to the Cinque Ports, but it did, remarkably, put 69 officers from Scotland Yard's Flying Squad on red alert at RAF Northolt, with instructions to board an air force transport 'plane and proceed to whichever resort put forward the strongest claim for assistance. Throughout Saturday and Sunday morning those policemen sat by Northolt airstrip. Sunday lunchtime came and went, and then, late on the Sunday afternoon, they were scrambled. Three or four fights had broken out in Hastings, where up to 3,000 Mods, and the obligatory few dozen Rockers, had been milling about all weekend. The arrival upon the scene of 69 hungry policemen warmed things up, and ultimately 18 young men were taken into custody—18 teenagers out of 3,000, and all on the usual tired old charges. 'He was one of a group of 400 people racing along the foreshore,' Inspector Stanley Russell told Hastings magistrates' court, to explain the arrest of a 16-year-old—'he was seen to throw beach stones.' But it was Hastings, and how the sub-editors had been praying for Hastings. You cannot, after all, do very much with Clacton or with Margate, but slap the two words 'Battle Of' before the name of Hastings and what folk memories are roused from their fitful sleep, what vague impressions of invasion and despoilment by an alien force are strewn from coast to coast? There were five arrests at Brighton and ten in Great Yarmouth on that August Bank Holiday, but they were merely footnoted beneath the glorious 69 who flew from RAF Northolt to Hastings in defence of England's honour.

As if to indicate that it was uninfluenced by party politics (Harold Wilson's Labour Government came to power in October 1964), this giddy circus moved from town to town throughout 1965, and as it did so the original spirit of Mod slowly sickened and died. The pretexts for arrest grew thinner with every Bank Holiday, and the sentences more severe. A common punishment for 'wilful obstruction' at Brighton that year was one to two weeks in police custody while 'inquiries were made', followed by three months in a detention centre or in prison, or a heavy fine. 'Do you call this justice?' shouted 17-year-old Phillip Britten of New Cross at the Brighton magistrates' court after being sent down for three months for 'obstructing the police'. 'Do you call this British justice?' he asked, hammering his fist against the side of the dock as the officers took his arms and led him back to the cells.

Those who were not arrested were penned in by policemen

on shingle beaches, ring-fenced from the cafés and the promenades, and escorted out of town at the first signs of frustration. It was not much fun to be a Mod any more, at Brighton, or Margate, or Hastings.

And the style which Mod had espoused, the slick and speedy elegance, was becoming lost in this sordid round of fisticuffs and nights in damp police stations. There had been a dandy element in original Mod; there had been a sense of continental European *chic*; there had been a substantial acceptance of men who would come to be known as gay; and a genuine curiosity about black culture. There had been good clothes and fast-talking, excellent music and skilful dance, and aesthetics which did not square with firing sawn-off shotguns into the chest of people like Buttons . . . *even* people like Buttons . . . or with carrying short, heavy hammers for self-defence to the Bank Holiday meets. By then, by the time that Buttons was shot outside the Bonanza Amusement Arcade in 1965, the end was in sight.

Young men and women who called themselves Mods would be seen on the streets of the cities in 1966 and even into 1967, but they were few and they were out of their time. By the end of 1965 the inspiration of Mod had expired, not at the hands of Henry Brooke, or George Simpson, or the police forces of the south-east coast, or—perish the thought—of Rockers, but rather, because the creative elements of the independent youth culture which Mod had done so much to broadcast had flowed in other directions. There was new and better fun to be had in other clothes, to the sound of different music, with wholly fresh ambitions, and under the influence of strange, untested drugs.

CHAPTER THREE

DOPE

You couldn't touch anything in Goodman's house in Seven Kings 'cos you'd trip. You'd open the fridge at this house and there'd be bottles and bottles of acid. There'd be more acid in the fridge than food, and Boss likes his food. You had to be really careful what you touched—you'd be sitting there and you'd touch furniture and you'd get contact.

STEVE SPARKS, FRIEND OF DAVID 'BOSS' GOODMAN

'We have watched them patiently through the wilder excesses of their ban the bomb marches. Smiled indulgently as they've wrecked our cinemas during their rock and roll films . . .' So said the Scottish *Sunday Mail* in the May of 1964, suggesting that Great Britain's patience with its upstart teenagers had worn uncommon thin, and a good job too. Even considering its distant northern redoubt, the *Sunday Mail* is not to be excused for its assumption that the young men in Edwardian suits who slashed cinema seats during showings of *Rock Around the Clock* in 1956, were still teenagers on weekend outings to Brighton in 1964 and 1965, or for its assertion that the eager, earnest youngsters who carried banners from Aldermaston to Trafalgar Square in 1961, were running up and down Hastings beach chucking handfuls of pebbles at each other three years later.

But the *Sunday Mail* was not alone. After all, hugely important questions were there to be answered: who were these young people? Where did they come from, what did they want, how much were they about to destroy? There *had* to be a link . . . 'You can expect it [riots] every weekend now—it will go on just like the [Aldermaston] marchers,' warned one south-coast councillor. 'Now that the Aldermaston marches are finished, you have all these kids running around with nothing to do,' echoed a youth leader. Even Bernard de Vries of the anarcho-communalist

Amsterdam Provos advised the British left that Mods could, given the opportunity, turn into a force for the New Order.

De Vries was more percipient about Mods than he knew. His error was in assuming that when the great conversion came, Mods would still be Mods. Mods had not taken part, as Mods, in the marches from Aldermaston because such activities were not their style. Getting wet, wearing out the soles of shoes, and sitting down in the road in front of the Ministry of War did not fit into their posing, strutting, self-absorbed sensibility. (They would also have disliked the accompanying music, the guitar-strumming and the early protest songs, traditional jazz and hymns of solidarity.) Despite being excoriated and legislated against in parliament, despite having their clubs regularly raided and their friends arrested and imprisoned on trumped-up charges, despite the nervous wooing of the fledgling New Left, Mods remained adamantly apolitical. There were, after all, principles and principles, and the over-riding Mod principle was the principle of style.

On the face of it, Mods had some things in common with another phenomenon which was causing the authorities concern in the first half of the 1960s. The Beats, unlike Mods, were neither numerous nor working-class nor an indigenous, British movement. They took their cultural lead from the 1950s Americans of Jack Kerouac's generation, and from the remnants of those foot-loose lyricists, Lawrence Ferlinghetti, Allen Ginsberg and William Burroughs. Within their European context the Beats leaned upon the radical avant-gardes of France, Holland and Italy, and they did largely adhere to the politics of CND. Not all of this was entirely outside the scope of Mod. Faces in the early Mod ensemble liked to show an intelligent interest in the films of Jean-Luc Godard. They would smoke Gitanes, drink cappuccino, and carry a French newspaper under their arm. Teenage girls could gain a cachet by entering the Sombrero coffee bar in Brighton and taking a George Orwell paperback from their bucket bags. Mod, at its best, was a broad, tolerant and curious church. And there was an item in the inventory of both Mod and Beat which held them together even before they realised it, and which helped them—when the time became right, as it very shortly would—to squeeze into the same cubicle and to emerge, shockingly, as one body, as a shared reincarnation wearing garish clothes and smiling placidly. Mod was united with the unkempt, existentialist Beat; and they were both anathematised by the executives of the Young

Conservatives, Young Liberals, Young Socialists and Young Communist Leaguers of their day thanks to one simple, wildly important detail. Both Mods and Beats bought, sold, and used illegal drugs. Unashamedly.

They were not always the same drugs, of course. Beats, being none too interested in dancing all night, had little use for speed. Theirs were the soporifics and woozy depressants, the mild hallucinogens and the serious narcotics: alcohol, marijuana, very occasionally heroin and, for one or two early settlers on the distant boundaries of society, lysergic acid diethylamide-25, which was already known by the acronym which became famous: LSD.

Just as not all Mods owned a scooter or spent every weekend sleepless in Soho, so only a minority of those who could broadly be classified as Beats dabbled in the stronger drugs. Heroin was used by William Burroughs and by Alex Trocchi (whose *Cain's Book*, published in 1960, was utterly and appallingly frank on the subject of addiction)—and the summer of LSD was yet to come. But in the years between the last great march from Aldermaston in 1963 and the final despairing disturbances at Brighton in 1965, the dried leaves and the processed resin of the plant *Cannabis sativa* began to find a constituency among the young which would spread so incorrigibly that, before the decade was out, a sizeable proportion of the population of Britain was living in contempt of the law.

The distribution and consumption of hash and grass made some quaint bedfellows in the early 1960s. Christine Keeler's impulsive friend, Lucky Gordon, rubbed shoulders on the stairways of houses in Notting Hill Gate with the young, white, Bohemian intelligentsia; the publishers of roneoed art and poetry magazines scored from the same dealer as Michael de Freitas, who later, as Michael X, became London's most troublesome Black Power leader, and was hanged in Trinidad for murder.

And that is the way that the market in illegal drugs for recreational use might have stayed, a prerogative of urban blacks and of the dabbling, daring few among the bright young things of the metropolis. It might have remained a world as remote and as hermetically sealed from the bulk of the young of the rest of the country as had been the world of opium and cocaine use in Edwardian times and in the 1920s, if it had not been for that trade, which had grown strong and supple in the clubs, in the coffee bars, and on the seaside promenades; a black market whose function had originally been to provide the working young with amphetamines to see them through their leisure hours, and which, when the time came, was flexible enough to extend the range of its wares. The youth culture of the 1960s, the various strands which came together in the middle of the decade, which found a broad consensus of taste in clothing, music, vocabulary, reading matter and even—however loosely—in its extra-parliamentary politics, was knitted together more than anything else by the shared use of illegal drugs.

The bedrock of this sub-culture, the small beer of its everyday life, was hashish. Many young whites may have been initiated into the sacramental use of marijuana by casual acquaintanceship with immigrants, and the children of immigrants, from the West Indies. But the fondness of young blacks for joints the size of howitzers, skilfully constructed out of several dozen cigarette papers ('skins', in the argot), and containing only marijuana leaves, did not transfer itself for long to the art schools, the clubs and the bed-sitting rooms. Hashish, concentrated resin, which could comfortably be accommodated, with tobacco, in a rolled cigarette little larger than a king-size Marlboro, and which could be transported in bulk in a hold-all or a rucksack, became the white person's preference. It could be sold in tiny quantities (a 'quid deal', the typical Saturday-night takeaway would, in the middle of the 1960s, when a pound of hash might cost £50, be roughly the size of an Oxo cube). The dealing of hashish quickly became the most successful self-contained commercial enterprise in this youthful counter-culture. It made some people a lot of money, and gave a great many others a form of regular income which, in its nature, did not affect their claiming of unemployment benefit. The movement of hashish from its native lands inspired and financed travel, and the shared use of the drug became a point of reference for the young people of two continents. Hashish, for a few years, came very close to being an alternative currency.

Pills, amphetamines and barbiturates, uppers and downers, Mandrax, Valium, and speed of various kinds, found their way into the portable pharmacies of the professional dealers of the mildly habitual hashish; but it was two other, hotter, heavier products which were to ring the changes in and after this strange period. One was unpopular at first, widely recognised as dangerous, even ostracised by purists and by the educated, and contrarily its use, when the 1960s were over, was destined to reach epidemic proportions. The other dictated to the popular art forms of the second half of the decade, its occasional use became a crucial rite of passage, very few suffered or died from it, and when the 1970s dawned, it slipped from fashion as quickly as it had arrived. The first was commonly recognised for what it was: destructive of life and of personalities, uncontrollable, a power-brokers' drug. The second was largely manufactured, marketed and controlled by members or friends of the sub-culture, and in its brief period of popularity it could light up the plainest of lives like a firework display. The second was LSD, and the first, the sad survivor, was heroin.

Lysergic Acid Diethylamide-25, also known as lysergide (and bought and sold and taken from Salzburg to San Francisco as, simply, acid), was first synthesised in Switzerland in 1938 by two chemists who were investigating the possible therapeutic effects of compounds of ergot, a parasitic fungus which is sometimes found on rye and other grains. Ergot alkaloids are not normally psycho-active (which is to say that they do not normally cause halluci-nations), they have a long history of medical use, and LSD-25 seemed, after its early tests on animals, to have no particularly original effects. It was not until five years later that one of the chemists, Albert Hofmann, accidentally discovered for himself what his guinea pigs had gone through in 1938.

Hofmann got some powdered LSD-25 on his fingertips in the afternoon of 16 April 1943, and unwittingly swallowed it. 'I was seized by a peculiar sensation of vertigo and restlessness,' he recorded later. 'Objects, as well as the shape of my associates in the laboratory, appeared to undergo optical changes. I was unable to concentrate on my work. In a dreamlike state I left for home, where an irresistible urge to lie down overcame me. I drew the curtains and immediately fell into a peculiar state similar to drunkenness, characterised by an exaggerated imagination. With my eyes closed, fantastic pictures of extraordinary plasticity and intensive colour seemed to surge towards me. After two hours this state gradually wore off.'

Having become the first human being to take an acid trip, Albert Hofmann determined also to be the second . . .

'I decided to get to the root of the matter by taking a definite quantity of the compound in question. Being a cautious man, I started my experiment by taking 0.25 mg . . . After 40 minutes I noted the following symptoms in my laboratory journal: slight giddiness, restlessness, difficulty in concentration, visual distur-bances, laughing . . . I lost all count of time. I noticed with dismay that my environment was undergoing progressive changes. My visual field wavered and everything appeared deformed as in a faulty mirror. Space and time became more and more disorganised and I was overcome by a fear that I was going out of my mind. The worst part of it being that I was clearly aware of my condition. My power of observation was unimpaired . . .

'Occasionally I felt as if I were out of my body. I thought I had died. My ego seemed suspended somewhere in space, from where I saw my dead body lying on the sofa. It was particularly striking how acoustic perceptions, such as the noise of water gushing from a tap or the spoken word, were transformed into optical illusions. I then fell asleep and awakened the next morning somewhat tired but otherwise feeling perfectly well.'

Seeing sounds and hearing colours, the death of the ego and the merging of space and time . . . Hofmann's diaries remain the best advertising copy written for LSD-25. But the drug had a long and winding road to take between Switzerland in the rage of World War Two, and *Sergeant Pepper's Lonely Heart's Club Band*.

While some well-meaning souls, such as Abraham Hoffer at the University of Saskatchewan in Canada, spent their 1950s exploring the beneficial effects of LSD-25 as an aid to psychotherapy (their experiments in this field were to prove fruitless), the drug was falling into more sinister hands. At the end of World War Two the American Central Intelligence Agency launched a research programme which they named 'ARTICHOKE'. This programme pre-dated, in many ways, some of the more subversive ambitions of the 1960s counter-culturalists, in that the CIA slipped LSD and other hallucinogenics to unprepared and often unwitting soldiers and other citizens.* Enthused by their success in rendering normal, upright, rational individuals down to a wide-eyed,

---

* It was a former US Army officer, Captain Alfred Hubbard, who helped to introduce the British writer Aldous Huxley to LSD. Huxley, who was by then in his sixties and had settled permanently in California, was entranced by the drug and wrote a celebrated essay, *The Doors of Perception*, which extolled its merits. The quotation ('If the doors of perception were cleansed everything would appear to man as it is, infinite') was taken, of course, from another British writer, William Blake, who died more than a century before the synthesis of LSD-25 but whose capacity to see such things as 'a World in a grain of sand,/And a Heaven in a wild flower', granted him a kind of posthumous shamanism in the acid generation. One of the better rock groups of the 1960s, *The Doors*, was to lift its name from the Blake/Huxley line.

Extraordinarily, it appears that Huxley also took LSD with the *Time/Life* magazine magnate, Henry Luce, his wife Clare Boothe Luce, and yet another British writer, Christopher Isherwood. Luce subsequently claimed to have met God on a golf course. The secret life of LSD in 1950s America is, if anything, an unopened door . . .

gawping vestige of their former selves, the CIA began to picture, with a dawning apprehension, the effect that small quantities of this substance could have on the populations of whole cities. Of whole *Russian* cities. Or how an undesirable presidential candidate might appear on the campaign trail, if his morning coffee had been spiked with 0.25 mg of LSD. Or how otherwise intransigent interviewees might, with all ego gone, all temporal concerns cast to the multi-coloured winds, embrace their interrogators and sing like canaries in paradise.

The CIA financed its second LSD programme in 1953, and they code-named it 'MK-ULTRA'. This project resulted in the first recorded acid casualty, and in the conception of the spirit of 'Hippy'.

Dr Frank Olsen was a biological warfare researcher who made the mistake, one evening in the 1950s, of attending an 'informal work conference' with other army technicians in Maryland. The CIA, keen as ever to open the doors of perception, doctored all the drinks. Olsen never recovered. He became paranoid (if his subsequent claims of harassment by the CIA can justly be described as paranoia), heard voices, sunk into deep depressions, and after some weeks he offered up his resignation. The CIA took Olsen to a psychiatrist in New York, and during his period of counselling he threw himself through a closed window on the tenth floor of a Manhattan hotel. Ten years later, when it had become politic for the agencies and disinformers of the state to spread dire warnings about the effects of LSD-25, the story of the death of Dr Frank Olsen would be told as if it were a commonplace: LSD makes its users jump out of windows. Poor Frank Olsen. There should be a memorial.

In 1959 the MK-ULTRA programme came to the attention of a young writer named Ken Kesey, who had arrived in California the previous year to attend Stanford University. By 1959 MK-ULTRA was based at the Veterans' Hospital in Menlo Park, San Francisco. The days of dosing unsuspecting biological warfare researchers had passed, and the Vets' Hospital was offering $100 a time to anybody who would come in, swallow a hallucinogenic, and answer questions about the experience. Kesey enjoyed himself (he was later to reveal that large parts of his first, bestselling novel *One Flew Over The Cuckoo's Nest*, which was published in 1962, were written while he was under the influence of hallucinogenics). He took some of the substances home, and shared them with his friends. Two years later, Kesey's overnight success as America's brightest literary hope dramatically broadened his social circle: the old lions of the Beat scene descended upon his Californian home; suddenly Neal Cassady himself (Dean Moriarty from Jack Kerouac's *On The Road*) became part of a group which referred to itself as the Merry Pranksters—a group whose subsequent activities entered the folklore of the 1960s, who were lionised by Tom Wolfe in *The Electric Kool-Aid Acid Test*, and who, like all great legends, operated only partly in the realms of reality . . .

For Kesey had come up with A Great Notion. A bus, a 1939 International Harvester school bus, was purchased. Its interior was converted into living and sleeping quarters, and its traction was customised to the requirements of the demonic driver, Neal Cassady, the outrider of the freeway. A turret was installed upon the roof of the bus to serve as a viewing platform; a platform was attached to its rear to hold a generator; a refrigerator was filled with LSD-25 and other drugs; the bus itself was painted in swirls and filigrees of primary and pastel colours—the kind of shapes and colours that you could *hear*, the patterns and shades that would shortly decorate the walls of apartments and squatted houses across the western world—and on 14 June 1964, 14 Pranksters, this wonderful confusion of born-again Beats and prototype Hippies, with Neal Cassady lined and laconic at the wheel and the country-boy bulk of Ken Kesey on the bridge, left La Honda, California, to make a circuit of North America, searching for the cool place in a psychedelic bus with just one word painted on its destination plate: the word 'FORWARD'.

The journey took just two months. In that time the Pranksters travelled south through Arizona and Texas, north to New York, where they met with Kerouac, Allen Ginsberg and Peter Orlovsky, the tribal elders of Beat, westwards into Canada, and back down to Big Sur, California. The bus hosted a score of fellow-travellers during its stoned pilgrimage, from Ginsberg and the acid gurus Timothy Leary and Richard Alpert, to the anonymous hitch-hiking forerunners of the gypsy young. It was a short, exuberant and massively effective metaphor. An ostensible purpose of the trip, a faltering, throwaway attempt to justify what was only ever intended to be *experience* through some resultant *product*, was to shoot a moving picture on the road. Miles of 16mm film were indeed used up, but the results were predictably dreadful. 'I watched about 20 hours of their films,' remembered

Hunter S. Thompson, 'and I'm glad he [Kesey] is writing again, because he wasn't a great film-maker.' Three years later, in 1967, the Beatles' first attempt at making their own moving picture resulted in a film called *The Magical Mystery Tour*. Its setting was a psychedelic bus, filled with eccentric characters, on a tour of Britain. Even in Britain, by 1967 it was past its time. It was way past its time.

Kesey's bus, in contrast, was bang on schedule when it pulled into La Honda again in August 1964. LSD-25 was still legal (possession of the drug was not made a criminal offence until 1966 in both the USA and Britain), and a former radar technician from Berkeley University was devising plans for the mass production of top quality LSD. His name was Augustus Owsley Stanley III, and in 1965 Owsley (as both he and his beautifully synthesised psychedelics came affectionately to be known) put his idea into operation. It will never be assessed how many doses of LSD were shovelled onto the illicit mass market by Augustus Owsley Stanley, only that they numbered many millions. Owsley's production line turned out a million and a half acid trips per batch, and he devoted the entire spring of 1965 to flooding the United States, Canada and western Europe with lovingly processed psychotropics. The CIA's perception of the fantastic potential of LSD-25 had gone horribly off the rails. It was indeed distorting the sensibilities of a substantial number of the inhabitants of half of the cities of the world. But they were *our* cities. They were *our* inhabitants. And they were swallowing the stuff voluntarily. They were losing touch with the base metals of everyday life and stumbling around in the nether world *because they wanted to*. They were doing it for fun.

The influence of LSD-25 over the rest of the 1960s was so profound that, even three decades later, no television programme, no scholarly dissertation, no magazine article about the period would be issued without its whorled titles and their exaggerated Arabic serifs, in mauve, green and red against a background of crude optical illusions or naïve paisley. At the time, one lick of the stuff seemed sufficient to transform a workmanlike purveyor of rhythm and blues in the pubs and clubs of the suburbs, into a sweetly-spoken cherub with a sitar in his lap and a geranium above his left ear. It was possible, in fact, for the transformation to be completed without the transformee ever having tasted Dr Albert Hofmann's synthesis; so substantial was its impact on his colleagues, on his surroundings, on his generation. Popular music, clothing, the jacket design of paperback books, all suddenly seemed to be marketed on the assumption that each and every potential customer was in a state of—or at least familiar with—psychic disorder.

There were bad trips and there was bad acid. LSD-25 enhanced painful as well as pleasurable sensations. Overdoses of the drug induced a form of catatonia, or hysteria and panic. Not many young people followed Dr Frank Olsen on his despairing (or was it overly optimistic?) flight through a tenth-storey window, but many had to be cared for by friends or by knowledgeable strangers. Special tents were erected at music festivals to cater for the shivering casualties. A drug which was, after 1966, necessarily almost always manufactured by part-time chemists in amateur laboratories, was liable to contain impurities, and those impurities occasionally had wicked effects.*

In its cleaner forms, LSD-25 was responsible for a small proportion of the most remarkable work by British rock bands and for some of the most innovative magazine design of the twentieth century. But it was probably worth it, when all that the tabloid press could set against that was the cautionary and probably apocryphal tale of a Soviet seaman who, newly arrived in an English port, purchased and gulped down several hundred tablets of LSD, and spent the following week standing quite still in an unused doorway, gazing out at the infinity of Southampton harbour.

LSD-25 could slip from the public's affection as quickly as it had arrived because, of course, it was non-addictive.† The same

---

* Possibly the most extravagant mass 'bad trip' of the decade took place late in 1969, at a party held by the newly-launched London edition of the American rock magazine *Rolling Stone* to entice advertising from the music industry. The drinks served at the party had been laced with LSD, and the LSD had in its turn been laced (unbeknown to the *Rolling Stone* staffers) with strychnine. There were several hospitalisations, and the singer Marc Bolan had to be carried home in a condition that would have interested the CIA. ('He started to put his hands in his mouth,' his wife, June, later recalled. 'I said, "What are you doing?" and he said, "I want to eat myself" . . . [later, he was] screeching his head off, he's scarlet, he's purple, he's dribbling, he's crying . . .') British *Rolling Stone* was closed down shortly afterwards by its American proprietor Jann Wenner—his partner and co-investor in the project, Mick Jagger, lost an estimated £20,000.

† It would be false to suggest that LSD-25 fell into complete oblivion at the end of the 1960s. At the time of writing (1992) British police forces were reporting a 400 per cent annual increase in the LSD trade since 1990. The size of that increase indicates that use of the drug had, previously, been at a very low ebb—but also that a substantial number of contemporary initiates, their appetites possibly whetted by experience of such minor hallucinogenics of the 1980s as Ecstasy (another with its origins in the exploration of psychotherapy), had come forward. The trouble with synthesised chemicals is that, like nuclear weapons, it is impossible to disinvent them.

could not be said of the drug which in part preceded it and which was wholly to supplant it as an escape route for young whites.

Heroin filtered slowly, almost imperceptibly, into the arteries of the 1960s drug culture. Unlike LSD, it had been there at the beginning, and also unlike LSD, it was to be there, fatally there, at the end. But initially heroin enjoyed no great boom in popularity. It just stuck around, it maintained a presence. Like any aristocratic narcotic, heroin was not lightly to be shaken off. Most soft drug users did not, contrary to official pedantry, take happily to narcotics. There was a time when it was not possible to force a *beer* down the throat of a self-righteous high priest of LSD. But this did not trouble heroin-users. Heroin's time would come.

Heroin was not, in the 1960s, a new drug; it merely leeched upon a new and susceptible distribution network. It had first been synthesised out of morphine by C. R. Wright, an English chemist, in 1874. Wright named his concoction diacetylmorphine, and tested it on dogs. When the dogs exhibited 'great prostration, fear, sleepiness . . . and a slight tendency to vomiting', this sensible man dropped his project. Unfortunately, his recipe fell into the hands of Bayer, the German chemical cartel, who launched the drug on the world market in 1898 under the trade-name 'heroin'. Bayer advertised heroin, in 12 different languages, as a panacea. It was prescribed for tuberculosis, rheumatic pains, neurotic stress and— extraordinarily—in China as a cure for opium addiction.

Bayer sowed heroin and reaped profit unrestricted for 26 years. By 1924, when the United States Congress outlawed the import and manufacture of the drug, there were a conservatively estimated 200,000 addicts in the USA alone. Most of the rest of the world's governments promptly followed the congressional example, but heroin was a stayer. Heroin, one of the most consistently profitable commodities that capital has ever bought and sold, had stamina.

But even the trade in illegal narcotics was not immune to the ravages of world war. By 1945 heroin smuggling (and consequently addiction in the western world) had reached its lowest point since the turn of the century. The embargos on trade and the strong national security which were demanded by a state of war had incidentally blocked the movement of non-martial illicit goods. The huge American addict population fell to less than 20,000. The war, however, effected other incidental changes.

As a sign of their gratitude to the Mafia for assisting in the

Allied invasion of Sicily and southern Italy, the American government flew the Mafia *capo*, 'Lucky' Luciano, from his stateside prison to a life of freedom and enterprise in Italy. Luciano wasted little time in starting to supply that skeletal force of 20,000 junkies across the Atlantic. Initially he worked simply as a middle-man, comfortably diverting the legal supplies of the Italian pharmaceutical company, Shiaparelli, to his own market. This cosy arrangement was exposed and (apparently) stopped in 1950—by which time Luciano had built up enough laboratories and Middle Eastern contacts of his own to import crude blocks of morphine base and process them into heroin without the assistance of Shiaparelli's employees. Luciano's Italian mafia, dismayed by the publicity which accompanied the exposure of their links with Shiaparelli, and ever anxious to extend their operating base, determined to set up shop in another *entrepôt*. They chose a city whose criminal underground had been allowed to exist, even to prosper, for the most disgraceful of reasons. They chose Marseilles.

Ten per cent of the post-war population of Marseilles (some 70,000 out of three-quarters of a million people) were first- or second-generation exiles from that most intractable of French provinces, the island of Corsica. The emigrants from this under-privileged place had traditionally served in the police force, in the army and in the menial labour ranks of mainland France. They had also re-formed into a mafiosi hardly less effective, if not so well publicised, than that of Luciano in southern Italy. Bound by its fierce clannishness and its impenetrable Italo-Iberian dialect, the Corsican community in Marseilles was a power to be acknowledged before, during and after the German occupation (when many of them collaborated with the Vichy government).

Marseilles was also, in contrast, the home of the best-organised communist *maquis* in France. Their strictly disciplined cells did the dangerous and subversive work against the Nazi invaders. As a political party and power within the trades union movement Marseilles's communists were without equal in the late 1940s and the early 1950s.

In 1947 they took 80,000 workers out on strike to protest about a drop in living standards. The Central Intelligence Agency of the United States of America, taking a break from spiking the drinks of employees of its government with hallucinogenics, developed a strong interest in the south of France. They contacted the Guerini brothers, the heads of the most powerful Corsica mafia family, and supplied them with arms and cash for use against union leaders and against picket lines. The Corsicans pitched in with gusto, and the strike was broken by the end of the year.

In 1950 Marseilles dock workers began to boycott freighters which were supplying the French Indo-Chinese war zone (the same war zone, of course, into which the Americans themselves were to be sucked throughout the 1960s). The boycott spread, via communist and socialist union chapels and officials, to the Atlantic ports of France, to the metal industries, the mines and the railways.

The Guerinis and their fellow mafiosi quickly found themselves to be the recipients of no small amount of patronage and protection from any political grouping, or any subterranean power-broker, with a stake in seeing the Communist Party of southern France brought to its knees—and that camp ranged from the CIA through the Gaullists to the corrupt Marseilles Socialist Party of Gaston Deferre. The Guerinis did not bask idly in the warmth of this affection. Inspired by Luciano and his Italian colleagues, they bought in the junior chemistry sets and the bricks of crude morphine, they memorised the five-part recipe, they gathered together their bottles of acetic aphydride, alcohol, ether, and hydrochloric acid, and after a brief period during which one or two garages and apartment blocks in downtown Marseilles were inexplicably subjected to explosions (the final stage in the processing of pure powdered heroin involves, in semi-skilled hands, the possibility of the kind of lethal explosion which still sporadically shakes the foundations of tenements in Hong Kong), the Corsican mafiosi had joined Lucky Luciano in the heroin trade.

Luciano handled the United States' wholesale and retail side of the business, and the Corsicans supplied Europe. The CIA had been faced with a choice between ignoring the flow of heroin into western Europe and the United States and stamping on communism, and ignoring Mediterranean communism and stamping on the traffic in heroin. If there was a middle way, they did not find it, and they chose the former. For two decades, until 1970, when internecine warfare and growing public outrage resulted in Barthelemey Guerini receiving a 20-year prison sentence and in the Marseilles heroin industry collapsing*, the strike-breaking

---

* The second of John Frankenheimer's remarkable *French Connection* films, which purported to show a thriving heroin manufacture and export trade in Marseilles, was, by the time of its release (1975) anachronistic.

Corsicans of southern France supplied the cities of Europe with a steady flow of 'number 3' and 'number 4' heroin: the cheaper, impure, workaday powder and its more refined cousin, the *foie gras* of junk. By 1970, the heroin industry in Marseilles had willing and able successors in Rome, Naples, Amsterdam, Hamburg and Brussels.

This was the high road to eminence taken by a drug which hung like an ominous cloud over the 1960s, occasionally dispensing drizzle. It is a wonder, and a small credit to the young of the period, that it did not break until the hopeless winter of the decade, because the climate for its pandemic was—almost—perfectly right.

Ritual played a strong part in what the works of reference and the government reports came to describe as the 'non-medical use of drugs'. Ritual came in many forms in the 1960s, from filling a cylindrical pottery chillum with grass or hashish and passing it around, to melting opium on heated aluminium foil and sucking its fumes through a straw; from experiments with the smoke-filled cardboard centre of a toilet roll, to arcane tricks involving jam jars and sewing needles. The ritual of recreational drug use is, in itself, a diverting experience. That is the origin and appeal of the cocktail-shaker.

It was so with the banknote, the blade and the mirror. The ritual of chopping grains into powder upon a mirror, carving the powder into lines and snorting (sniffing into the nostril) those lines through a rolled-up note, had been practised casually in the sub-culture of illicit drug use for a number of years, chiefly as a method of ingesting amphetamine sulphate or cocaine—two other drugs which, at the time, were encountered only occasionally. Nonetheless a new ritual was introduced into the drug culture. And the banknote, the blade and the mirror could be used, once the simple technique had been mastered, to snort any powder, once that powder had been drawn out into lines and offered—offered honourably, in the sharing tradition, just one step sideways from passing around a joint of hash; there were, after all, no disgusting *needles* involved here—and it was no longer a foreign ritual. Even if the powder was heroin, which, increasingly as the decade drew to a close and the 1970s began, it was.

In the absence of any dependable advice and informed instruction about drug use from the straight society whose law enforcers were persistently arresting them, framing them, sending them to prison and, now and again, beating them up, the young of the 1960s had to find their own way through this lucky-dip barrel of psychotropics which had suddenly been laid at their feet, a cornucopia of amphetamines and barbiturates, hallucinogenics and narcotics, opiates and hypnotics. It was not *fashionable* then, as it was to be for their equivalents of a later, more sensible, generation, simply to say 'No', to reject all mood and mind-changing substances in favour of a clear and clean sobriety. It was not fashionable, and how could it be desirable, when chemicals were being synthesised by the minute which could introduce their taker to Prince Siddhartha Gautama in person, or make Unidentified Flying Objects visible (regularly visible) to the naked eye, or indicate that some long-playing records contained the meaning of life ... or which could simply relax the user, after a long day watching the tulips in the municipal park turn into miniature, teeming planets?

It was impossible for this generation to take seriously the laws and social restrictions concerning drugs. It was an empirical time, a time of trial by error, and no practical assistance was available from a society which considered marijuana to be as threatening as amphetamines, which saw no difference between LSD and heroin, and which determined that alcohol and tobacco were preferable to any of them. Slowly, it dawned upon those young people that they knew more about drugs than did their parents; they knew more than the legislators, more than the doctors, more even than the CIA. They knew more, possibly, about drugs than any previous group in western society, with the creditable exception of druids, witches, and the Claudian women of Ancient Rome.

And so, besieged on the one side by the forces of law and order, and on the other by the efforts of the murderous criminal underworld to create and monopolise an addict market in narcotics, the youth culture of the 1960s evolved its own mechanisms of drug import, production, wholesaling and retail; formed its own organisations to regulate, protect and educate its own people, organisations such as Release and BIT; and eventually, through its own printed media, was able to tell more of the unembroidered truth about the non-medical use of drugs to its own trusting generation than had previously been available anywhere else, in any form. It was no coincidence that the decline of the underground press and the collapse of the 'alternative' society's creaking, jerry-built infrastructure, as the era came to its end, preceded by only a few short seasons the spread of a poly-narcotic epidemic in Great Britain.

The youth culture, counter-culture, alternative culture, sub-culture, drug culture of the second half of the 1960s—the titles are interchangeable and essentially synonymous—carried some responsibility for that plague. Ultimately, it proved unable to control what it had borne. For too many of its scions the *knowledge* of drugs, the undoubted awareness of their dangers as well as of their benefits, was assumed to levy control over their habit-forming, deadly effects. They knew that heroin was addictive, therefore they were proof against addiction. Their understanding of drugs gave them, they dreamed, a Faustian power, a supernatural defence against falling into thrall. It *was* a dream. Unlike the Devil, heroin has no favourites and they fell, too many of those favoured sons and daughters, those flirts with sweet morphine. They fell along with the uneducated and the innocent into the grey fog of junk time.

And over the years the distribution system grew rotten and corrupt. A network which had originated in the supply of uppers to the all-night clubs and of hash to drowsy parties, which sustained a degree of relative integrity throughout the late 1960s; a network whose retailers became trusted men and women within their youth community, recommending high quality soft drugs to their customers, and spurning both narcotics and inferior produce; a network of people who were uncomfortable with big profits and were willing to plough some of the proceeds from their sale of hash and LSD back into the fund-raising benefit events of their community—this network was almost a reality in the late 1960s. But then a police and custom crackdown on the smuggling of hash resulted in a swift trebling of its price and in a scarcity on the British market. Many dealers went out of business, and too many of those that remained chose to diversify their range of products . . . and began to favour the easily transportable, easily hidden white powders which carried a high mark-up and, after a while, a guaranteed demand. And the ritual of the banknote, the blade and the mirror had its day, before it too was replaced by the ritual of the tinfoil and the tube, and by the black mass of the shared hypodermic syringes . . .

But that, as Mods left home and began to smoke hashish, as those smart and sharp young people turned inexplicably (to the outside world) towards the gormless drapes and chiffon scarves of Hippy, that was a generational failure which lay beyond a far horizon. More immediately, there was a Summer of Love to be getting on with.

CHAPTER FOUR

LOVE

For a few he wove long answers of fairy-tale fancy—nonsensical but sharply amusing. If anybody had been tempted to lose his patience, it was Dylan. Dylan tries without conceit to explain that he's a watcher, embroiled in nothing ... but the publicity people these days demand nonconformists who are conforming nonconformists.

REPORT IN THE *Melbourne Age* OF BOB DYLAN'S 1966 TOUR OF AUSTRALIA

The images, like flashbacks in a romantic film, are faded and vaguely blurred as if by heat-haze, but instantly, nostalgically identifiable. On the worn grass of some public park in Amsterdam, London or California groups of young men and women are arranged in a series of tableaux beneath a warm afternoon sun. The men, naked to the waist and with hair that straggles to their shoulder-blades, are floating a frisbee to and fro with variable expertise, their bell-bottomed loons flapping gracelessly as they sprint to make a catch or to collapse, laughing, onto the ground. An unkempt, collarless mongrel is loping excitedly about—perhaps the same dog which will later cause Amy to freak out when, while tripping on acid, she caresses him and discovers his matted coat to be crawling with fleas. But for the moment Amy is sitting cross-legged on the turf with the other women, attached ('old ladies') and unattached ('chicks'), and she is complacently rolling a joint for the company. Her hair is braided and a little girl burbles and plucks at the hem of her purple and mauve paisley frock. When they converse, they speak in gentle, soothing tones, as if each and every one of them was a patient in intensive care, and their dialect is interwoven with bastardised expressions from black American hep and with the innocent interjections of the strip cartoon. They are self-contained; they take no notice of the passers-by in pressed shirt-sleeves and slacks who eye this little

73

band politely, almost nervously, and with something close to bafflement.

In California they might have whiled away the previous night at the Family Dog's Tribute To Dr Strange, a seminal acidhouse party held at the Longshoreman's Hall in San Francisco, where under the startled, interested and increasingly sympathetic eyes of Allen Ginsberg and the music pundit Ralph J. Gleason (who was to become the godfather to Jann Wenner's *Rolling Stone* magazine) hundreds of stoned young people were dressed like extras from a score of Hollywood historical dramas: as pirates, cowboys, and Victorian ladies; they danced a swirling, communal dance made epileptic by the strobe lights; while Jefferson Airplane played and Grace Slick and the Great Society admonished them to 'remember what the Doormouse said . . .'

In New York they may have attended the Grand Opening Night of Timothy Leary's Spiritual League at the Village Theatre, a multi-media representation of an LSD experience which packed 2,000 people into every showing. Leary sat and narrated at one side of a massive screen, upon which were projected, according to one witness, 'fiery red and orange membraneous images that floated across the screen to pictures similar to a newsreel done at double time . . . psychedelic explorations of our molecular compositions, sex fantasies, murder, and finally the death of the mind . . . represented by a flashing spotlight on a grey screen, followed by shrill laughter, after which a series of gentle kaleidoscopic images drifted across the screen . . .'

In Stockholm they had for their entertainment the exhibition of 'She, the Woman as Cathedral', the immense caricature of a female body which lay on its back, legs akimbo, for three months in Sweden's Museum of Modern Art. 'She' measured 90 feet from her gross, brightly be-socked feet to the crown of her head. There was an art exhibition in one leg and a slide in the other. Entry was via the doorway of the vagina, immediately inside of which was laid a pond stocked with goldfish. One of her breasts contained a planetarium, and in her heart sat a man watching a television while being fondled by a host of androgynous hands. There was a soft-drinks bar in her stomach and a Greta Garbo film showing endlessly in one arm . . . or there was the Fylkingen Congress's showing of the South African premier's imagined destiny, 'Dr Verwoerd's Arrival in Inferno', an event which had occurred (Verwoerd was assassinated in the South African parliament building in Cape Town in September 1966) according to this state-sponsored troupe of Swedish musicians, to the accompaniment of black African music and with a colourful backdrop of 'puppets of heathen gods, toothbrushes, all giving war threats, unsullied simple joy, ancient beliefs, threats of annihilation . . .'

In Amsterdam they could have drifted along to the opening of Sigma Centrum at the building at Kloverniersburgwal 87 which had been, until 1941, the home of the Jewish Theatre Company. Sigma Centrum was born with a performance of Jean Genet's *The Maids* by New York's Living Theatre Company, followed by a party which lingered until dawn with the help of a rock group and five girl dancers. The function of the revitalised venue was, according to its director Olivier Boelen, to enable visitors to dance, have fun, meet each other and discuss the direction of the new world order in the amenable surroundings of a theatre workship, a psychedelic-experience room, and a platform for plays, poetry readings, dance demonstrations and musical events. Sigma Centrum would be a 'day and night, international multi-cultural area for the fusion of new ideas, and spontaneous transla-tion into activity . . .' Transport to and from this haunted place was simple for the young and fit. Throughout Amsterdam white bicycles were to be seen leaning against walls and railings. They were distributed by the remarkable Provos, and they were avail-able for use by anybody, so long as punctures were mended . . . and the user did not expect to find the bicycle where he had left it, on the following morning.

And in London, which had been declared by *Time* magazine in a special issue in April 1966 to be 'The Swinging City',* a label which hung like an albatross around the stiff neck of the embar-rassed, grey old capital of Empire for the remainder of the 1960s, even in London strange things were happening—if you knew

---

* *Time*'s encomium to London was titled, with providential ambiguity, 'You Can Walk Across It On The Grass', and consisted largely of a survey of the capital's theatres and artists. It was accompanied by a map of part of the city which was headed 'The Scene' and covered an area from the Victoria Sporting Club on Edgware Road to the north, the Chelsea clothes shop Granny Takes A Trip, to the south, the Royal Festival Hall in easterly Lambeth, and Biba in Kensington to the west. Buckingham Palace was, according to *Time*'s cartographer, central to The Scene, being just around the corner from 'actress Leslie Caron's home' and Christies of St James. Signs pointed out of this desirable quadrangle towards Portobello Road ('antique shops'), and inset was a map of the rest of England, which showed how all the population centres of the midlands and the north (especially 'Liverpool, Home of the Beatles') gazed towards The Scene like starstruck teenagers squatting in the stalls.

where to look. And in the early sixties you had to look hard. There was little or no street culture in this metropolis outside the parks and the open-air markets. To find events, exhibitions, happenings, music, dances, drugs, to find like-minded souls you had to look in attic flats and disused warehouses, you had to look in basements, you had to look . . . well, *underground*. A parallel, subterraneous evolution of dissatisfied youth was taking place in Manchester, Liverpool, Newcastle, Edinburgh, Birmingham, and within the different postal districts of London; this phenomenon was connected (and prompted) only by a curious shared interest in music, clothes and drugs. When the sub-culture surfaced, back in those formative years, it did so in the distorted descriptions of the Fleet Street press. It was not shy, but it was nervous of attention.

It was no accident, therefore, that the first two grand public expressions to be heard in the course of those elusive summers of love were largely organised by Americans and continental Europeans. It was no accident, and it was significant, because those two events in 1965 and 1966, both of which were held in that coliseum of the British Imperial establishment, the Royal Albert Hall, marked the beginning of the end of the insular British youth culture of the 1960s. The metamorphosis of Mods, art-school Beats, lingering Teds, and even Rockers into the mid-Atlantic clone which became known to outsiders as Hippy was by the beginning of 1967 almost complete. And, almost, above ground.

The first of those Albert Hall extravaganzas was, in fact, as much the valedictory of Beat as it was the heralding of a new, transcontinental order of youth. It was, of all things, a poetry reading—but a poetry reading on such a scale, with such wired and gibbering ambition, and staffed by such holy fools that it turned upon its head the received meaning of the words 'poetry reading'. It was a poetry reading which seriously considered the possibility of levitating Queen Victoria's monument to her dead husband. It was a poetry reading, in other words, on LSD.

A flurry of American beats passed through London in the early summer of 1965. Following a couple of readings by the likes of Allen Ginsberg in such inadequate venues as the basement (the *underground*) of Better Books, an American film-maker/hip entrepreneur named Barbara Rubin asked some English friends for the name of the biggest hall in town. She then picked up a telephone, booked the Albert Hall on 11 June for £450, and commenced ringing the newspapers. June 10th, 1965, was a quiet day in the national newsrooms, and the event—promoted by Rubin as an international gathering of poets—was given space on the BBC's evening bulletins. No fewer than 7,000 people turned up at the Albert Hall on the following evening, to see Ginsberg, Ferlinghetti and Corso as well as such home-grown talent as Michael Horovitz, Christopher Logue, Adrian Mitchell and George Macbeth. They were also treated to a lot of tedious stream of consciousness; to the sight of the Dutch activist Simon Vinkenoog, flying on LSD, seizing the microphone and addressing them in Dutch; to a group of genuine, certified schizophrenics who had been released for the night by Dr Ronnie Laing and who created havoc in the front row of seats; to compère Alex Trocchi, happily chaotic on heroin, to Harry Fainlight, so zipped on amphetamines that he began to introduce a poem, and could not stop the introduction, the introduction went on and on, it became the performance, and the poem, the poem never happened . . . They missed John Latham and Jeff Nuttall, whose experimental covering of their naked bodies in blue gloss house paint went badly awry, blocking their pores with the result that they had to soak in a backstage bath (the same bath, simultaneously), but they did hear Adrian Mitchell, powerfully exhorting the absent common enemy to 'Tell me lies about Vietnam'. And they did, those gallant, occasionally bewildered 7,000, more than cover the booking fee of the Royal Albert Hall. 'The Albert Hall,' considered Michael Horovitz many years later, 'brought a lot of the things that were happening together . . . all over the world there were other people in similar situations; that changed things and it became more international.'

Filling the Albert Hall, covering its booking fee, would be routine for the entertainer who performed there one year later, on the nights of 26 and 27 May, 1966. He was not, however, accustomed to having half of his audience stalk out in pique during his performance—the half with duffle coats and CND badges, the half which was confronted, on those epochal May nights, with the fact that the fast, glib, electric youth culture of the decade had kidnapped their dearest icon and was not even asking for a ransom. In his spring tour of Great Britain and Ireland in 1966, Bob Dylan cut loose from orthodoxy, lost for ever the beards and the black woollen polo-necks from his extended circle of devotees, and won over most of the rest of western youth. In a series of tense and dramatic concerts which echoed with bitter rebukes and even—occasionally—angry back-biting between the stage and the auditorium, Bob Dylan took up the baton dropped by the poets at the Albert Hall in 1965 and announced through amplifiers the ascendancy of a weird, anomalous era of swirling, drug-inspired images, imprecise dissent, and an arbitrary kind of love.

More than any other western artist, Bob Dylan called the tune of the 1960s. His 1963 and 1964 LPs, *The Freewheelin' Bob Dylan* and *The Times They Are A-Changin'* could have been written as much for the Aldermaston marches and the anti-nuclear movement of Great Britain as for the civil rights activists of the United States. This gaunt, refractory young man who composed and delivered the theme tunes of the decade, would never see his success and his influence measured by chart success, by the top ten hits so dear to Tin Pan Alley and its successors—and that was, in large part, why he, his acoustic guitar, his harmonica, his arch and assured nasal command of lyrical sarcasm, that was partly why they were all hugged close to the jealous breast of bijou Bohemia. Bob Dylan was just too precious to be shared with the broad and common and ideologically unsure outside world.

Let us briefly go back to the spring of 1965, when, just a month before the international poetry jamboree at the Albert Hall, Dylan's first tour of Britain had been something of a sensation. His concerts sold out from Newcastle to Liverpool to Leicester and, of course, the Albert Hall, where a second booking was hurriedly made. He was courted by the hip British aristocracy and by the major British pop groups of the time: Manfred Mann (who had cut an electric version of 'God On Our Side'), the Animals, the Rolling Stones and the Beatles, who told their fans to take especial notice of this troubador prophet. His aeroplane landed in London to a startling sea of expectant faces. He won over the Communist *Daily Worker* ('his magnetism ... power to hold an audience captive, his perfect timing') and the Conservative *Daily Telegraph*, which decided that 'There are better singers, better guitarists, better harmonica players and better poets. But there is no other 23-year-old who does all these things with even a semblance of the power, the originality, or the fire ... this haystack-headed young American has achieved in an age of more and more pictures, and less and less text, of emotional noises rather than meanings, an astounding popular victory for the word.'

There were some carping voices, such as from those who wondered why he lodged at the Savoy while preparing for concerts which would damn the world of money and power ('I can't live in a shack!' snapped back Dylan, and was later comforted to learn that John Lennon inhabited a house which had 22 rooms), but the young singer was largely delighted by his reception. 'In England they're more ready, y'know,' he mused after the second Albert Hall concert, for which the tickets were all sold within an hour and a quarter (excepting those which were withheld for the Earl of Harewood and Robert Morley) and still thousands were turned away. 'People don't grow up the same way,' he considered. 'In England they are more ready, the young people. Over there, you could get killed for having long hair, if you're in the wrong part of the country. You could actually get killed for saying something out of place . . . I think England's more open-minded.' (That was a judgment which, twelve months later, Bob Dylan was given reason to amend.)

At the end of June, 1965, Bob Dylan returned to the United States. In July he was booked to make an obligatory showing at the Delphi of progressive American folk music, the Newport Festival. He arrived in Rhode Island to find himself scheduled to appear on the final Sunday evening as part of a line-up which the doyen of American guitar-and-mouth-organists, Pete Seeger, had promised would deliver 'a message from today's folk musicians to a new-born baby about the world we live in'.

This fayness would have been too much for almost any young iconoclast; it was certainly too much for Bob Dylan. He sought out the electric guitarist Al Kooper, and three members of the Paul Butterfield Blues Band. He took them to rehearse in a nearby house, and on Sunday evening, wearing black leather and carrying an electric guitar, he walked onto stage before them and their banks of speakers, and he proceeded with rock versions of his acoustic protest snarl, 'Maggie's Farm', of 'Like A Rolling Stone' (which had been conceived and written purely as an electric number), and of 'It Takes A Train To Cry'. Backstage, Pete Seeger 'turned a bright purple and began kicking his feet and flailing his arms'. Frontstage, the audience shrieked abuse, calling 'Sell out!' and 'This is a folk festival!' Somewhat shaken by the vehemence of the audience reaction, Dylan went off for his acoustic guitar and returned to perform 'Mr Tambourine Man', before closing with the information to Newport that 'It's All Over Now, Baby

Blue'. His former lover, Joan Baez, watching from the bleachers, took refuge on the arm of the emphatically *non*-electric British folk singer, Donovan.

By the time of his 1966 tour of Britain and Ireland, Dylan had consolidated his electric act (signing up a Canadian rhythm 'n'blues band called The Hawks for support—The Hawks would shortly be better known as The Band), repeated his Newport Festival outrage in August, 1965 at the Forest Hills Music Festival in New York (to cries of 'Traitor' and 'Where's Ringo?'). He had also released two LPs, *Highway 61 Revisited* and *Blonde on Blonde*, albums of such stylish musical genius and obscure, egregious lyricism that they confirmed, finally, that the young Turk of American folk had left the world of Pete Seeger and Donovan far behind. To a man who was nursing a baby heroin habit, the world would never again be a place of blacks and whites.

When he arrived in Dublin on 5 May 1966, therefore, the old guard knew what to fear and what to expect. They also knew, from reports which had crossed the Atlantic, how they themselves were expected to respond. Dylan played for 50 minutes upon his guitar and his harmonica, and followed it with a 45-minute electric set in front of the band. In Ireland, they shouted 'Traitor!' and 'Throw out the backing group!' In Bristol, five days later, letters were written to the local *Evening Post* which captured the disillusion of a folkie spurned. 'I have just attended a funeral,' mourned one castaway. 'They buried Dylan in a grave of guitars. My only consolation, Woody Guthrie wasn't there to witness it.' On 16 May his concert at the Gaumont, Sheffield was delayed by a bomb warning. At Manchester Free Trade Hall on the following day, one of the finest live concerts ever to be delivered by a rock'n'roll band* was punctuated, halfway through the electric set, by a desperate, panicked and utterly memorable screech of 'Judas!' from somewhere in the humming auditorium.

And at the Royal Albert Hall on 26 May, this failing cry of retribution reached its climax, and then disappeared with those who walked out into the street to escape the amplified clamour,

---

* A tape recording was made of this concert which, when surreptitiously cut onto vinyl and released as a bootleg LP, became one of the best-selling albums of the late 1960s. It was incorrectly titled *Bob Dylan Live at the Albert Hall*, and the error was probably deliberate, the later concert having attracted most publicity, and the words 'Albert Hall' carrying more cachet, in the classless alternative society, than 'Manchester Free Trade Hall'.

and it was never heard again. At the Albert Hall, his voice slurred with fatigue and heroin, Dylan talked back to his detractors. The very sight of The Hawks' equipment lined up on the Albert Hall stage after the interval sparked yells of 'Rubbish!' and 'Woody Guthrie would turn in his grave!' (causing Lennon, McCartney and Harrison to shout 'Leave him alone—SHUT UP!' from their box).

The small, weary figure in a houndstooth check jacket paused before breaking into the violent opening chords of 'Rainy Day Women Nos 12 and 35', whose key, repeated line is 'Everybody must get stoned'.

'I'm not going to play any more concerts in England,' Bob Dylan told the Albert Hall. Then he rambled, briefly, as people in his condition will . . . 'I'd just like to say this next song is what your English musical papers would call a drug song. I never have and never will write a drug song. I don't know how to. It's not a drug song, it's just vulgar.'

Having protested too much, and with the audience passably attentive, he reached the point. 'I like all my old songs,' he said. 'It's just that things change all the time. Everybody knows that. I never said they were rubbish. That's not in my vocabulary. I wouldn't use the word rubbish, if it was lying on the stage and I could pick it up. This music you are going to hear . . . if anyone has any suggestions on how it can be played better, or how the words can be improved . . . we've been playing this music since we were 10 years old. Folk music was just an interruption, which was very useful. If you don't like it, that's fine. This is not English music you are listening to. You really haven't heard American music before. I want now to say what you're hearing is just songs. You're not hearing anything else but words and sounds. You can take it or leave it. If there's something you disagree with, that's great. I'm sick of people asking "What does it mean?" It means nothing.'

It means nothing. You're hearing nothing but words and sounds. However identifiable the masters of war may once have seemed, they were truthfully only chimerae. It *was* a form of apostasy. Tend your own garden, Bob Dylan said, the time of easy answers is gone, the clearly written labels have been peeled away. In an experimental world, there are no certainties. This is a time of mysterious complexity, of confusion and blurred images, of imprecise hatreds and dissent, and of uncertain love.* Believe only what you see and hear and swallow, be *empirical*, he told a generation, and they would respond as though each and every one of them had been present at the Royal Albert Hall on that stormy night in May, in person instead of merely in their dreams.

In his sweet, stoned artistic prudishness, Bob Dylan was probably right to tell the Royal Albert Hall that it was 'vulgar' to write drug songs. It was self-indulgent to do so, and it pre-excused slovenly work, and it was—finally—trite. But no matter: everybody did it. In 1967 the Beatles, by a series of odd deeds and the issue of a long-playing record called *Sergeant Pepper's Lonely Heart's Club Band*, announced to the world that they had taken LSD and that they had liked it. 'I had it one time in some flat in Eaton Square after a club,' Paul McCartney remembered later . . .

'We'd all rolled back there as you would do after one of these clubs. Somebody said, "Has anyone ever had acid?" It was a slightly upper-class crowd. (The crowd separated itself into all us working class and the Lord Londonderrys and that kind of people which Mick and the guys were always into and still are. I never disliked that crowd but I never just found myself in with them.) So that was who had it, someone slightly upper-class. And it was on blotting paper, you just cut it up into little squares and you had one each. So it was like "Wow, right . . . who's game for a bit of a . . ." so we all had it and it was okay. I was actually conscious of having a dirty shirt on, which was weird for me.

'Before this John and George had been spiked. They had a dentist friend and he spiked them one evening. I think he wanted naughty sex games, 'cos they had all their wives there, and he sort of said, "Does anyone fancy a little bit . . ." and they said, "You fuck off, mate! But we'll have a coffee . . ." They went to a club after the coffee, because they didn't really know what would happen to them. And they got to the Ad Lib Club and it appeared to be on fire, and they decided they'd get away from that, and they drove back at about 20 miles an hour, hugging the kerb, apparently, out to Esher, where they ended up at George's house,

---

* An immediate and illustrative casualty of this sudden renunciation of form was the disappearance, almost overnight, of the intricate and lovingly devised dance movements of the Mod era. The Ska, the Dog and the Shake became as suddenly outdated as any waltz, and were replaced by the unstructured undulating from tip to stem that characterised that hippy dance: a kind of freeform squirm like a snake coming out of its basket, or (which was more likely to be in the practitioner's mind) a pliable shrub disturbed by the wind.

and these huge big friendly trees were waving at them . . . It was a kind of mixed experience.

'What we had heard about acid was that it would change you irrevocably. You would never be the same. I remember driving round Hyde Park Corner and we were all in a taxi and we were discussing this and one of us—John or George— said, "I hear you're never the same after it," and that made quite a big effect on me, and I thought, "Okay, I could change and everything, but maybe I've got something going here that I need to preserve, maybe I don't need to take a leap back into the dark on this one." So I did resist quite a lot. They said to me, "Come on . . ." but I backed off, and that was peer pressure of the highest variety . . . your fellow group members. There you really have got to do what they do, 'cos you're group members, it's like being members of a commune or something. But I resisted and said, "Well, you know . . ." because I could see what it was doing to them. And what it was doing to them basically was making them sit around very dopey and making them hear noises I couldn't hear, from miles away—"Listen to that!" and I'd go, "What . . . ?" '

But the experience was unavoidable for Paul McCartney, as it was unavoidable for apparently hard-headed products of the Mod era such as the Rolling Stones, as it was unavoidable, of course, for Bob Dylan, for Donovan, for the Pink Floyd, and for the increasing number of less affluent young people who no longer considered that they had to get up for work on the following morning. 'She comes in colours,' sang Jagger, and that, surely, was something not to be missed.

From the Summers of Love, staggered across the international time-zones, emerged the gaudy array of products which appeared to give credibility to the notion of an alternative society of western youth. Product, retail outlets, music, clothing, food, publications and such consumer durables as stone chillums and metal roach-clips (a roach being the dying end of a marijuana joint, the clip being necessary to smoke it without burning one's fingers): these were the acid-painted lawful manifestations of the time. There may have been a brief, hot summer when, as Chris Rowley, the young assistant to a Japanese artist called Yoko Ono, remembered, 'Notting Hill was really a little paradisical . . .' with fairy-tale hippy weddings in Hyde Park, celebrations modelled loosely on the works of Tolkien, 'this atmosphere of trees, golden haze, an aura of decadence and mellowed out young people' after which the moneyed got back into their white Rolls Royces and the unenvious poor, the lumpen hippies, strolled hand in hand through the warm enveloping dusk back down Ladbroke Grove. There was, for many, a period in which the routine passage of time appeared to have been derailed, in which the whole of society faced a series of tomorrows which were so bizarre, so unprecedented, and so daunting that one might as well face them with a hole in the head—which is why Joe Mellen, a songwriter for the folksinger Julie Felix, decided one London morning in 1966 to trepan himself. Gathering together medical equipment to the value of £20, Mellen got to work at 6 a.m. on a Sunday. He taped a green eyeshade onto his brow to prevent blood from obscuring his everyday vision, and by 9 a.m. he had carved into his forehead a hole the size of a sixpence and was awaiting the advent of a permanent state of heightened consciousness ... this was not product. It was strange, it was iconoclastic, and it seized the attention, but it was not for sale. Mellen, unlike Richard Branson or Andrew Lloyd Webber, was not about to become rich.

A respectable number of the entrepreneurs who launched themselves, more or less incautiously, upon the surf of the Summers of Love saw their income multiply. Branson and Lloyd Webber, with their student magazines, their chains of progressive record stores, and their dreadful hippy musicals, were never properly of that time (as each, now, would cheerfully agree) if only because they were nagged by the certainty that there was a tomorrow, and that in that tomorrow—as in all of Britain's yesterdays—there was money to be made, and that he who had made money would not be forever regarded as a laughable pariah by his acid-educated peers. They had, in other words, no faith.

Somewhere in between Branson and Joe Mellen lay the broad consensus of the children of those gilded summers. They were vague communalists operating within a liberal free market. Profits were to be, if not actually despised, at least guilt-edged. Clothes shops such as Granny Takes A Trip were expected to employ 'members of the community', many record companies felt obliged to subsidise the 'underground' press through sympathetic advertising, rock bands which did not perform in benefits and fund-raising concerts could expect to be pilloried and regarded with suspicion, and artists took the images of psychedelia onto the front covers of the most unlikely publications of Penguin Books. It was a period when *Time Out* refused to run listings of soccer matches because professional competitive sport seemed too much the apotheosis of the tired old straight society which the magazine's editorial was purporting to replace. When the laconic American brothers Craig and Greg Sams established their macrobiotic restaurant 'Seed' in the basement of the Gloucester Hotel, they defused the inevitable criticisms of 'hippie capitalism' by advertising 'The Free Meal' on the menu, a dish of rice and vegetables and green tea which was always available to those who professed themselves unable to pay. 'At times our patience was tried,' Craig Sams recalled. 'People would come down, have the free meal, and then say "I'll have an apple crumble", and we'd say that the apple crumble wasn't included in the free meal and they'd say, "Oh, that's all right," and whip out a fiver.'*

Self-absorbed, aggressively collectivist, and usually concerned more with the exploration of some uncharted (and possibly non-existent) middle Earth within themselves, that group with the frisbee and the joints in the public park idled in a political no-man's land. Harold Wilson's optimistic lowering of the voting age from 21 to 18 made no more impression upon them (and consequently, upon his political fortunes, as the Conservative victory in the 1970 general election showed) than if they had been Quietists. They held those giant, accommodating doctrines—capitalism and communism—equally responsible for the decline of the quality of human consciousness and they said, with Mercutio, a plague on both your houses.

Such cynicism about both the consumer society and the state ownership of the means of production and distribution, should have made this little band potential recruits to the British Labour or Liberal parties. And, to do them justice, if there was one thing that routinely they were *not*, it was Conservatives. There might be an element of cool in some aspects of socialism, there may have been something neat about the liberal fondness for banning bombs,

---

* Under the watchwords 'you are what you eat', diet was in fact to become a seminal style statement of the time. Young people who wished to replace the red-meat mentality of their parents were adjured to spurn the processed foods to which their mothers' generation had turned with relief, and to treat food as a sacrament. 'Food is more important than a poem because food makes a poem and is a poem,' ran a tract of 1968. 'Treat every meal as a pleasure. Give every meal its proper time even as you would give music its proper time . . . The man who rushes carelessly through his meal is caught up in the web of Maya, ensnared by delusion, he is convinced that he is important, indispensable, and that without him the world will perish . . .' The small enterprises of the brothers Sams, incidentally, grew from such acorns into the health food empire of Ceres and Harmony Foods.

but the British Tories, in this time of style and hedonistic law-breaking, had very little to commend them. When the drug-bust protection agency Release, in an idiosyncratic attempt to draw attention to its non-affiliated base, broadcast the fact that one of its employees voted for the Conservative Party, the wonder which rippled through the alternative society was two-fold. It was partly that Release should even have considered *boasting* of such a thing, and it was partly . . . who *was* it? Which one of those office-workers in tie-died T-shirts and ankle-length paisley skirts, who spent their ill-paid days arguing for the legislation of cannabis resin and attempting to achieve amnesties for drug-users who were serving prison sentences . . . which one of them nursed a secret passion for the politics of Edward Heath and Robert Carr?

They were unrepentant extra-parliamentarians, extra to *any* established political body or school of thought. A few years after those Summers of Love, when the residue of typesetters and designers on the underground press was courteously approached by the print unions (courteously, but with the strong hint that without union membership their work could be blacked by union print chapels), there was a deeply felt if short-lived resistance to the notion. It was not that they were opposed to solidarity, more that *that* kind of solidarity smacked too much of the old, failed order, too much of tea and biscuits in Downing Street, of shady deals and rigged ballots, of association with the people who set in type the scurrilous attacks on long-haired youth. They did not, largely, accept Allen Ginsberg's injunction that in order to influence an institution for the better, or even to engineer its decline, it was necessary to join that institution. They were a constant source of irritation to the extra-parliamentary organised left, which seemed often to be dancing with dismay at the sight of a whole generation of apparently susceptible young people being steered by drugs and abstracted musical shamans and sloppily uncommitted publications outside the realm of political action. These people, who the former *IT* columnist Jonathon Green described as 'the ideologues of the New Left, who in turn took on certain hippy trappings, but from a cautiously mandarin perspective', were fated to spend a good part of the 1970s denying that they had ever had anything to do with the 'youth culture' of the 1960s, except perhaps the penning of an occasional article in *Oz* deploring the selfish apoliticism of hippies—much as they were doomed to spend the 1990s denying that their school of thought had ever been truly influenced by Eastern bloc communism.

No, any quest to get to the bottom of the political meaning of the apparent rejection of their parents' society by a conspicuous proportion of the western young during the second half of the 1960s was destined to fail, as surely as were the several attempts to understand and to explain the lyrics of Bob Dylan's songs. Those adolescents had their roots in Mod and music, not in the Committee of 100 or in the debating societies of Oxford, Cambridge, or the Young Communist League. A big and merry game was afoot, whose largely middle-class players pretended the rejection and eventual replacement of society while they survived upon society's excess fat. It was a game which, when played at its lowest level, rewarded panhandling, begging and theft; but which occasionally, briefly, flew like symbols on a flimsy kite images of a society more tolerant of those who live and think in diverse ways, of those who worshipped different gods, who practised different sex, who had (naturally, for racism was anathema to the generation which grew out of Mod) different colours of skin, and of those who preferred to take stimulants other than alcohol and cigarettes. That, as the prosecutor Brian Leary was to say to Felix Dennis during the trial of *Oz*, was just about the size of it. It was a game which had few eventual losers (few *serious* losers), few eventual winners (*serious* winners), and a great body of loosely affected contestants who, after the final roll of the dice, simply picked up their lives and continued, with alarming ease, along the steady pathway towards employment, family and home. They went back to the brandy and cigars.

Yet the image which has come to characterise the era, if not the entire decade, is the image of flower-power, the iconography of the Summer of Love. Young men with large and vivid flowers in hair which had only just started to grow, wearing embroidered Edwardian jackets and ruffled shirts, flared trousers and sandals or bare feet; young women in kaftans or granny blouses or naked from the waist upwards, swaying in some festival field, their bodies painted by an art school drop-out with a day-glo pen. Such people, the picture books tell, spent the best part of ten years dressed in this manner and behaving in this way. But nobody's Summer of Love lasted for a summer in Great Britain, and few people's lasted a halcyon day. The image is in fact a collage, a fantasy congealed from many single sunburnt afternoons. There never was a Haight Ashbury under these grey skies (in California, indeed, there was only such a mythic place for less than a year). There were Saturday afternoons on Primrose Hill and down upon the King's Road; there was the Rolling Stones performing live in Hyde Park, Jagger in a dress, releasing butterflies and reciting Shelley in that exaggerated south London accent; there were hippy weddings in the balmy afternoon, with the photographers from the tabloid press jostling for shots of bra-less brides; there were even cowbells worn by the inspired few (with the clappers removed) . . . but that was just about the size of it.

That, and the product which it released: the clothes and music stores, and the peculiar phenomenon of an entirely amateur publishing network which appeared from nowhere to sell, within a couple of years, up to 150,000 copies per issue of its combined magazines, which employed as many as 200 people from Devon to the north of England, and which died as quickly as it had been born within eight short years, sinking suddenly from sight as the last fond fading memory of the Summer of Love vanished into the denser atmosphere of the 1970s.

CHAPTER FIVE

UNDERGROUND

IT might have been a radio station, a television network, a mass extra-sensory communication machine . . .

International Times, OCTOBER 1966

The first and the last was *International Times*. *IT* was *early*, early enough to pre-date *Sergeant Pepper's Lonely Heart's Club Band*, early enough to proclaim itself (later, when its own significance sank in) as one of the first underground magazines in the *world*, never mind Great Britain, early enough to be able completely to ignore phase four of the Labour Government's heretical Prices and Incomes Act which, in October 1966, gave Harold Wilson the power to freeze wages and prices. *IT* was so early, in fact, that its first five issues were published by the hot metal and not the offset litho printing process.

Lithography was the making of the underground press. The virgin litho presses of the 1960s became the playthings of artists, designers and typesetters who discovered, with enormous delight, that the making up of publications for print could be as unrestrained, as easy, as colourful and as much *fun* as they chose. Litho was *flexible*. Litho would print *anything*. Litho would treat a thumbprint with the same lack of prejudice as a column of justified Times Roman. Hot metal letterpress had demanded individual blocks for every illustration, single metal slugs for every full-stop, and the presence of a highly qualified artisan before a single line could be transferred onto newsprint. Litho, on the other hand, would (and occasionally did) translate the hand-written opinions and scrawled cartoons of a schoolchild into tens of thousands of copies of cheaply-priced magazines. And litho, before the price of paper inflated in the 1970s, was cheap. Offset litho was technology heaven-sent to the youth culture of the 1960s. There was no masonry of litho printers, no arcane management of the ink-ducts.

Across the country, jobbing printers installed the new technology, sent their reluctant hot metal men on retraining courses, and then leaned back to watch, with greater and lesser degrees of benignity, as long-haired young entrepreneurs grasped and exploited the wonderful fluidity of the process before failing—as often as not— to pay the bill.

Most underground magazines would never have existed without the availability of a local litho printing press. *International Times* was different. Litho may have saved it from an early grave, and litho certainly extended its life beyond a decent, natural limit, but *IT* had a cultural and not a technological birth. *IT*, in October 1966, was waiting to happen; it was the first and the last legitimate media child of that ephemeral Summer of Love. It did not even, until rather later in its short life, employ the false, embarrassing, vaguely political but, finally, indispensable term 'underground' when talking of itself, of its sister publications, and of the broad church of which it became the parish magazine.

Even within the wonderful museum of British subversive publishing, *International Times* had no logical antecedence. It was not a piece of scurrilous pamphleteering and it was not a Fabian tract. The mantle of Claud Cockburn's mimeographed magazine of the 1930s, *The Week*, had partly been donned by *Private Eye* (although two of Cockburn's sons, Andrew and Alexander, would later work for and contribute to *IT*). It was not even entirely an arts magazine of the anarchic left, despite the fact that three of its small band of founders had earlier produced exploratory collections of writing and slash'n'burn art: Barry Miles and John Hopkins having collaborated on *Long Hair*, and Jeff Nuttall having produced, from the wilderness of south London, *My Own Mag*. Its first editor, Tom McGrath, was a veteran of *Peace News*, but *IT* was not a production of the Campaign for Nuclear Disarmament. Its character was formed as much by the party which was held to celebrate its launch, as by any editorial predetermination.

The launch party of *International Times* was held on Saturday, 15 October 1966, at a disused railway depot in Camden Town, a large and rickety circular building, like a flaking prototypical astrodome, which the playwright Arnold Wesker had envisaged as Centre 42, his breeding ground of the accessible arts, but which would be better known, then and now, as the Roundhouse. About 2,500 people made their way to the Roundhouse on that cold and wet October evening, to hear the new acid bands Pink Floyd and the Soft Machine, to watch Kenneth Anger movies projected on the damp walls, to be given imaginary sugar cubes of LSD, to frolic in a large bowl of jelly, and to be in real danger of incineration from the free-form oil heaters.

'It was a new kind of celebration,' remembered Mick Farren, who was later to edit *IT*. 'The Roundhouse, then, was a vast, filthy, circular building. Loose bricks, lumps of masonry and old wooden cable drums littered the floor. Slide and movie projectors threw images on a screen of polythene sheeting that had been hung at the back of a rickety, makeshift stage. The only way into the building was up a single flight of shaky wooden stairs. At the top Miles and Hoppy (John Hopkins) passed out sugar cubes. According to legend one in twenty was dosed with acid. Mine wasn't.

'Somebody gave Joy and me a load of speed, which we swallowed. A bottle of Scotch was passed round. A Jamaican steel band played on stage. It was plenty jolly. It was all those freaks we had seen at all those parties. Paul McCartney came by in an Arab suit. For the first time in my life I saw joints being passed round openly in a public place. The steel band left the stage, a poet came and went. A band called the Soft Machine played from the floor as a weird biker rode round and round them. Another band, called Pink Floyd, took possession of the stage. They played music that sounded like a guitar solo by The Who, only it was a solo without any song to go round it—like a sandwich without bread. They honked and howled and tweeted, clanked with great concentration. They were very loud with no musical form save that every forty minutes or so they stopped, paused a while, and started again.

'Across the room an Italian film crew filmed a couple of nubile starlets stomping in a mess of pink emulsion paint. As we lurched into shot we were told by the producer: "Fuck off, you're spoiling the spontaneity." We stumbled off to watch a bunch of freaks dragging an old horse-drawn cart around the building.

'Out of my head on speed I wandered around the railway tracks at the back of the Roundhouse, hoping vaguely I wouldn't be run down by a train or step on a live rail. The one thing I was acutely conscious of was that back inside was something more than a new rock and roll show.'

Indeed, it was a new rock'n'roll event which paid the band

with the light show—Pink Floyd—£2 10s more than the band
without one (Soft Machine), and which raised almost £1,000 for
the *International Times* ('Pop Op Costume Masque Drag Ball Et
Al', read the poster, '5 shillings in advance, 10 shillings door'). *IT*
was launched on its first, letterpress, volume, in a fantasy of fake
acid and swirling lights.

The origin of its name is a matter of dispute. Miles claims
that a woman from Louisiana named Bobo Legendre, who was
staying at the time in a Mayfair apartment, stopped dead an early
editorial meeting by marching across the room and suggesting
they call it, *IT*. Miles's wife of the time, Sue, insists that the idea
was her own. The two letters could be short for almost anything:
Intergalactic Times, *Intravenous Times*, or the *International Times*
which led the proprietors of the London *Times* into a half-hearted
and shortly unsuccessful lawsuit, the first of the British underground press's busy legal agenda.

Those two letters also resulted in one of the most abiding
images of the 1960s. The magazine's logo, it was agreed, should
feature the word *it* in lower case, alongside a bleached photograph
of the It-girl of the 1920s, Clara Bow. Understandably unsure of
early cinema history, the designer got the wrong girl. Instead of
Clara Bow, Theda Bara's hooded eyes stared steadily out from the
front cover of the first and all succeeding issues of *International
Times*.

The number of copies of that first issue which were printed
and sold is also a matter of minor dispute, ranging from 15,000
with only a few returned, to 2,500, most of which never left the
magazine's Holborn offices. It was produced in a fashion which
never left *IT* and which became standard throughout the underground press: hurriedly, haphazardly, and late in the day. At 10.45
on the morning of 12 October 1966 Tom McGrath sat down to
write *IT*'s first editorial, three days before the magazine's launch
party and just 30 minutes before the first deadline. He was using a
typewriter which had been given to the magazine by Sonia Orwell
and which, according to popular rumour, had been used by her
late husband to write *1984*: '. . . days ago we were still uncertain
as to whether this newspaper would actually appear,' McGrath
confided in his readers. 'And if it did appear, what would it be
like? The editor's guess was as good as anyone's . . . I have a
feeling that *IT* will produce hot-cold reactions. If you're with us,

you'll know. And we'll probably be hearing from those who have no doubts they're against us.'

At this point McGrath was interrupted by somebody entering his office and removing the typewriter. The editor philosophically hunted around for another, and continued: 'Forget all that crap I just wrote above. *IT* is just for fun. Even when we're blasting off or being subversive, remember we're just in it because we like playing games . . . Yes, we're just a young, fun-loving newspaper. Remember that.'

Eighteen months later, *International Times* would be selling more than 40,000 copies of every issue. Using the 'pass on' formula adopted by fortnightly magazines of the established publishing world, this gave *IT* a readership of at least 200,000.

What was the editorial rock upon which such a circulation was built? Initially the magazine took the 'international' part of its title very seriously indeed. Reports were co-opted from all across Europe ('This year the 10th Warsaw Autumn International Festival of Modern Music displayed the triumph of performers, not of compositions . . .') and the United States ('Andy Warhol's Exploding Plastic Inevitables are back at the Velvet Underground with Supergirl Nico and the Man With a Snake'). There was an analysis of events in China, where the Red Guards, seizing Mao's exhortation to build a society in a state of continuous flux, had commenced the terror which became known as the Cultural Revolution. Regretting that the British, American and European press was devoting so little space to such astonishing, crucial events, Alex Gross reported: 'The Red Guards are being actively encouraged to act against party officials—something not even permitted to the Hitler Youth. The leaders of China have left the Class Struggle behind them and taken a gamble that they will be able to mobilise and control the tensions between conflicting generations. There is no precedent in history for this movement, unless it be the catastrophic Children's Crusade of the Middle Ages . . . These are some of the reports which continue to filter through—we can only hope beyond hope that they have been exaggerated.'

They had not been overly exaggerated. It was a curiously *balanced* line for a magazine of malcontented youth—albeit *western* youth—to adopt. And there were book and film reviews, which reflect as well as anything the identity crisis which was being endured by both the makers and the reviewers of the progressive arts in the middle of the 1960s. ('Visually more "artistic", but no less paroxysmatic, was a black-and-white film of Nietzsche's *Self-Destruction*. A man's face is caked with— dough?—which he pulls apart as if it were his own putrescing countenance, and agonises in a space-time continuum which recalls, now, a surgical operation, now a salt desert . . .')

There was Jeff Nuttall's cartoon strip, 'Alone In Swinging London, featuring Clifton de Berry and Vera Groin' ('Your first assignment, Vera my blossom, is to interview the visiting American poet Albert Hall'). Charles Mairowitz occupied most of the front page, and much of the back, of the first issue with a lengthy review of the Royal Shakespeare Company's treatment of the Vietnam War, *US*. 'If the double-entendre of the title means anything,' wrote Mairowitz, 'it means the Vietnam War, which is to say organised and accidental mass-murder, systematic torture, brazen deceit and chronic duplicity is *us*, rebounds on *us*, is answerable to *us* . . . It does not presume to press home a personal viewpoint, although even the fairest assemblage of facts cannot help but indict American Far East policy.'

And there was the *IT*-girl, the page-three hippy pin-up which was, before very long, to be cited as damning evidence of *International Times*'s overabundance of reckless testosterone. Those were the days before the second coming of twentieth-century feminism (a movement which grew partly out of the underground press and which, in its fledgling years, achieved some shamefaced coverage within those male-dominated magazines). The *IT*-girl, who became only an occasional feature by the spring of 1967, and was to be utterly abandoned before that year was out—although photographs and fantastic sketches of lubriciously decorated naked women wearing welcoming smiles were never entirely banished from the front covers, the feature sections and the advertising pages of the underground press—was not quite as bad as all that. When an understandably outraged Nigel Fountain accused the typical *IT*-girl of 'brandishing candles, bananas and transparent dresses', he was exaggerating. Invariably a friend of a member of staff, the average *IT*-girl posed demurely in such decorative dress as might have recently appeared on the London hippy marketplace . . . 'The *IT*-girl wears a new idea in jewellery made from dyed coral shells from the Philippines,' read the caption on page three of the first issue. 'This is not a money-catching project,' announced the jewellers. 'We regard jewellery-making as a craft.' Above this worthy nonsense stood a young woman draped in what appear to be foil-covered chocolate half-crowns. She would not have found shelf-space in the most moderate of Soho newsagents.

There was, in those early issues of *International Times*, little coverage of rock'n'roll. More space, indeed, was granted to progressive 'serious' music of the kind which was to be discovered at the 10th Warsaw Festival. A single column at the back of the paper was devoted to 'pop', and written by the archly by-lined 'Millionaire'. Having been fortunate enough to witness Ike and Tina Turner and the Rolling Stones on the same bill at the Albert Hall, *IT*'s 'pop' correspondent confessed himself disappointed with the sound system, although 'the power of Tina's voice almost managed to overcome the problems of the hall, and her dancing would overcome anything'. As for the Stones . . . ? 'I had not seen them work for almost a year and had got the impression from other reports that Jagger had, in this time, turned into an effective and dynamic stage performer. Far from it. Standing in a flowered jacket that glistened as with pearls or sequins, with his head between his legs and his arms outstretched, he looked more like a gymnast in fancy dress than he ever did.' That debilitating menu of underground press content, sex, dope and rock'n'roll, was not yet complete. The last course was to come, and play its part as a cornerstone of *IT*'s appeal.

But dope was there. From the very beginning, dope was there. To the outrage of parents and the displeasure of the law, the non-medical use of drugs informed most sections of the very earliest issues of *International Times*. 'Millionaire' regretted in his pop column a 'disconcertingly prejudiced article about pot in *Fab* magazine recently'. 'Vague, smiling acid-heads' were greeted on the front cover of the first issue as being certainly sympathetic to the new publication. The price of hash in the Greek archipelago, readers were informed, had reached £23 an ounce; and those nearer to home were warned to beware a 'pusher named Nigel in the Chelsea area, reportedly being supplied with anything he wants by the fuzz, in order to set people up. Has red hair.'

And the *International Times*, for all of its reports from Peking, its profiles of French philosophers, its details of dope prices in Ibiza, had London—the new, emerging London—at its feet. Almost accidentally, and certainly without lasting regard for the importance of their discovery, the editorial board had stumbled upon a city whose entertainment industry was experiencing rapid and remarkable change. The one weary listings magazine, *What's On*, had neither the will nor the capacity to monitor the performances of a score of psychedelic rock bands, experimental theatre groups, Op Art exhibitions, poetry and jazz sessions, and lectures in the ICA on 'The Nature of Perception'.

International Times, in its gauche and energetic youth, was anxious above all to create in the capital of Great Britain a 24-hour city, a metropolis which was capable of keeping pace with its young citizens. Along with an end to the war in Vietnam and the legalisation of cannabis, *IT* wanted an all-night tube service. As an adjunct, almost, to this campaign, as proof of the demand for public transport at four in the morning between Morden and Marylebone, *IT* began to fill its back page with lists of 'What's Happening . . . London, England, Europe, Night, Day, Continuous'. In doing so it fell, unwittingly, upon a marketing strategy. The diary service was free and it quickly burgeoned, becoming an intolerable nuisance to a staff which was 'just in it because we like playing games'. Eighteen months after the launch of *IT*, when a likeable graduate of Keele University—who had himself been selling 50 copies of *IT* a fortnight on his campus throughout the summer of 1967—called in and asked if the flourishing magazine would be offended if he took the 'What's Happening' section and turned it into a separate magazine, the staff gave Tony Elliott a grateful nod. Partly in the congenial spirit of the day, partly because the future belonged anyway to a widespread and co-operative underground press, and largely because of the unqualified relief which was gained by off-loading so much drudgery, Elliott and his notion of an events sheet with the name of *Time Out* were warmly greeted and helped on their way. By the end of 1968, *IT*'s 'What's Happening' section and its 40,000 fortnightly sale were both in irreversible decline.

Between the beginning and the beginning of the end, the magazine hosted some extraordinary editorial material. Barry Miles, a bespectacled academic character with a passion for the American beat poets, had discovered early in his career that the celebrities of the New Age, far from being aloof and unapproachable, were often just waiting to be approached by an intelligent interviewer. It made a pleasant change from listing their favourite foods and pet hobbies to *Fab* magazine. Miles had little or no interest in popular music—he was to claim that, when he first

Anderson, Neville and Dennis prepare themselves for the Central Criminal Courts and possible life sentences in prison

But would you wish your wife or servants to read it . . . ? The unexpurgated Chatterley, finally on sale (The Hulton–Deutsch Collection)

Freewheeling sexuality in the dock . . . Christine Keeler enters court (The Hulton–Deutsch Collection)

The art of hitch-hiking ... whether to display the palm of the hand, to look the driver directly in the eye, or to indicate aggressively in the desired direction ... ? (The Hulton–Deutsch Collection)

Reclaiming the planet—or at least the public parks—with vague, swirling visions of a new social order (The Hulton–Deutsch Collection)

A solitary Rocker, led to custodial safety at Margate, 1964 (The Hulton–Deutsch Collection)

I can go anywhere, at 65.3mph, for as little as £109.00 (The Hulton–Deutsch Collection)

Let me through, I'm a graphic designer . . . (BBC Hulton Picture Library)

Those radical Redgraves ... Vanessa addresses the troops. Grosvenor Square, 1968 (The Hulton–Deutsch Collection)

For a while the dream almost became reality, and the smell of marijuana mingled with CS gas above the cobblestone barricades of Paris, 1968 (The Hulton–Deutsch Collection)

Could an October Revolution be launched from Grosvenor Square? No
(The Hulton–Deutsch Collection)

What future here, for anybody's children? Desolation Row, the Isle of
Wight (The Hulton–Deutsch Collection)

*'By the end of the second meeting they wanted to change everything'—
the Oz triumvirate and their schoolkid editors*

*The days of not taking it seriously
... Inspector Luff removes the
evidence ...*

*... and Oz goes its merry way. 'We
knew he was in earnest when he
began removing the filing cabinets'*

came across the Beatles, he did not know anything about them, was entirely disrespectful of their enormous popularity, and could not tell John from Ringo. The Beatles liked Miles, and from that strange social circle a number of exclusive interviews found their way onto the pages of *International Times*. Four years later John Lennon was to grant Jan Wenner a couple of extensive, life-saving interviews in his struggling *Rolling Stone* magazine.* Between 1966 and 1968, Lennon and other British rock stars helped to establish *IT*'s editorial reputation—and, in the process, a new form of pop journalism—by talking freely and with confidence to the engaging Barry Miles.

Pete Townshend was one of the first. 'Well presented destruction is what I call a joy to watch,' he told *IT* readers through the medium of Miles. 'Just like well presented pornography or obscenity. Although destruction is not as strong as obscenity, it's not so vulgar but it's rare, you don't see destruction so often, not malicious destruction just for the sake of it, and so when you do you normally stop and watch . . . I'm not afraid of calling anything I do an art form . . . I go on and smash a £200 guitar and they go home and say, "Yes, they were quite good tonight!" When I first did it people used to come up to me and say, "You bastard! I've been saving all my life for a guitar a tenth of that price, and there you are, smashing it up on stage. Give me the bits!" and I have to say, "Calm down, it's all in the cause" . . . All I know, is that there's this beautiful land ahead where all the problems are answered . . .'

'We're Beatles, and it's a little scene,' said George Harrison to 'the only honest paper' in the spring of 1967 ('you can print your paper, you know that they can't touch you because you

---

* Lennon's support of the British insurgency was consistent and mostly anonymous. Many years later, in 1974, when I was editing the last issues of *International Times*, I received one day a telephone call from the Beatles' London promotional centre, Apple (which was also on its last legs), asking me to call down to their office. On arrival I was given a cheque for £1,000, told that it was a gift from Lennon, and that it was given on the understanding that no publicity would be attached. I agreed and kept my word until the morning after his assassination in December 1980. I was working then on a newspaper in the north-west of Scotland and when the news of Lennon's death came in I told a friend of his unprompted generosity six years earlier. That friend looked startled, and confided that when he had been a student in the early 1970s he had taken part in a demonstration against the South African rugby tourists in Edinburgh, which had resulted in several hundreds of students being arrested. Their massive total of fines looked set to bankrupt the students' unions which had organised the demonstration, until a cheque which covered the entire amount arrived in the post from John Lennon, along with an insistence that no publicity be afforded the gift.

know more than them'). 'We're playing and we're pretending to
be Beatles, like Harold Wilson's pretending to be Prime Minister
and you're pretending to be the Interview on *IT*. They're all
playing. The Queen's the Queen. The idea that you wake up and
it happens that you're Queen, it's amazing, but you could all be
Queens if you imagined it . . . they'll have a war quickly if it gets
too good, they'll just pick on the nearest person to save us from
our doom.'

'Our society is a white European race, an island kingdom,'
mused Mick Jagger in a 1968 issue of *IT*. 'As a race, not very very
old, but it's very proud, and it's quite old, and it's not been
changed around too much and it's been preserved, and . . . you get
five million black people in it, really change things. Because they
just are different and they don't live the same, not even if they
were born here they don't . . . And it breaks up the society, it
doesn't just break it up into black and white, it breaks the white
up into, like, getting on with black people and not getting on with
black people.' There was little hope, Mick considered, to be found
in an alternative society which, posited Miles, 'as it grew would be
the society itself'.

'They haven't got an alternative,' insisted Jagger. 'They've
still got all the things of the other society, in other words *their*
society . . . They're both the thinnest film on water, you can't
float a boat on it. I mean, but they're just veneers, they're looking
at each other and they're the same fucking thing! And they'll
degenerate to the same thing, they'll degenerate to putting helmets
on and fighting each other, and when they come out they won't
know who the fuck they are.'

There was to be internal feuding, and there was certainly to
be a crisis of identity, but in the short term *IT* was more concerned
with the aggressive attention of the law. On 9 March, 1967, the
day before the publication of issue number 10, 12 plain clothes
detectives entered the Southampton Row office carrying a warrant
issued under the Obscene Publications Act, 1959. They removed
every copy of *IT*, an address book, the accountant's briefcase, the
subscription list and file of distribution outlets, a large photoblock
of the next *IT*-girl, several books (by William Burroughs), and the
contents of every ash-tray. No charges were brought, but paranoia
ran quickly through the building. Tom McGrath delayed publication of the next issue in case it too was immediately seized, wrote
a long and nervous editorial—'the police seizure had done us one

favour in that it separated out those who are proud to associate themselves with *IT* when the praise and publicity are flowing but quickly dissociate themselves when the trouble begins'—and then left the building and the magazine for good. Others, most notably Mick Farren, a fast-talking aspirant rock singer with an afro hair style which, as Miles was to point out, made him a singular target for policemen at any public demonstration, quickly moved into the deserted citadel. With plaintive pleas for its subscribers to re-identify themselves, *IT* picked up the pieces.

In June one of the magazine's founders and favourite sons, the photographer John Hopkins, was sent to prison for nine months for possession of a small amount of cannabis. 'FREE HOPPY', demanded the front cover of *IT*, to no avail. 'When 1,000 teaheads can coolly take out 1,000 joints and smoke them in front of the Notting Hill police station,' a social worker named Jo wrote to the magazine, 'and when those 1,000 teaheads can be replaced by 1,000 more, that law will become a farce and will have to be changed. By that time Hoppy may be free—but action to change the law may save many others—you and me—in the future.' 'I am never,' editorialised Mick Farren, 'going to love policemen, whatever the hippies might tell me.' One week later Scotland Yard returned to Southampton Row the goods which had been seized in March—all of the goods, that is, except the cigarette butts. Somehow, in the smoke and the panic of the previous nine months, George Orwell's typewriter had disappeared.

It was an attractive life for the young and fit. It contained occasional brushes with the rich and famous, lively clashes with the law, a sense of danger and a froth of fun. There were free records, parties, concerts and drugs,* and the certainty of hovering about the arrogant edge of the new order which, whatever

---

* Occasionally the wages of the staff of *International Times* were paid in part or, sometimes, in full in the form of small blocks of hash. This was not regarded as unusual or undesirable by the employees, who correctly saw such remuneration as either a valid use of easily convertible alternative currency, or as a device which saved them the trouble of having to negotiate for their own weekly relaxants or, more commonly, as both. The economy of the underground would (and did) defy the most expert analysis. Taxes were never paid, advertising accounts were often settled with produce, be it clothes, meals or concert tickets. There was a widely debated theory that the whole network of mutually sympathetic enterprises existed for a number of years on a pool of about £500, the same £500 which found its way in dependable small percentages to and from the magazines, shops, restaurants, clubs and dope dealers, circulating in a mini-economy which was sealed almost hermetically from the world outside.

privileged cynics like Mick Jagger might suggest, was so obviously imminent. All this, and offset litho too . . . the underground press proliferated. By the end of the 1960s they were difficult to number: a host of hastily prepared broadsheets, linked by the Underground Press Syndicate (which forswore copyright within its membership, thereby gifting to its British members the invaluable, and frequently abused, claim to the published works of such American comic talents as Robert Crumb and Gilbert Shelton). There was in Manchester the persistent *Mole Express*, edited by a pessimistic, lugubrious young man named Mike Don. '*Mole*,' he would tell enquirers, 'hasn't got much sign of a future. It has a hairy past to live down. A history of mediocrity burdens us.' Yorkshire had *Styng* and its successor, *Horse* ('It's quite simple really. We're fighting a lunatocracy.'). *Grapevine* endowed the city of Birmingham—'There's so much dirt to turn over in this city, we're just feeling our way into it . . . the midlands may be the wastelands, but first we have to prove it.' There was to be the *Devon Snail* and the *Liverpool Free Press*, *Muther Grumble* in Durham and *Hod* in Leeds. Lacking distribution and lacking advertising, they burst keenly into life and fizzled, without exception, to the ground as the decade died.

Only in London, where the record company advertising executives lived, where Moore-Harness operated a non-judgmental distribution company, where young artists and writers gravitated, desperate to see their work in print, did the underground press find some longevity. There were brief candles in the city too: *Gandalf's Garden*, a magazine so committed to the acid generation that during its short existence it made parody of the underground press redundant; *Cyclops*, the first underground comic book; the English edition of *Rolling Stone*, which after its staff had excited the terrible wrath of US proprietor Jann Wenner and his main financial backer, Mick Jagger (chiefly through their holding of a publicity party which dosed record company executives and some of the rock industry's finer musical talents with bad acid—see Chapter Three) and been removed from their plush offices in Hanover Square, became an *ad hoc* venture based in the Portobello Road called *Friends of Rolling Stone*, and then *Friends*, and then *Frendz*.

But London was home to the twin pillars of the British underground press. *International Times*, the house magazine, diligently published every other Thursday for eight years, expertly trading in its publishing company for another each time a print bill could not be paid—so expertly that, by the end, its staff performed this trick without dropping an issue, without missing a step—*International Times* was one. The other was a dilettantish, impetuous thing which never kept a date in its life; a brash and colourful and thoroughly charming creature, absolutely its father's child; which was to become, for a few weeks towards the end of its life, the best-publicised magazine in Britain—too late, unfortunately, to help its beleaguered business manager.

Richard Neville first published *Oz* magazine in Sydney, Australia, on April Fool's Day, 1963. It was a satirical postgraduate publication, staffed by some of Neville's rebellious cohorts from the University of New South Wales and also, as it gathered pace, by some who were to join Neville in London, such as the brilliant designer Martin Sharp and Marsha Rowe, who would ten years later co-found *Spare Rib*.

Australian *Oz*, the *Private Eye* of the antipodes, quickly amassed a remarkable sale of 40,000 copies—assisted, naturally, by the fact that the very first issue was charged with obscenity and fined $40. By issue number six, which was published in February 1964, the Australian authorities had a gimlet eye firmly fixed on *Oz*, and were ready to pounce. The cover of number six gave them the opportunity to do so—an opportunity which seemed even then to be fatuous. The civic pride of Sydney in the early 1960s was the town's new P & O building, an expensive pile which was embroidered at ground level by a fountain. This fountain, considered Neville and his colleagues, looked like a urinal. It looked so much like a urinal that they had themselves photographed apparently pissing into it. The photograph appeared on the front cover of *Oz* number six and the editors were promptly arraigned before Sydney magistrates' court on charges of obscenity; they found themselves sentenced to six months' imprisonment with hard labour.

The sentences were revoked on appeal, but Richard Neville had had enough of New South Wales. He packed a bag and hit the hippy trail, north and west through Asia, towards the beckoning lights of Swinging London. Neville arrived at the London flat of his elder sister in September 1966, wearing an Afghan coat and ready for conquest. News of his Australian trials had reached the London media, and the *Evening Standard* shortly sent round a young reporter named Mary Kenny to interview Neville. 'I panicked at the sight of my first reporter in London,' he remembered. 'I thought, my God, how can I make myself *interesting*? Give her good copy? And of course, I started waxing lyrically on how we were going to start a magazine that would shake the city walls. And of course Mary Kenny went off and wrote it, and the next day the 'phone started ringing—the birth of British *Oz*.'

If *International Times* was the tabloid of the self-styled alternative society, *Oz*, which was launched in London in January 1967, quickly became its colour supplement. Shaking off an early interest in being a satirical media review (the first issues weakly lampooned, among other targets, the *New Statesman*—which had given Neville's venture a gentlemanly welcome—and *Private Eye*—which had warned him to steer clear of its precious readership), *Oz* achieved a style and a momentum of its own. The style was largely visual,* wholly experimental, obviously influenced by LSD, without precedent in magazine publishing and quite inimitable. *Oz* was mercurial; its logo, the fixed and sacred point of reader identification to all other publications (not least, of course, to *IT*), changed wildly from issue to issue, becoming buried, on one or two financially ruinous covers, in vivid artwork. Its shape and format altered, from vertical to horizontal A4, to tabloid, to being two feet square. Its content was thematic: there was a Flying Saucer *Oz*, a Travel *Oz*, a Cuntpower *Oz* (edited by a lecturer at Warwick University named Germaine Greer), and, reassuringly, a Granny's *Oz*. Neville's charm and wit and catholicity attracted to *Oz* a unique range of writers, from Greer to Auberon Waugh to David Widgery, but as often as not these diligent stylists were appalled to find their copy printed in yellow type over an aquamarine background, or reversed out of a rainbow

---

* Although the work of many of the artists and cartoonists who originally appeared in the underground press was within ten years to be seen liberally sprinkled throughout the publications of Fleet Street, the established press of the time was reluctant to seize upon this new talent. Part of the reason for this may lie in the salutary tale of J. Edward Barker. Barker, the designer of *IT* and a droll cartoonist, was asked in 1970 if he would draw a weekly strip for *The Observer*. 'I was introduced to David Astor [the editor/proprietor],' he recalled, 'and he smiled encouragingly and said, "I understand you're *funny*".' For ten pounds a week (more than his full-time *IT* wage) Barker proceeded to introduce the readers of the liberal Sunday press to the Largactilites, a collection of cone-shaped creatures who did very little and said less. That readership erupted in fury at the name of the animals, as the drug largactile was used in the treatment of the mentally ill. Barker adroitly changed them into the Galactilites, but his heart had gone out of his task, and a few weeks later he handed in a four-frame strip which consisted of four simple horizon lines. The strip was run (and consequently became the first cartoon to find itself in *Private Eye*'s Pseud's Corner), but a week later *The Observer* apologetically informed him that the experiment had failed, and he was paid off.

effect which had been created at some indulgent print shop in the stoned hours before dawn ('what happens if we put blue in this part of the duct, yellow here, and then ochre at the far end . . . ?'). The writers had a point. While not all of their articles were quite as illegible as they later claimed, *Oz* put its illustrators and its designers first. If most issues of the magazine had been produced in, say, the prosaic, copy-led style of the *New Statesman*, in simple, unyielding columns of grey type, it would indeed have been a mostly worthless and unnoticed publication. Instead, *Oz* became a champion, arguably *the* champion, of psychedelic style. Once or twice in that roller-coaster process—and only once or twice, for consistency was, by the magazine's own definition, undesirable—when an inspired Martin Sharp let loose upon its art-boards, an issue of *Oz* became as essential an experience to the commonplace hedonist of the 1960s as the taking of any psychotropic substance.

Richard Neville took a great and unselfish delight in the talents of others. A clever, disciplined and lucid writer himself, he recognised those qualities whenever and wherever they came into view, and would promptly be filled with a youthful enthusiasm to put them into print. He loved wit and incongruity in all of his contributors. He was an almost irresistible editor who believed that once the commission had been accomplished and the artist or the writer set to work, the job of the commissioner was to go to a party, or to a Mediterranean island.*

While *International Times*, responsible for a schedule and bound to its busy offices, responded to police and press hostility with bitterness and outrage, *Oz* ridiculed and exploited the enemy. Flippant, vagrant, flying by night from one printer to another,† incapable of being pinned down even to a publication date,

---

* And he saw copy in every situation. On one occasion when *Oz* magazine had taken refuge on the top floor of a West End office block, its staff found themselves to be the subject of a one-man picket line from a disabled person in a wheelchair who, having established that there was no lift in the building and that no secretary was prepared to carry him up four flights of stairs, blocked the entrance with placards which accused the underground press of discrimination against the disabled, and loudly harangued the central London lunchtime crowds. All pleas were in vain, until Neville arrived, discovered within five minutes that the demonstrator was fond of taking LSD, and sent him away to prepare a major feature for the magazine on the pleasures and the benefits of psychotropic drugs to persons who are confined within wheelchairs.

† By issue number 26, British *Oz* had worked its way through no fewer than 16 different English printers. Not all of them rejected the magazine entirely because of its content. One did so because, as its manager apologetically explained, 'we're rather close to the Palace, here, you see.'

Neville's magazine made an elusive target. In 1969 the garish Sunday tabloid *The People* decided to expose the underground press in all of its vile corruption. A reporter conducted a telephone interview with Neville before writing:

> Your kid may pick up a magazine in a discotheque or record shop. It will look way-out, switched-on and hippy. And it will contain precise details of sexual practices that make Fanny Hill seem as depraved as Goldilocks . . . That's the sort of literary freedom that the proprietors of the so-called 'underground' magazines, *Oz* and *IT*, are getting . . . Both *Oz* and *IT*, so far as I can understand them, contain political and social comment in a zany kind of way. Maybe they are published for ideological reasons. But there's no ideology in teaching kids to take drugs and mutilate their sex organs, as *Oz* does. I implore shop and discotheque owners: Don't help to spread this muck.

The People's article was illustrated with a photograph of a recent *Oz* front cover which had shown a Hell's Angel in full regalia being embraced by a lissom girl, an advertisement for the sex-aid suppliers Pellen Personal Products, and a photograph of a monstrously ugly, bearded hippy with matted, tangled hair, which was captioned: 'The kind of editor that *Oz* has . . . Mr Richard Neville.' *The People*, as *The Guardian* approvingly noted a week later, had been set up. Before the arrival of their photographer, Neville had pressed into service an itinerant, kenspeckle figure of the underground, a drug-besotted American named Lee Heater who had the single advantage in life of looking, smelling and talking exactly like a *People* photographer's preconception of the editor of *Oz* magazine. Heater introduced himself as Neville, Neville himself pottered unobtrusively about in the background, and the photographer did his undistinguished work. It was a game, a huge game . . . it was all just for fun . . . nothing was certain, nothing was real, if *The People* and its readers wanted Lee Heater rather than the personable Richard Neville to be the editor of *Oz*, then they should *have* Lee Heater . . .

The pages of *Oz* did not often urge children to 'mutiliate their sex organs', but they did contain—among the recipes for baked brown rice and David Widgery's exasperated polemics—a careless number of erotic drawings and photographs of woman-as-object, and they invariably included the most extraordinary advice column in British publishing.

Eugene Schoenfeld MD was, and is, a respectable Californian general practitioner, who moonlighted as 'Dr *Hip*ocrates', the 'Dear Marje' of the Underground Press Syndicate. His work was relayed from state to state, and was seized upon by *Oz* with glee. 'Where can I get myself *castrated*?' a reader might ask the good doctor. 'I'm tired of sex. I hate sex . . . Will a hospital do it? I don't mean just removing the tubes. I mean cutting off the dick and the sac . . .' or 'Am I gaining calories by ingesting my boyfriend's semen? Should I keep an account of this and add it to my diet chart?' Hipocrates' inquisitors were often unbalanced or naïve to the point of inanity, but his answers were a model of responsibility. ('I think you should call the Department of Mental Health of your county. Don't cut off your nose to spite your face,' was his advice to the first questioner; and 'it would seem likely that these felonies committed with your boyfriend lead to a net calory loss for both of you', his reply to the second.) To the average reader of *Oz*, Eugene Schoenfeld was both a comic turn and a gorgeous riposte to the trite and puritanical agony aunts of the established press. To *The People*, the policemen of the Obscene Publications Squad, and the Crown Prosecution Service, such writing in its bed of licentious artwork and drug-inspired design represented a calculated affront to public decency and to the dignity of the law. At the other side of London the editors of *International Times* were delivered an indictment to appear in court and answer charges of publishing illegal contact advertisements for the homosexual community, and then, for a couple of years at least, the authorities switched their gaze to Holland Park and the sidestreet terrace offices of *Oz*. Inspector Frederick Luff began to make his calls.

'Felix, Jim and myself greeted the harassment of *Oz* with only sporadic bursts of seriousness,' wrote Richard Neville in January 1971, 'as had many of our friends. It was instinctively assumed that we could ultimately establish in a court that *Oz* did not deprave and corrupt—even if it meant redefining the whole concept of obscenity. Notwithstanding the perpetual ransacking of our offices, we were aware that in less enlightened communities we would have been automatically jailed. But it has finally dawned upon us that the authorities in this country take our publishing venture more seriously than we do.'

Felix Dennis and Jim Anderson had arrived at *Oz* magazine from different perspectives. Anderson had trained as a barrister in

Australia, before dropping out, meandering the hippy trail through Africa, and arriving in London with the ambition—which he has since realised—to become a novelist. A tall, quietly-spoken, accessible man, he found himself organising the production and artwork of *Oz*—a job whose strain was never more apparent than on the morning when he fell asleep on an early tube and woke to find that the camera-ready boards for an entire issue, which he had been delivering to the printer, had been stolen. Dennis was a drummer with an indifferent rock band who, with the roughneck assurance that would make him a publishing millionaire before his thirtieth birthday, sat down one evening in his south London flat and dictated into a tape recorder a lengthy critique of *Oz* magazine, which he then posted to Neville. The two met, Neville charmed Dennis into selling copies of *Oz* on the King's Road, a task which the young Londoner performed with such aplomb that within months he was able to commandeer a managerial seat in the office and to complete the triumvirate which steered *Oz* into and out of the Old Bailey.

In 1969 the British underground press was approaching, as a confederacy, its corporate apex of magazine sales and advertising revenue. It was also running out of ideas. Its original constituency, the Mod generation which had, along with Bob Dylan and the Beatles and even, eventually, the Beats, discovered LSD-25 and electric acid rock and had briefly considered that they might somehow fashion a new society from the two, was growing old and starting to squabble. New and fiercer drugs were entering the magic circus ring—drugs which the underground press stoutly resisted, drugs which, they warned their readers, could be as lethal as tobacco or alcohol, but drugs which would be tested and taken by the empirical generation which the underground press had served and encouraged. The citizens of flower power, insofar as they had ever existed, had vanished from the streets as sharply as had the missionaries of Mod.

There was disillusion in the air. Women such as Marsha Rowe at *Oz* and Rosie Boycott at *Frendz* were waking to the fact that when it came to visual proof of the sexual revolution, it was most frequently their sisters' genitalia which figured in the evidence, and were talking of beginning their own, feminist imprint. The rock'n'roll music which, for a while, had been the province of the underground press, was revealed with every day that passed to be nothing more than another product of the international entertainment industry. Three of its practitioners, three Americans who were innocently perceived as likely to confront these contradictions, Janis Joplin, Jimi Hendrix and Jim Morrison, choked to death before their mother decade was herself cold in the grave. The better rock writers of the underground press would soon be tempted, like Indian scouts with their secrets, to the providential pages of *New Musical Express* and *Melody Maker*.

'In the formative stages of the counter culture,' Richard Neville stated to the nation, 'it was possible to draw inspiration from the open behaviour of Albion's children. It was tempting, if naïve, to hope that with the intake of id liberating rock, lateralising dope, the emerging group tenderness, communal living style and an intuitive political radicalism ... that from all this a qualitative change in the conduct of human relationships might develop. But ...'

But ... 'we must organise real people and actual organisations, not a series of publicity stunts and press openings with the same old cast,' replied David Widgery in the following issue.

Real people? Actual organisations? There was still *fun* to be had, trails to be followed, youth to be tapped. As 1969 turned into 1970, Neville, Dennis and Anderson inserted a small advertisement in *Oz* 26. 'Some of us at *Oz*,' it read, 'are feeling old and boring. So we invite any of our readers who are under 18 to come and edit the April issue. Apply at the *Oz* office in Princedale Road, W11, any time from 10 a.m. to 7 p.m. on Friday, March 13th. We will choose one person, several, or accept collective applications from a group of friends. You will receive no money, except expenses, and you will enjoy almost complete editorial freedom.'

Six months later, when detective inspector Frederick Luff of the Obscene Publications Squad arrived at Princedale Road with a warrant allowing the seizure of Schoolkids' *Oz* in his hand and the certainty in his heart that *this* time *Oz* had gone too far, Richard Neville happened to be on the telephone to the office from the island of Ibiza. Then, as so often, a backwater of the trail was probably the best place to be.

CHAPTER SIX

HITCHING

There were nine young people in Crete busted for possession and use of hashish. Arrested very randomly, they were woken with machine guns, pulled off the beach and from their own cars, taken in unmarked cars and held for two days without food, clothes or communication privileges and for six to seven days without formal charges. While this is acceptable Greek arrest procedure, the amazing thing is the attitude taken by the Embassy in Athens— 'they deserve what they get'.

NEWS ITEM IN *IT*, AUGUST 1969

Arne and Shershtin drove their customised Volkswagen minibus south through the liberal suburbs of Stockholm on a summer's morning in the second half of the 1960s. They had prepared for this journey for months. The interior of the minibus had been gutted and then rebuilt to an open plan, draped with paisley patterns, carpeted with mattresses and stuffed with enormous bean bags. A stick of joss, wedged into a window frame, burnt slowly and dripped its pencil of ash harmlessly onto a shelf crammed with tins of food.

The outside of the bus had not been extravagantly decorated. Arne and Shershtin were not desirous of attracting much attention. They were carrying two passports each, one for Europe and the other, stamped with enough recent European seals of entry to make the deception work, for Asia, so that on the way back from Afghanistan the six customs posts which they would have to brave between Turkey and Sweden would have no way of knowing that they had been in the lands of the cannabis growers. Carrying two passports each is illegal, and Shershtin kept the spare ones, the passports to be brought out in Asia, in a neat little leather pouch which hung around her neck. They smiled at each other a lot as they drove towards Halsinborg and the Denmark ferry, he tall and thin, she shorter and gregarious, each of them with long blond hair which had frequently to be tossed out of their eyes. There was some danger ahead of them on this hippy trail, but the reward for a successful journey would be substantial: enough hashish loaded behind the panels of the minibus to keep them comfortable in Stockholm for a year or more. And they were young and, like so many of their contemporaries, they were contemptuous of the forces which might try to arrest their progress. If it came to trouble, Arne at least was certain, they could outstrip trouble. They could levitate above it. Shershtin was confident that by simply adopting a certain, uncomplicated frame of mind, they would not encounter trouble in the first place. They had done nothing wrong and they were not planning to do anything wrong. Their kharma was good.

They drove through Denmark and West Germany. South-west of Munich the *autobahn* reached the border with Austria, at the top of a high and sprawling hill, half-covered still with forest, from whose summit the spires of Salzburg seemed a short but comfortable walk. There was nothing on this hilltop but the border guards, customs officials, several carparks, a beerhouse and, on either side of the desolate borderline, lengthy queues of young people waving their thumbs at both north- and south-bound traffic. Each and every one of those young hitch-hikers had been taken in a lift to the border but dropped off before the barrier by drivers anxious not to be delayed while their passengers were searched for drugs, or to be held responsible themselves for anything found upon them, or to discover that the cushions of their car-seats had been used as a temporary dope caché. Some of the hitch-hikers had been there for days, sleeping at night in the woods or in the backs of lorries whose accommodating drivers were awaiting clearance to take their goods into or out of Germany.

Arne and Shershtin would pick up one or two of these stranded youngsters, but they would exercise discretion. They wanted no straights. On the Austrian side of the border they cruised slowly down the line, finally spotting two disconsolate, longhaired Englishmen. Arne slowed to a crawl and wound down his window.

'Where to?'

'Anywhere. Out of here. Yugoslavia? Greece . . .?'

'Instanbul? Afghanistan?'

The two young men threw in their bags, and the minibus set off towards the Austrian Alps, towards Klagenfurt and Yugoslavia. Halfway up an Alp, in the middle of that night, the throttle cable which ran from beneath Arne's right foot to the engine at the rear of the vehicle, snapped in the middle of the undercarriage. One of the two Englishmen pronounced it unrepairable, but wedged open the carburettor with such precision that the minibus, lodged permanently into first gear, was able to crawl the steepest of the moonlit Alps, occasionally reaching the summit with all three passengers pushing and the driver walking alongside with one hand on the steering wheel, like muleteers with a reluctant beast. As the descent began they would all leap aboard—all but Arne, who, with an Englishman at the wheel, preferred to climb onto the roof-rack and lie howling gleefully at the mountains and ravines while the minibus freewheeled down around precipitous curves towards the Yugoslav border. He was always still there at the bottom, dropping down onto the tarmac, windblown and exhilarated as another climb began.

On the western outskirts of Ljubljana they came across a roadside garage. Arne bought a throttle cable and borrowed a tool-chest from the mechanics, and handed them to the Englishman with the frizzled, ginger Afro hair and the Fu Manchu moustache. When it was fitted Arne threw the tool-chest in the back of the vehicle and drove away at speed. It was booty, legitimate booty; an endowment of the trail.

Between Zagreb and Belgrade, along the meandering banks of the Sava River, Arne stopped again to pick up two more young men. They were Danes, each with long, straight, light-brown hair and high back-packs. They spoke quietly to each other in the back of the minibus. They were intensely serious. They were, they explained, on their way to India. 'It is possible there,' they explained in the English which became the currency of the vehicle, 'to live without spending any money. Not just for a day or a week, but for years. You can go to people's houses and they will feed you, for *nothing*! It will be a good life.' Arne and the Englishmen exchanged uneasy glances. Arne did not believe in living for nothing. Arne believed in trade.

The party was held up at the Bulgarian border, 30 miles from Sofia, by officials who were plainly anxious to discourage them from entry. In the town of Plovdiv, while Arne negotiated the minibus through hectic traffic in the cobbled central square, a traffic policeman blowing furiously upon a whistle approached the vehicle and demanded to see passports. They were handed over and, without looking at them, he planted them firmly into a back trouser pocket and, holding out an open palm, demanded the spot payment of a fine which, it was quickly calculated, amounted to less than two pounds sterling.

'No,' said Arne, firmly. Shershtin, after looking anxiously through the dashboard tray, began to speak to him urgently in Swedish.

'No,' he repeated.

Shershtin turned despairingly to their passengers. 'I gave him the wrong passports,' she said. 'He has the Asian passports.'

'No,' said Arne to the policeman, getting out of the minibus. 'It is a bluff. They do it all the time. There is no fine.' He put an arm around the official. '*Polizei stazione*,' he said, pointing down the main street while obstructed traffic honked and drivers shouted all about. 'We go to the *polizei stazione*.' Grudgingly, the policeman handed back the passports and waved the minibus away. On the long straight road out of Plovdiv towards the Turkish border, the bus came up behind a Bulgarian Army staff car with two grizzled, brown-coated and red-starred officers in its back seat. The white lines down the middle of the road were newly painted and rubber bollards had been planted neatly between them. Arne swerved out to overtake the staff car, crashing through the bollards, and, once in the left-hand lane, drove alongside it for half a mile, catching bollards with his offside bumper and expertly sending them spinning into the side, or into the path, of the stately staff car. There was no response, no sign of recognition or of anger, from the set expressions of the senior military men and their chauffeur.

Before leaving Bulgaria they stopped at a village to buy yoghurt and milk and bread. The people of the township crowded curiously around the minibus, smiling, and when the representatives of western youth joined the queue to the dairy, a queue which stretched out of the shop and down the dusty street, they were laughingly pushed to the front. By the time that they left, a hundred villagers had gathered to inspect them, children perched upon their fathers' shoulders, old women in black clucking and beaming and answering in kind the waves from within the Volkswagen minibus.

They stopped for an afternoon in a wooded grove by a lake,

while the Danes lit a fire and boiled handfuls of a dozen varieties of dried beans and pulses. They swam naked in the torpid water, emerging with cattle-leeches fixed to their limbs, and dried in the hot sun while Arne and Shershtin retired to the empty minibus; buffalo-drawn ploughs worked distant fields, and the unsoaked beans simmered without softening throughout the drawn-out day.

The two Englishmen disembarked in Istanbul. Arne dropped them outside the Pudding Shoppe, a small café which was patronised almost entirely by the itinerant young, which sold cakes, sweet tea and coffee and advertised upon its walls lifts offered or desired to the east or to the west, which informed the newly-arrived where their friends were staying or if they had already moved on.

Arne and Shershtin drove eastwards, with the Danes, through Armenia and Iran towards Afghanistan, collecting and depositing long-haired pilgrims as they went. They arrived in a Kabul which the writer Murray Sayle described at the time as 'the end of the line, the roughest stop in the great hippy trail which girdles the earth from San Francisco to Nepal.'

'Rooms run to 150 afghanis (approximately 75p) a night, plus food,' reported Sayle, 'although most of the young guests prefer for budgetary reasons to eat out—a meal of grilled mutton or goat, carrying a fair risk of stomach ailments or hepatitis, can be had in many wayside street cafés for the equivalent of 3p, while the standard Afghan diet of sweet tea and Afghan bread costs only 1p.'

Drugs of every kind were available in Afghanistan; opiates and amphetamines could be bought over the counter in Kabul's back street pharmacies. There were no formalities such as prescriptions or drug registers, and any minor hitch could easily and instantly be overcome by the production of a 100 afghani note, worth 60p. The hillspeople who were to become internationally famous, ten years later, as the Mujahaddin resistance to Soviet occupation, controlled much of the country beyond the city pale. 'Savage tribesmen,' said Sayle, 'who, in a system which dates from the days when Afghanistan was an unwilling British colony, are paid subsidies by the government to behave themselves and refrain from killing people on certain roads. Since the tribesmen can muster 200,000 picked riflemen on an off-day the police never go into the tribal areas and the army only in large numbers. These tribal areas happen to be the places where the best hashish reckoned by connoisseurs to be the finest in the world is grown. The tribesmen often bring hashish to Kabul with them and are willing to sell it to tourists, along with their guns, their sisters, and anything else on which they can raise a little cash.'

Sayle met a young American woman, who told him with wide china-blue eyes, of the beauty of the Afghani-based hashish industry. 'We run no risk at all . . .' she said, explaining how hashish was bought for between eight and 18 dollars a kilo and shipped in false-bottomed suitcases to Amsterdam by hippy 'runners' who were paid $1,000 for the cargo, whose bulk value in western Europe was $2,000 *a kilo*.

He also attended the funeral of Joseph William Morris, a 24-year-old from Hatfield, England, who was found dead in a Kabul hotel with a needle of cheap morphine still hanging from his arm. 'He was the ninth young British traveller in search of adventure or illumination to have died an untimely death in Afghanistan in the past eight weeks . . . The graves are temporarily unmarked while the Embassy in Kabul attempts to collect instructions from parents about headstones and funds to erect them with. If both fail a row of simple wooden markers is planned.' Joe Morris was known by no British official in Kabul, by no vice-consul or clergyman, and he had made the acquaintance of but a few of his fellow westerners. He was a withdrawn and haggard youth. 'He just did not care any more,' a girl who stayed in the same hotel told Sayle. His body was discovered by the postman, who was attempting to deliver to Morris a letter and a postal order from England.

The two Danes left Arne and Shershtin in this place of cheap deals and occasional death, and moved on towards the milk and honey of the Punjab. The two Englishmen failed to find, even upon the walls of the Pudding Shoppe, a lift southwards into Asian Turkey, so they crossed the Bosphorus and took a train to Izmir. They were robbed of all but their clothes, their passports and their money while bathing in the peaceful bay of Kusadasi, and travelled onwards, barefooted, in rattling omnibuses, through the stricken villages and the gypsy-lands of south-western Turkey, through Milas and Mugla to Marmaris and the open boat to the island of Rhodes.

Rhodes, and in particular its outlying township of Lindos, was a backwater of the trail. Like Mykonos and Ibiza, like Hydra and Formentera, it was a seasonal rendezvous for many of the travelling young and a permanent settlement for the envied few. Scattered among its indigenous population and its centres of tourism were small white houses, scented, in the Mediterranean warmth, with patchouli oil, joss and marijuana smoke, echoing with the thin sound of a transistorised tape recorder playing Bob Dylan cassettes and with the shouts of a few small children named Sunshine and Aquarius, houses with loosely-clothed, soft-eyed young men and women lounging upon their terraces or upon the shoreline rocks below, houses which were left, to a large degree, alone and unperturbed by the native islanders. The occupants of these houses were often American, occasionally rich and famous— Leonard Cohen wrote many of the classical dirges of the 1960s on the Greek island of Hydra—and always fully aware that their lot and their lifestyle was more enviable by several degrees than that of the occupant of a west London squat. More enviable, that is, until the law-enforcement officers of Generalissimo Franco or of the Athenian military junta arrived to make their investigations.

The two Englishmen booked into a cheap pension in the centre of the old town of Rhodes, where they found themselves sharing a decuplet room with a secretive and frightened young American. Just one week earlier the villa in which he was staying in Lindos had been raided by the Colonels' police. He had been away at the time, but his two friends were searched, discovered to be in possession of a small amount of hashish, beaten, chained together, driven north to Rhodes, and marched in manacles through the centre of the town to the police cells, the police court, and a one-year prison sentence which they had just commenced at a small jail on the eastern coast of the island. His absence had been noted by the authorities, who had publicised the fact that if he was to reappear he might anticipate the same fate. He shivered in the warm evening, wondering when it might be safe to sneak onto the ferry to Athens, and the two Englishmen wondered if the villa was still empty.

It was. They requisitioned the building and the blankets which had been left behind. They admitted a German couple who took fond comfort from the fact that after the revolution, everybody would have such a house by the sea. They were visited by the local Lindos police, who spoke of the harm that hashish did to young Greeks, and then left without disturbing the vestigial furniture. They in their turn visited the two imprisoned Americans, their unwitting hosts, taking paperback books to their small enclosure by the sea. Sitting on deckchairs in the sun behind a deer fence which was electrified in its topmost wires, the Americans seemed surprisingly settled. They might, they said, be out in nine months. And in the meantime, this was not *too* different from a summer in Lindos. The Englishmen ran out of money and dived for sponges to sell to the daily coachloads of tourists. And then they caught the ferry to Athens, where an accommodating Embassy official stamped their passports for confiscation at Dover and repatriated them in the car of a similarly stranded Brixton mini-cab driver. Two months after their return they received in the post an envelope bearing a Stockholm postmark and containing half an ounce of resinous black Afghani hashish.

Such was the commonplace of the hippy trail. The trouble with the trail, says one student of the subject, 'is that it was just one story: went to Goa, caught hepatitis, woke up one morning to find somebody's run off with all my cash, got airlifted home . . .'

There was usually (although not always) a little more to it than that. Young people—'freaks', as they had come to dub themselves, in mockery of their parents' disgust—hit the trail for several different reasons. The wholly amoral dope-runner took the same road as the placid young person in search of a yogi. The pendulum of colonial attitude took a reverse swing in the 1960s. Although many of those who claimed to prostrate themselves before the wisdom of the east were financially as exploitative and uncaring as any tea-planter of the Raj (and in the case of those who sought to knock on the door of a Pradeshi hovel in search of their evening meal, arguably more so), there were plenty who clung to a real desire for the kind of enlightenment that might only be delivered in Monkey Temples, in ashrams, and by Tibetan Lamas. The courting by the Beatles and their entourage of the quaint and beaming Maharishi Mahesh Yogi was both the product and an affirmation of this mood: it was in no way remarkable to the children of flower-power. Western society had plainly failed, western values were transparently corrupt, and western thought was in receivership; what could have made better sense than to turn to the wisdom of older cultures—particularly as it transpired, delightfully, that those older cultures also considered marijuana and hallucinatory experiences to be no bad thing?

And so the levitating brahmin and the saddhu on his pole, the Marrakeshi fire-eater and the Atlas Mountain percussionists received for a while an unexpected pilgrimage of devotees, and for all of them, it was a strange and salutary congregation. On the ground of a temple in Nepal there are two copper seals, remembered Neil Rock, a veteran of the trail; 'one of them bears the seal of Solomon and the other one bears the Hindu cow with all the holy parts of the body. All round the courtyard are small replicas of the stupa in stone, also sleeping quarters for the monks and a small chapel with a large brass buddha, surrounded by all kinds of copper and brass utensils . . . It was night time. I went there with someone else and we were both interested to see what was there. I happened to stand on one of these copper seals. I looked at it and thought of it as a terminal. Well, my body turned green all over. I stepped off it and onto the other one and my body turned red all over. Then I stood in between them. There were hundreds of bugs flying in the air and I watched them fly through me, going through my hands. I turned to the person who was with me and said, "Have you seen?", and he said, "I'd rather not speak about it."'

What price, after that, matins at St Biddulphs?

The most practical users of the trail were drug smugglers and Australians migrating to London. They were less interested in trans-substantiation than in getting somewhere. The one usually travelled well, by aeroplane or by car, the other went steerage. The first was the seed of an international drugs trade which was to become so broadly based as to be uncontrollable, and the second was the origin of that more respectable phenomenon: the independent traveller. A serious trafficker of drugs would rarely if ever have hitch-hiked. Everybody else, for at least a part of their journey, did so. Hitch-hiking was, of course, not an invention of the young of the 1960s, but it was clasped dearly to their hearts. Hitch-hiking became the subject of style, a matter of principle and the stuff of legend. Did the hitch-hiker look the approaching driver squarely in the eye, or gaze modestly at the road? Should the thumb be waved expansively, palm outwards, from the left hand, or pointing in the desired direction from the right? Hitch-hiking was not just morally defensible, in a world of finite resources and so many half-filled motor-vehicles it was surely the only righteous way to travel. The Amsterdam provos issued stickers to drivers who wished to declare their willingness to give lifts. Stories circulated the camp-fires of the trail, stories of Istanbul to Calais in under 24 hours, of journeys diverted, by way of a fortuitous lift, from some tame European jaunt into the mystical beyond, of sleepy drivers who promised their passengers

116

a seat only for as long as they were able to keep talking in an interesting manner (and of the passengers who, as a result, sustained an unfaltering monologue between Frankfurt and Jaipur), as well as stories of rape and theft and murder.

There were dangers on the trail, apart from the prospect of being found dead in an Afghani hotel with an armful of bad morphine. There was the danger of brutal prison sentences in Middle-Eastern jails for those, like the American Billy Hayes whose experiences were dramatised in the film *Midnight Express* or the 14-year-old English boy Timothy Davie, who were caught in possession of even the smallest quantities of hashish in countries which were at the time nervously petitioning for American aid. In Iran in 1970, 125 people were shot by a firing squad for smuggling drugs. And many people simply disappeared, succumbing to disease and malnutrition in forgotten corners of the world, destroyed by bandits in the Anatolian hills, or falling into the hands of such as Charles Sobraj, the Indian serial killer who preyed remorselessly upon the hippies who came his way.

And there was the danger of being discovered in an unguarded moment on the streets of Kabul by a public school housemaster acting on behalf of the Anti-Slavery Society, or by a photographer from the British tabloid press. Mr Peter Willey of Wellington College reported to the Society in 1971 that: 'The hippies who have set out with their dreams and fantasies of reaching an illusory promised land have become broken, smashed and empty like so many garbage cans. Such is the effect of hashish. These young men sell their possessions, their bodies and those of their girlfriends to buy their hash. Those who may not descend so far return psychologically and physically addicted. The embassies, understandably enough, largely disown them, and can do no more than send them back home by the shortest and cheapest route, if they are willing to go . . . the United Nations should be informed of the true state of affairs in parts of Afghanistan.'

'*Britain's begging hippies treated as weird pets*', echoed the London *Evening News*. 'WHERE ENGLISH GIRLS ARE SOLD FOR DRUGS . . . Young English hippies are begging like dogs for scraps of bread and drugs in the streets of Afghanistan. They are selling their bodies and those of their girlfriends to buy hash. They live in sordid, tawdry houses, often treated by Afghans as weird human pets.' The *Sunday Mirror* followed Willey's revelations by sending a cameraman to Kabul and giving prominence to his work: a photograph of several western youngsters cavorting in the narrow streets. You thought your children were pursuing a summer course in Oriental Studies, the unwritten caption read, well, take a look at *this* . . .

Most returned, of course, alive and moderately fit from the hippy trail. They may have failed to change the world, but they certainly changed Mykonos. The violinist Yehudi Menuhin had a holiday home on that island which he visited in 1976 after an absence of nine years (he had honourably refused to enter Greece during the military dictatorship). Menuhin was stunned to find Mykonos overrun by 'naked Beatniks of all sexes'. He wrote to the mayor, explaining why he would no longer be holidaying in the fallen idyll, and his letter found its way into the Athenian national newspaper *Kathimerini*. He spoke of 'locusts' invading Greece, and of Mykonos in particular becoming 'an island of ill fame'. In less than a decade, Menuhin lamented, 'your noble Mykonos, where the visitors came for its own uniqueness and its proximity to the sacred island of Delos, has acquired the reputation of a place for all and every kind of decadence', a decadence which was 'costing you the best kind of foreigner'.

Yehudi Menuhin's 'best kind of foreigner' might never again dominate the Mykonian tourist industry, but neither would the hippy locusts. Their trail became a four-lane highway, and their backwaters developed unchecked into space-cities of self-catering apartment blocks and bars with English beer on tap. The issue of a more prosaic age would barter time-share schemes instead of dope and, with charter flights leaving hourly from their neighbourhood, would neglect the gentle art of hitch-hiking. There died with that decade, thankfully or not, the tourist who would set off for Yugoslavia with every back issue of *Oz* magazine under his arm (for use as subversive currency) and report from the Balkan highlands that 'the oldsters have what we would term "longhair mentality"—and they grow their own. The local hash was outasight! They have two nice habits while they're smoking. One is watching the horizon and the other is sitting in the sun with a hat over the eyes. And they could teach Zappa and Hendrix something in the way of farout music!' He disappeared, that youth, before even the Prosperos of the Crna Gora heights and their red Montenegran hash.

CHAPTER SEVEN

Mobs

'What do you want to do—start a war?'
SINGER JONI MITCHELL TO THE PART OF THE AUDIENCE WHICH
HAD BROKEN IN THROUGH THE FENCES OF THE THIRD ISLE OF
WIGHT FESTIVAL AND WAS SKIRMISHING WITH SECURITY GUARDS

'Tariq Ali's crowd,' said *International Times* in the first week of October 1968, 'are calling for a demonstration. Before you go shooting off there, think about this. Why are you going? What is going to happen there? Numbers alone are enough to make the police paranoid . . . will the police and their horses act/react against the crowds? Will women and children be hurt?'

'Tariq Ali's crowd' was the Vietnam Solidarity Campaign, and the demonstration for which they called was the third and final march upon the Embassy of the United States of America in Grosvenor Square to protest against the escalation of American efforts to bomb that indomitable country back—as a US general had memorably expressed it—'to the Stone Age'.

IT, for all of its apparently superior popular support among the young, had got it wrong, and placed itself in danger of disappearing up a circuitous internal trail. Tariq Ali, a man of unflinching resolve and dedication to the cause of international proletarian revolution, had got it right. Vietnam was *the* political issue of the 1960s. Along with long hair on young men and the universal flirtation with illegal drugs, opposition to America's war in Vietnam was uniform among the masses of disaffected western youth—it could be argued that the war in Vietnam helped to create so many freaks and oddballs, so many who were contemptuous of the western democracies which had bred them. Opposition to the Vietnam war was the flip side of the special relationship. British troops were never sent to south-east Asia, but Harold Wilson's government maintained an uneasy, if not craven,

posture of support for the cousins across the Atlantic, and as the
young of America split their country in two, as they dodged the
draft, burnt their call-up cards, ran underground, or to Canada, or
even to Britain, as they marched upon the Pentagon, stuck flowers
in the barrels of the rifles of nervous troops, fought with police or
were shot dead by the National Guard—*their* counter-cultural
relatives in Great Britain found the issue of that war impossible to
ignore. Vietnam succeeded where most other political matters,
domestic or international, failed; Vietnam united the hippy and
the hard left, it brought together the rock star and the libertarian
socialist, it polarised society into the bad guys and the good, into
those who were (as a catechism of the time had it) part of the
problem, and the ecumenical hordes of youth who were part of
the solution.

The horrific images which issued from Vietnam (images
which were ultimately to sicken America and to end the war) were
propagandist gifts to the alternative society. The cover of *Oz*
number 10 featured a photograph which was almost as shocking
as a bare-breasted hippy woman, a picture of a South Vietnamese
army officer blowing out the brains of a prisoner of war in a
Saigonese street. Vietnam was black and white. A self-sufficient
peasant army, historically independent of its powerful Communist
neighbours, which successfully resisted the American war
machine, had surely to be applauded and supported to the bitter
end. In the high summer of 1968 Soviet troops entered Czechoslo-
vakia and crushed the reformist government of Alexander Dubjek,
but the incident left hardly a mark on the consciousness of western
youth in comparison to what was happening in Vietnam. Martin
Luther King and Robert Kennedy were shot dead in April and in
June of the same year, and their violent ends seemed if anything
to be *linked* to Vietnam, to be part of the same psychosis, part of
the same eclipse. If the starry-eyed and starry-badged, beret-clad
figure of Ernesto 'Che' Guevara was the sexy image of guerilla
warfare for the time, Vietnam was the apocalyptic backdrop to the
whole of western society. The war may have been opposed from
different perspectives: the hippy may have seen in its vileness the
dark side of every human soul; the member of the International
Marxist Group may have identified a routine attempt by the
western military-industrial complex to crush a small but worthy
attempt at socialism; and the young Liberal might have feared a
conflict which could lead to nuclear war; but opposed it was,

passionately, tearfully, and violently, and in Great Britain that opposition found its loudest voice in the three protest marches on Grosvenor Square.

The first took place on 22 October 1967, in tandem with demonstrations in Washington, Paris and Berlin. To the surprise of its organisers and of the police, 10,000 young men and women found themselves gathered behind the flags of the North Vietnamese National Liberation Front in Trafalgar Square. They marched northwards, singing and chanting, up South Audley Street to the steps of the United States Embassy ... to discover that the building was virtually unprotected. After some excited discussion a few demonstrators walked through the thin police cordon and up to the Embassy doors before being dragged away and dispersed. It had been *that easy*. The titan was vulnerable. It would have been possible to storm his redoubt, with better planning and a few hardier souls, to loot his filing cabinets and send sneering messages down his telex. Tariq Ali and the Vietnam Solidarity Campaign returned to their apartments and began to plan the next demonstration.

It took place on 17 March 1968, and this time the police were ready. Ali recalled arriving in Trafalgar Square 90 minutes before the march was due to begin, and finding the place full. The 25,000 people who set off for Grosvenor Square that spring were students, hippies, trades unionists, West German radicals, and members of the Redgrave family. 'If the conversations of those who came that day had been recorded,' Tariq Ali reflected later, 'I am sure that the overwhelming majority wanted more than just a victory in Vietnam. We wanted a new world without wars, oppression and class exploitation, based on comradeship and internationalism.' Certainly so, but the Metropolitan Police, embarrassed by the 1967 demonstration and unnerved by the size of its successor, were equally anxious that such qualities should not be advertised in Grosvenor Square. Nevertheless, in the late afternoon of 17 March, all hell broke loose in south-west London.

The demonstrators arrived at the square to find a line of policemen blocking its entrance. Those in front of the march could not resist the pressure of those at the back, even if they had been of a mind to do so, and the police line broke. Mick Farren remembered stumbling onto the grass in the centre of Grosvenor Square, smiling in the sunshine, and mentioning to a friend that 'It's like a fucking love-in,' when 'there was an alien sound, thundering hooves, and a line of mounted pigs hit us. It was like a nineteenth-century battlefield. Men and horses ran through the middle of us, the pigs striking out at everyone they could reach with the long batons, like wooden sabres, they carried.'

Tariq Ali watched as 'a hippy who tried to offer a mounted policeman a bunch of flowers was truncheoned to the ground.' Some demonstrators had accepted the advice of continental radicals and carried along pockets full of children's marbles. They were supposed to be rolled along the ground to destabilise police horses; in the panicked event many of them were thrown, and the police redoubled their assault.

'A young woman beside me went down with blood streaming down the back of her head,' Farren remembered. 'Her friends dragged her away unconscious. The cavalry wheeled at the far end of the square and charged back through the crowd, again hitting out at everything they could reach. Those of us who could, took shelter under a tree, where the police couldn't wield their clubs on account of the low branches.'

The police lined up before the embassy steps, and infuriated demonstrators began to throw rocks, bottles and lumps of earth in their direction. 'As the rain of garbage continued to fall on the police ranks,' Farren says, 'a few of the mounted section appeared to freak and rode full tilt into the crowd lashing out indiscriminately with their clubs ... A snatch squad would detach itself, now and then, from the lines of police on foot, and charge into the crowd, either to rescue one of their mounted buddies who had got himself into trouble, or to grab a few demonstrators at random. They evolved a neat technique for transporting those they had arrested. If the victim put up the slightest struggle he or she would be knocked down, then five pigs would lift him, two holding arms, two legs, while the fifth supported the victim's head and shoulders by hauling on his hair.' Hanks of long hair, complete with their roots, were indeed discovered, and photographed on the sward of Grosvenor Square in the hours following the demonstration. Two hundred and eighty demonstrators were arrested in the battle of Grosvenor Square. 'Then we all went home,' said Farren, 'to see ourselves described as thugs and malcontents on television.' Mick Jagger went home to write a song called 'Street Fighting Man' which, upon its release by the Rolling Stones later in that year, was banned from airplay by the BBC. The Metropolitan Police gathered from the ground more than a hundred watches, coats and odd shoes, and invited their collection from West End Central Police Station. There was a small response to their generosity and the residue was burnt at the end of April. P. O'Rourke wrote to *International Times* to complain that 'Fuzz harassment in both our private and public lives is great enough: surely the amount of violence at Sunday's demonstration did nothing at all to discourage any increase in further interference. Perhaps when you—as you no doubt will—state the cause of fuzz brutality, you should state that the underground's policies are not only based on freedom of speech and expression, but also based on love for our fellow human beings. And, let's face it, even the fuzz are human.' Less conciliatory sentiments appeared in the columns of the Fleet Street press, where the return of the birch, the return of conscription, and the return of Tariq Ali to Pakistan were judged the most efficacious methods of preventing a repeat of the performance in Grosvenor Square.

Ali and his colleagues on the Vietnam Solidarity Campaign were criticised also from some quarters of the hard left (the Communist Party of Great Britain rarely regarded such populist explosions with anything other than a grudging respect, and more often condemned them outright), and from the people that they dubbed the 'lotus-eaters': the mass of young detritus from the days of love, the insistently pacific stylists of wilting flower-power. The VSC was told that it was 'both impractical and immoral to throw an unarmed, untrained mob against a symbolic objective like an embassy', particularly as nobody had demonstrated any clear idea about what was to have been done had the embassy fallen. Rumours swept the streets of armed US marines stationed inside the US Embassy, who were briefed to show no mercy to any intruders. Tariq Ali had, however, spent time in a North Vietnamese village when it was under attack by American B-52 bombers, he had seen the agony of the aftermath, and he was largely unmoved by allegations that the impressionable young people of Britain were being used by the organised left as cannon fodder. His was an understanding of what people look like when they have *really* been used as cannon fodder, and he and his comrades set about organising a third large demonstration and march on Grosvenor Square.

Between the two marches of 1968 there were many changes. Deep divisions began to make themselves apparent, in what their elders had assumed to be a scruffily united army of the young.

The splinter groups and entryists of the Trotskyite left had not realised (or perhaps, deep in their hearts, they had begun to realise only too well) that this popular revolution which fell so easily from the lips of their contemporaries was, after all, nothing more than a *cultural* rebellion, a thing which had little substance other than its style. It was diet and clothing, drugs and music; and the creation of a new order *incidentally*, as the result of everybody eating much more brown rice, listening to the Grateful Dead, smoking hash rather than drinking beer, and making sexual love in a loose-limbed fashion. Hard-nosed realists of the new dawn found themselves banging their foreheads on hippy indolence, woke up to the discovery that they themselves, and not the hippies, were the true romantics, for it was they who harboured dreams of changing the whole of society, the political institutions, and the government of Britain; while the longhairs, the freaks with their peace-signs who turned up to swell the numbers of the anti-war marches, were interested only in changing themselves and leaving all else to wither or to grow on the vine. The product of Mod had been, after all, simply style with added pretension. Some of the organised left, some student bodies and young idealists, who had expected the glowing evidence of the death of western capitalism to comfort them in their autumn years, grew to hate the hippies for this betrayal, to despise them with a bitterness that not even Fleet Street could match. But before that hatred had much of a chance to realise itself, before the Vietnam Solidarity Campaign's third march through London, before the seekers on the hippy trail were able to prove that with Zen patience and oriental application the Pentagon could be levitated and the frame of mind of the South African parliament could be entirely altered, before any of those things could happen, Paris caught fire, and it seemed for a few brief days as if everybody might be able to test and experience his and her own personal, unique, and contrasting variety of revolution.

Few enough people in France, and almost nobody in Britain, had anticipated the uprising which began at the Sorbonne University on 6 May 1968. From the Vietnam Solidarity Campaign to the *International Times*, experienced monitors of the pulse of youth consciousness were taken entirely by surprise, firstly by the acceleration of events across the channel, and then by the speed of their decline. Miles of *IT* was holidaying with his accountant in the south of France when the telephones began to behave oddly, the garbage to pile up, and the two men realised that something was amiss in the state services of France. They drove quickly back to London, a special 'ALTERNATIVE SOCIETY—NOW!' issue was released, and just as suddenly France was back to normal. Gary Kahn, an English student with a holiday job selling encyclopaedias in Normandy, threw away all of his produce upon hearing the news and rushed to Paris to join the barricades, only to discover that the barricades had been dismantled and he had nothing left but a dishevelled suit and a sense of disillusion.

But while it lasted, Paris in the May of 1968 seemed to offer the blueprint for the alternative society of the young and its replacement of the corrupted state. The revolt began with the young, with students from Nanterre who occupied first the Sorbonne and then the entire Latin Quarter of Paris, fighting pitched battles with the police to keep those areas within their control. Despite the absence of the established left (who were, ultimately, to negotiate the uprising out of existence), factory and agricultural workers quickly went on strike, until an estimated ten million people were engaged in disrupting the French state, in refusing to maintain the telephone system, collect refuse, or build cars. They too were, by all accounts, urged on by their younger workmates, baited into action by their children.

'We have shown,' said Jacques Tarnero of the seminal March 22nd Movement from Nanterre University, 'that we are not children at play but people who consciously reject their social conditions. We have shown in the streets and at the barricades that our revolt is effective ... American youth has been polarised by the Vietnam war but there must be consciousness of the unity of the struggle between the youth of all of Europe and of America, both to reject the present socio-economic conditions and to destroy the crushing bureaucracies of East and West. This is not a dream. There are already radical and dynamic student movements in Germany, Holland, France, Belgium—in fact, in all the countries of Europe. This is a common struggle. It is young people who are most sensitive to problems concerning the future structure of society. It is this which is our hope for the future.'

But it was a dream. There was, for a short time, rock-and-roll music played above the cobblestone barricades of a European city in revolt, the smoke of marijuana joints mingling with tear- and CS-gas, there was the easy sexual love which historically accompanies such thrilling chaos, there were New Age graffiti on the walls of Paris—'Freedom is the consciousness of our desires', and 'I take my desire for reality, because I believe in the reality of my desires'—and there were governing committees of the young.

But it was a dream, the notion that such a state of affairs could last. By early in June the Communist Party of France had negotiated its own members back to work, and in hurriedly called elections a shaken bourgeoisie swept General Charles de Gaulle back to power. It was a dream, but not a bad dream, the events of Paris in the May of 1968. Rather like the first visit of 10,000 demonstrators to Grosvenor Square, where they had discovered that the door to the embassy lay open and unguarded, so the Paris revolt offered to the whole of western youth the lesson that the citadel could fall ... and, with patience, and with planning, it could possibly be held ... next time ...

The third mass demonstration against the war in Vietnam was planned for 27 October. In the heated atmosphere of 1968 it was spread about that this could be London's answer to Paris in May: an attempt to march to the heart of the system and indulge in some wholesale evisceration; another October Revolution. In the event, it turned out as a relatively orderly affair. The Communist Party for once gave their blessing to the Vietnam Solidarity Campaign, sending a few burly dockers to bodyguard Tariq Ali (whose ability to dodge the hands of the police on such occasions was the cause of some wonder and no little envy among his contemporaries), and a route was agreed with the authorities which avoided Grosvenor Square in favour of delivering a petition to Downing Street. Up to 100,000 people left Trafalgar Square in a carnival mood. Ali handed a scribbled note over to a prime ministerial doorman, and the mob filed dutifully into Hyde Park— with the sterling exception of a few die-hards, who broke the police lines and entered Grosvenor Square, only to be surrounded, isolated and given a mild lesson in obeying orders by the metropolitan police. And that was it. Young people wandered amiably about the familiar turf of Hyde Park, speakers lambasted the Labour Government, street-sellers distributed the underground press, theatre groups performed symbolic mimes, and John Lennon made his presence obvious. A mere 38 people were arrested. Despite its promising preliminaries, such as an arson attack on the Imperial War Museum on 13 October (which led the London *Evening News* to suggest, tantalisingly, that urban guerillas were preparing to ignite the capital), despite a *Times* story in

September that an 'army of militant extremists' was amassing weapons and Molotov cocktails in preparation for assaults on the Ministry of Defence, the BBC and the Stock Exchange, nothing at all happened. Fleet Street photographers complained to demonstrators that they could not even find a suitable tableau of a policeman being kicked by young hooligans. Despite the fact that those 100,000 people represented the rainbow coalition which had been anticipated for so long, and from which so much was expected in some quarters—a starburst of the feckless young, students and hippies, rock stars and Maoists, trades unionists, eminences of the left (hard, new, soft, and libertarian) and old-fashioned, good-natured anti-war liberals—the October Revolution died a polite, apologetic death.

'We failed,' wrote Peter Cadogan in *International Times*. 'Callaghan gave both the police and the demonstrators a pat on the back. Wilson and his US complicity are as firmly in the saddle as ever ... A demonstration is insurrection in embryo or it is nothing.'

'We thronged the streets,' added Peter Stansill, 'to show our politico-emotional solidarity with the Vietnamese people and instead used the opportunity to express our solidarity with some of the basic thinking of our spiritually and politically mortgaged elders. The demonstration was a failure simply because it was *understood*. All the prongs of the Establishment (from press to police) know about political activism. It's a part of the popular static notion of history, which conveniently obliterates the possibility of there being a popular humanistic view of the world.

'They know the mechanics of political activism, all its possibilities. They can take precautions against it, pamper it, contain it, crush it ... Politics has been exhausted of its slogans—indeed, this was painfully clear on the march, where the force of potential joy was shadowed by the thick, heavy words of other decades and other situations. No banner represented a frontal conceptual attack on established mediocrity and habitual thinking—with the exception of the International Situationists'* banner, which read:

---

* If any quasi-political group was emblematic of the 1960s it was the Situationists, if only because it is difficult to imagine their existence in any other decade. Formidably enigmatic, they had been founded in France in 1958 in pursuit of a belief that provocation of every glorious kind—the provocation of thought, the provocation of hostility, the provocation of a breakdown in order—was, if persistently applied, the only way to combat the establishment's insidious co-option and dilution of spontaneous rebellion. The International Situationists and their remarkable slogans ('In our spectacular society [continued]

"Storm the Reality Studios: Retake the Universe" . . . The level of protest has got to change inside our heads before it's taken to the streets. Then we can attack the soft underbelly of the public consciousness, and create new realities for it to contend with.

'Guerilla culture, street theatre, National Ecstasy Days, urban graffiti, the gradual but purposeful loveplay with the gnarled old organs of England, which will finally result in the conception of a new-style post-economic Albion, where people smile fondly at the memorials to the Labour Party.'

This was not an argument which was likely ever to win fond smiles from most sections of the organised left, but it proved a seductive line . . . the state could be not overthrown, but simply made redundant, without bloodshed and without resistance and without—even—too much hard work or planning. The world could be changed by *style* and by *love*, by *sex* and by *fun*, rather than by the disciplined application of political analysis. Discipline, in fact, was to be spurned at every corner. Discipline was the tool of school-teachers and the police. Discipline led to a massive demonstration taking an autumn afternoon turn around Hyde Park. Nobody quite knew where the absence of discipline led, but there would, surely, be laughs along the way.

If there was to be no Paris springtime for the students of Great Britain, there was no shortage of minor excitements. Throughout the later years of the 1960s university chancellors could hardly leave at night without their administrative blocks becoming occupied and their filing cabinets ransacked, their walls daubed with slogans and their plans for higher academe being held to ransom by a belligerent mob of scruffy malcontents who, having been persuaded to abandon their insurrection, invariably left the stubs of marijuana joints in the provostory ash-trays. Students at the London School of Economics, that radical think-tank which had been established earlier in the century by Beatrice and Sydney Webb and the Fabian Society, were the first to show the way when, in February 1967, they occupied their premises in protest against the appointment as director of a man whose previous post had been in the University College of the

---

where all you can see is things and their price, the only free choice is the refusal to pay') brought colour and consternation to the time. It is comforting still to know that if I have misrepresented them in this brief sketch (which is more than likely), they are unlikely to complain, not just because they no longer exist but also because confusion and a concealed identity are, after all, revolutionary weapons.

renegade apartheid state of Rhodesia. Hull University was subsequently taken into student care when its members discovered that the authorities were banking with Barclays, who in turn invested large sums of money in South Africa. Six students from Cambridge University were given prison sentences for rioting outside a hotel in the town, in which local dignitaries were being entertained by representatives of the Greek military junta.

The students of Hornsey College of Art, however, took over because they considered that they could run the institution along better lines than had their elders. The Hornsey occupation, which lasted for six weeks between 28 May and 8 July in 1968, seemed more than any other to be groping towards an actualisation of the misty theories of an alternative society of the young. It started as a prosaic dispute about the rights of the students' union to spend its own funds in the manner which it thought best, without guidance from the college authorities. The students arranged a 20-hour teach-in which would, in its nature, disrupt the academic agenda of the college, and then they simply stayed, outwith the régime of the principal, the governors, and the education department of Haringey Borough Council, running the canteen and cleaning services themselves, producing (over the six-week period) 63 study papers and statements of intent, interviewing reporters on the college campus, and attracting to the madcap, racy *style* of the affair a small number of tutors and lecturers.

For a while they thought, at Hornsey College of Art, that they were on to something, and for a while it seemed that they were right. Alderman Cathles, the chairman of Haringey's education department, assured the media that 'the rule of law will be restored', as if he were the district commissioner of some insurgent province of the Raj—and then he disappeared from view and from the tabloid headlines, as surely as if he had been withdrawn from duty by the high command. The students were left to formulate their own courses and hold their own lessons, clearly recognising their strengths and the weaknesses of the opposition.

'To use too much force too crudely or too publicly', they announced at the time, 'disqualifies the normal mechanisms of servility. It permanently damages the mystification. If they had rushed the fuzz up Crouch End Hill instantly to battle in front of the TV cameras and pressmen, nobody would ever have "consented" to anything again. As for the watching world . . . how soon would LSE have struck in sympathy, how many other art colleges would have been affected.'

They knew that, like Paris in May, it must end, but this knowledge became a part of their peculiar strength. 'Sooner or later a vacation will come along,' they accepted, 'the impetus of the revolution will slacken, people will become tired and have the feeling of getting nowhere; then "the rule of law" will be restored, quietly and easily . . . then, the trouble-makers can be dealt with, the agitators will have their contracts ended, or their grants stopped, the children will have had their fun and things will go back to "normal". In Britain, authority may agree to lose a battle now and then, precisely because it is so profoundly sure of winning the war.'

There was such prescience and articulacy among the Hornsey rebels that it was difficult to dispute their claim that they could run their college in a superior manner. It was actually proven that they ran a healthier canteen: in one hilarious incident Haringey Council, in an effort to get the occupied canteen closed down by the law, sent along their Health Inspectors. The inspectors were obliged to report that the canteen (into which they had been warmly welcomed) was more hygienic than before the occupation. The students and their scores of tutorial supporters called for an end to 'O' level requirements for entry, an end to the grant scheme whereby students were assisted only in relation to their parents' income, and for joint government by students and staff.

In early July of 1968 their occupation ended, as they had predicted, with a whimper rather than a bang. Having survived a police seige, they conceded to the promise of an independent commission of inquiry into their grievances.* As they had also predicted, Haringey Borough Council exacted its revenge: 28 students were not readmitted and 50 members of staff found their contracts at an end. The little counter-cultural light at the top of Hornsey Rise went out, but not before—as the short-lived 'Association of Members of Hornsey College of Art' claimed in its

---

* Much hope was naïvely invested in this inquiry. 'To fight for reforms is one thing,' said a sensible student named Prue Bramwell-Davies, 'but to carry them out is even more demanding. The sit-in was pure joy because we learnt we all felt the same . . . we were totally involved. Now it's a case of making things work that we believe in. It's a subtle, marvellous change.' But when those students who were allowed back in finally did return, they found that all of the ground-floor windows of the college were protected with prison bars, and that even the drainpipes had little skirts of sharpened metal. Any International Situationist who happened to be watching would have nodded knowingly.

dying days—'a microcosm of society changed totally, the people who took over had to change the inner organisation, to change its relationships with the outside world, and to change themselves. Revolution of thought and feeling is the only permanent revolution. A structure can only work so long as it grows out of feeling. The only magic wand was our imagination. Anyone, anywhere, can create this revolution.'

In such microcosmic testing grounds, in occupied places of further education, in urban Free Schools, in meeting places known as Middle Earth and UFO, did those who took the time to think about these things assume that the groundplans for an alternative society were being drawn. And niggling at the back of the minds of the movers and the shakers of the British counter-culture was always the feeling that the biggest microcosms of them all should be the rock festivals. Here the music, which they claimed to be revolutionary, was combined with freedom, fresh air, the easy movement of drugs, and vast quantities of the young. The sense of the enormous potential of such gatherings was inevitably succeeded by despair, only to grow again as another summer approached and the rumours spread of plans to attract unprecedented numbers of rock-and-roll bands to one vast open-air site or the other. It was a strange phenomenon, indissolubly linked to the topical notion that music and lifestyle could together build a new Jerusalem, and it had its roots firmly in the semi-mythological events which took place in the August of 1969 on a dairy farm near the town of Bethel in upper New York State.

The Woodstock Art and Music Fair had looked set to become just another disastrous festival until the morning of its first day. Originally scheduled, as its name suggests, to take place in the artists' colony of Woodstock, its organisers were chased from one upstate burgh to another until they found a resting place on the 600-acre farm belonging to Max Yasgur.

The first indication offered to its organisers that things might, after all, turn out well, was the fact that not a single one of the impressive bill of booked performers cancelled. The Who, Jimi Hendrix, Joni Mitchell were all willing to helicopter into Bethel, put on their act, and helicopter out again. And the first indication offered to *anybody* that this festival might become a memorable affair was the number of young people who trudged along dirt-track roads, ploughed gaily painted vehicles through churned up fields, who hopped, skipped and danced their way towards Max

Yasgur's dairy farm. The organisers had expected 50,000 young-sters. By the end of the first day they had 100,000, and by the middle of the second a quarter of a million people had assembled at, or were converging on, the Woodstock Festival. Food supplies were quite inadequate, the portable toilets exploded under the strain, causing a health hazard, the drugs of the time were abundant, the *New York Times* fiercely and hurriedly (and to its later embarrassment) condemned the event, and the authorities considered declaring Bethel—which had become, overnight, the third-largest centre of population in the state of New York—a disaster zone.

And then it dawned upon all who were present, from the indulgent country cops to the organisers, from Max Yasgur to Jimi Hendrix, that something strange was happening in that muddy bowl of countryside. Nobody was starving, food was being shared. Nobody was mugged, raped or murdered. A child was born in the arena, and upon the announcement of this fact the masses roared and laughed ecstatically. When put to the test, it seemed, these young people could deliver. In hunger, they shared their food. In rain and cold they shared their shelter. They had changed a time of what could—what *should*—have been great travail and distress, into a triumphant celebration of their new way of dealing with each other and with the world about them. Had they been right all along? Had all of those mystical polemics on lifestyle and 'id liberating' music been more than pretentious waffle?

Woodstock Nation was declared immediately—a new state, said the jack-in-a-box American activist Abbie Hoffman, a new state *of the mind*. Woodstock Nation recognised no boundaries and imposed no taxes. Its citizens were free men and women of the world, and when they gathered together, wherever and when-ever they gathered together again, then the world would become as Max Yasgur's dairy farm between 15 and 17 August 1969.

Four months later, at a concert thrown by the Rolling Stones in the Altamont Speedway east of San Francisco, those citizens found themselves briefly to be inhabiting the dark side of the moon. There was murder and mayhem at Altamont, and it could not be blamed upon the pig state: it was the fault and the doing of members of the alternative society. The Hell's Angels, those renegade motorcyclists who were often oddly cast as the counter cultural police force, had been naïvely employed by Jagger and company as security guards at Altamont (the kind of work which was often suggested to them in the vague hope that it might elicit some sense of social responsibility, much as an errant schoolchild may be made a prefect) and they celebrated the occasion by clubbing a young man to death with sawn-off pool cues directly beneath the stage. Most of the 300,000 people gathered in the speedway bowl were unable to hear the music through an inadequate system of amplifiers; almost all of them were unaware that down in the darkness, where the Rolling Stones dithered and protested and played with half a heart, a monotonous series of ruthless beatings was being inflicted—nemesis had come to call, in the last month of 1969, on the youth culture of the democratic west.

Altamont soured but did not destroy the sweet dream of Woodstock Nation. Altamont had, surely, been little more than an aberration, a stumble on the road to Jerusalem. Woodstock showed what could be done, and it was the job of all—even across the Atlantic—to repeat that sizeable microcosm and brandish, once again, that flawless banner.

But where, in the wetlands of the western European seaboard? In 1968 and 1969 two large festivals had been held near the town of Ryde on the Isle of Wight. The second event had been contemporaneous with Woodstock and had attracted Bob Dylan back to Great Britain. About 130,000 paid for entry, outnumbering the local police by 1,000 to one and more than doubling the population of the island. Those 130,000, reported *International Times* approvingly, 'created a shanty town of tents and makeshift lean-tos, marquees, shops and facilities containing more people than Bournemouth.

'The man everyone had come to see was of course Bob Dylan, but the main attraction of the festival, in fact of any festival, was the opportunity of living one's alternative lifestyle, free from police, straight neighbours or any authoritarian moral restrictions, if only for a few days. Most people went to see Dylan but came away with memories of old and new friends and in many cases with new and long-lasting relationships. The pop festival has replaced the large demonstration such as Aldermaston and contains all the same feelings of friendship, comradeship, respect and awe at "our own numbers" and the sheer energy of such a mass of turned-on people assembled in one place. From that angle Dylan and the other fine groups were important but not essential.'

A third Isle of Wight festival, featuring The Doors, The Who, Hendrix and Joan Baez, was planned for the August bank holiday weekend of 1970. The abiding problem with such mammoth events was, in many eyes, that they were controlled and exploited by the marketeers of hip. Their gate receipts and their franchise profits went into the bank accounts of the new entrepreneurs and burnished the apparently gilded lives of those who had already become rich from the tastes in entertainment of the rebellious young. Early in 1970 *IT* had been badly stung by the fines which resulted from its gay contact advertisements court case (a case which they had lost despite the services of a Tory barrister named Leon Brittan, and which was to cause the magazine, once again, to do a moonlight flit from one holding company to another). The staff of *IT* determined to plough some easy money back into a worthy cause—their own publication—by holding their own festival.

Phun City, whose main musical attractions were to have been the British groups Free, the Edgar Broughton Band, the Pink Fairies, and the MC5 from Detroit, was advertised to begin in a field near Worthing in Sussex on Friday, 24 July 1970. On 14 July lawyers acting for West Sussex County Council sought an injunction to prevent the festival from taking place. On the following day its financial backers pulled out. On the day after that the injunction was withdrawn. On 17 July the man behind Radio Caroline, the early 1960s pirate radio station, Ronan O'Rahilly, agreed to buy some notional film rights, and site construction began with a week to go, and with a steady trickle of hippies arriving, finding a convenient stretch of woodland, and disappearing into it to build a hidden city of indeterminate population, whose inhabitants would occasionally emerge to forage for supplies, mutter complaints to the festival organisers, and pass dark comments about staying in there for ever. This hobgoblin workforce was put to use when, on the day before the festival was due to start, the stage had to be moved . . .

'The stage had been built willy-nilly,' remembered David 'Boss' Goodman, one of the organisers, 'and all of a sudden I start to notice—just as the roof was about to go on—that running above it is the main electricity pylon. So I asked around and took advice and, yes, it would be fucking dumb to have a whopping great PA directly below the main electricity cables, especially if it rained. This little guy who put the stage together couldn't believe it, the thought of dismantling it all, but I said: "No, man, we'll carry it," and he said: "Impossible", and I said: "Rubbish. We'll get all the hippies out of the woods and we'll go one-two-three and lift, and we'll carry the fucker and put it over there." So we went into the woods where there were at least 500 hippies camped out, and I said: "Can you do us all a favour? The stage has been put in the wrong place, we've got to move it. They say it can't be done." So everyone goes, "Let's go". and I say "One-two-three", the fucking hippies lift the stage and we carry it 100 yards across the field.'

The British Hell's Angels under the command of Buttons, quite reconstituted after his brush with a Mod's sawn-off shotgun in 1965, appeared and offered to police the event. One car had its windows smashed with a sledgehammer as the result of its driver looking at Buttons in a funny way while the commander was on traffic duty, and a drugs squad detective in plain clothes was tied to a tree in the cover of darkness, but there was no repeat of Altamont. No more than 3,000 people went to Phun City, and most of them appeared to be small-time drug dealers who spent the weekend trying to sell hash to each other. Nobody paid to enter, and none of the bands could be offered any money (a fact which they all—with the interesting exception of the group named Free, who left immediately—took good-naturedly). A reporter from *The People* was offered and accepted LSD, mounted the stage and addressed the wondering crowd. In a polo-necked sweater and neatly pressed jeans, and pointlessly holding an acoustic guitar by its neck, he confessed to having been despatched to invent untruths about this new way of life, but now . . . why, he was handing in his notice and joining the revolution. On the Monday after the festival 100 members of the West Sussex Constabulary arrived in columns of buses and cleared the woodland of its vestigial population. Three people were arrested for the possession of illegal drugs. *International Times* profited by not a penny.

One month later half a million people took the ferry to the Isle of Wight, a mere six years after the 'Battle of Hastings', for 'five days of peace, music and love'. The comparative attendances at Phun City and the Isle of Wight presented harsh, mocking evidence that this new constituency of the young was not, in fact, as interested in experimenting with new ways of living, as it was interested in being the audience for internationally famous musical acts. They were, and the majority of them always had been, consumers: passive consumers whose shanty towns of tents and lean-tos were less the model of Gandalf's Garden than they were simple techniques for temporary survival. The third Isle of Wight festival was a tiresome occasion, fraught with broken promises and bitter with recriminations. 'It seemed,' said Mick Farren, 'more as though a concentration camp was being built than a rock festival.' Security guards with alsatian dogs patrolled perimeter fences, outside of which groups of penniless youngsters set up their tents in dismal bivouac and erected signs which read, after the Bob Dylan song which was supposed to caricature the old and not the new society, 'Desolation Row'. French anarchists and British radicals who styled themselves the 'White Panther Party' attempted to tear down those fences, and skirmishes ensued with the security guards. 'You bastards,' screamed one of the organisers as the fences tore apart and the blood began to flow, 'you ruined everything. I'll see you in hell before you come onto this island again.' Even the Young Liberals, who had set up a tent in the middle of the battlefield like some latterday Salvation Army, felt obliged to make representations to the authorities concerning the insufficiency of basic services which were available to the tired, wet and hungry masses. Scores of people were arrested for the possession of cannabis, and suspected plain-clothes policemen were turned upon and beaten. One of the collaborators on Schoolkids Oz, which had appeared three months earlier, turned to Richard Neville and sobbed 'You realise this thing's over?'

'I'd been to the Woodstock movie,' remembered Charles Shaar Murray later, 'read all the stupid books and I thought life could be an endless free rock festival. At the Isle of Wight I realised that it couldn't be and that it was dishonest to carry on claiming that it was feasible. I had bought the whole package, as much as I could swallow.'

Even Buttons was disgusted. Having spent an afternoon tearing Hell's Angels' insignia from the backs of motorcyclists from the Midlands who were not, in his judgment, qualified to wear the winged death's head, Buttons and his few colleagues joined the anarchists toppling the fence. He sustained injuries to his head during the counter-attack of security guards, but shortly 'the guards limped off, carrying their wounded comrades to safety. The French moved in, followed by about 50 freaks who had merely stood by and watched the action.

'The whole panorama of the event was completely frozen and

stupefied when those on the inside, who had paid, *rushed to keep the fences up*. I just couldn't believe what I was viewing! I thought I'd gone crazy! I asked people on the hill overlooking the festival if they wanted to get in. They said yes, they'd certainly like to get into the concert free, but were content to remain half a mile away on their hill . . . That was it. I'd had enough. I learned my lesson. The ride home was much colder and it gave me plenty of time to think. From now on my club was going to have nothing to do with the alternative society.'

Buttons was not alone. Others looked down from Desolation Row as the third Isle of Wight festival ended on Monday, 30 August 1970, looked down at the wretched youngsters filling polythene bags with garbage for a guaranteed 9d per sack from the organisers, looked up at the police helicopters still circling the site, saw the large celebrity marquee gingerly dismantled, the marquee which had hosted so much champagne and caviar and kept comfortable so many of the stars and their velveteened friends, and then wandered away from the smell and the squalor and the routinely unpaid accounts, wondering what sort of a future was there here, for *anybody's* children.

CHAPTER EIGHT

SCHOOLKIDS

I recall the military gentleman who thought of enrolling his nine-year-old son as a pupil. 'The place seems alright,' he said, 'but I have one fear. My boy may learn to masturbate here.' I asked why he feared this. 'It will do him so much harm,' he said. 'It didn't do you or me much harm, did it?' I said pleasantly.

A. S. NEILL, *Summerhill*

The American folk singer Joan Baez gave a press conference on the third day of the 1970 Isle of Wight festival, to rectify false stories which had appeared in the tabloid press suggesting that she had asked for an inflated fee and for a yacht to be made available for her, at anchor in the Solent. She regretted the poor conditions which her young spectators had been obliged to endure, and opined that festivals were probably, by 1970, things of the past. Her fee, she said, had been £8,000, which was in line with the other top-billed performers, and she had asked for no yacht. She did *not* reveal that she had given the entire sum to a small independent school in Suffolk called Summerhill.

Summerhill School anticipated the 1960s by some 40 years and, unlike almost all of the institutions which were flung up during that decade, was to find itself approaching the twenty-first century in a state of rude good health. It was not a product of that temporary turbulence but it became, for a few brief years, both a lodestar to, and the single working model of counter-cultural values. Throughout the later years of the 1960s this small settlement became a place of pilgrimage for many who went away convinced that, if the garden was ever to be built, then it would look, sound and feel something like Summerhill School. Those notions were never much encouraged by its hard-headed founder and his harassed staff, but they were—and they remain—inescapable.

The conscientious rock stars, moneyed liberals and hitch-hiking freaks who wound towards Summerhill in their eccentric droves throughout the late 1960s, found a place of striking, promising scruffiness. Sequestered in the orderly marches of rural Suffolk, the school's main building, an elegant late-Victorian country house clad in runaway ivy, easily met their expectations. It was corralled by jerry-built classrooms, timber dormitories and disused railway carriages roughly converted into sleeping quarters. It had a 'visiting parents' camping area', and a volleyball net stretched haphazardly across its unkempt central green. There were bicycles, cracked windows and graffiti.

Since its establishment in England in 1924 Summerhill had enjoyed some renown as a seminal and quite uncompromising 'free school'. Alexander Sutherland Neill, its founder, had a reputation in educational circles as a serious philosopher, a daunting iconoclast, and as a man who had chosen to put his radical theories into form, rather than leave them mouldering in print. Neill's witty assaults on sexual repression and bogus morality were heaven-sent, however, to the contagious ideas of the later 1960s. Above all, here was something that *worked*, that had been deliberated over and recorded and visited by government inspectors and which, after all of that, still appeared to confirm the acid dreams. Summerhill became a protégé of the new generation and A. S. Neill, to his minor discomfort, was acclaimed as one of its patrons.

So A. S. Neill died in 1973, one month short of his ninetieth birthday, at the end of the era which made him famous. His belief, which had been only strengthened by years of headmastership, that there was no such thing as a problem child, only a problem society from whose constrictions children must be released before they can properly develop, had become common currency. His books sold suddenly in extraordinary numbers. The volume *Summerhill* sold two million copies upon its release in 1970 in the United States alone; and between 1969 and 1972 the same book, exhilaratingly retitled *The Theory and Practice of Anti-Authoritarian Education*, sold one million in West Germany. In Britain, Penguin Books had refused to issue it until 1968, when they promptly found themselves flooded with orders and forced into further impressions. The school's roll swelled with younger members of the Age of Aquarius, and by 1971 the number of visitors each 'open' Sunday was so great that the pupils' council, to their headmaster's enormous relief, voted to ban them.

Neill, ever pragmatic, welcomed the extra publicity, pupils and income but remained gently (for the most part, gently) sceptical of the whole kerfuffle. He held out no great hopes for a world governed by former hippies. 'Those who seek freedom now will many of them be Goldwaterish by the time they are 50,' wrote the man who had seen other bright, rebellious generations come and go. 'A cynic might say that all this challenging is fine, but in 20 years the flower and hippy boys will be staunch conservatives.'* He had some sympathy with the trials of the underground press and with the tribulations of other educationalists, but thought the former too frivolous by far to be a worthy *cause célèbre*, and the latter naïve in encouraging state-educated children to attempt real changes in their schools—'how can a kid challenge a bad teacher when he has been moulded to obey and fear?' Above all, he could not embrace the violence of the militant leftist factions which emerged throughout Europe and America. 'Sabotage is not the answer,' he said wearily, 'in 50 years of self-government my pupils have spent much time condemning the sabotage of unbalanced children.'

And then he died and the 1970s were born, and many assumed that the school would die with Neill and with the decade which had so comprehensively embraced his philosophy. It had become, for some years before his death, a broadly accepted wisdom that Summerhill would, Summerhill *must*, follow A. S. Neill to his grave. Even Neill himself, by preference an optimist, was occasionally disturbed by fears of the school throwing itself on his funeral pyre, or—more likely—of forces of the night, emboldened by news of the old warrior's death, crawling armed with closure notices from their corridors. These fears had little to do with the fatuous notion that the school should fold, like an underground magazine, because a generation no longer found it

---

* Neill's deep well of patience with those who wished to love, understand and identify themselves with Summerhill was dredged, at times, almost dry. When I published an article which focused on a recent arrival, the precocious 14-year-old son of a Californian draft dodger who boasted of his fondness for hashish, I received a letter from the old man which patiently explained that he would rather I had chosen a more amiable child, there being plenty on the premises. When on another occasion I invited him to share my brilliant deduction that Summerhill represented nothing less important than the first and definitive exposition of post-scarcity anarchism, Neill said that he had never understood what anarchy meant, and gazed bleakly out of the window before sighing and offering me a drink.

fashionable. Summerhill had been through that before: it had been seen once as just another product of the inter-war intellectual left, as part of that equally amorphous radical grouping of Book Clubs and Leagues and Friends Of and Fellowships whose pamphlets and poems and prayers for a new order were sundered on the hills of Catalonia and in the maelstrom of the 'necessary' war.

Rather, the perceived weakness of Summerhill School was what turned out to be its enduring strength: its stern, uncompromising, *unfashionable* individualism. Unlike the ventures which foamed around its heels in the 1960s, Summerhill was not dependent upon the vagaries of radical fashion, any more than it was dependent upon the orthodoxies of the Church and the State. If it had been so dependent then it would indeed have been swept away, with all the detritus of the decade, when the tide turned. But Summerhill School was the creation of a man possessed, above all, of a supremely unfettered mind.

A. S. Neill had an antibiotic aversion to orthodoxies of any kind, most obviously in the areas where orthodoxy was most demanded of him: the fields of psychology and of politics. He was not without favourites in the former enclosure; his deep respect and affection for Homer Lane and, later, Wilhelm Reich, was unwavering in the face of the scandals and trials which slurred the reputations of both men. The greater part of the rest, however, including the efforts of some young 'progressive' psychologists who pleaded with him to join their ranks and who called him snobbish when he did not, went out with the dishwater.

Politics often demanded more complex reactions, if only because politics could affect the life of his school in a very real way, by terminating it. Neill's inclinations were naturally to the left, and he abominated the right. In 1948 he wrote to a friend that 'ultimately communism will give freedom to youth. I want to speed up the process.' Diplomatically, he shrank from making such statements in public, but this did not stop the United States government from identifying him as a fellow-traveller and banning him from their country (where he had undertaken the occasional lecture tour) in the 1950s. He lived to see both Margaret Thatcher and Ronald Reagan achieve political office (she as Secretary of State for Education, and he as Governor of California) and viewed them both with despair. Shortly before his death he told a friend that 'fascist' Reagan made him 'tremble for the future'.

Thatcher's ascendency to cabinet office in 1970 presented the old man with a familiar conundrum. He could not pretend a fondness for her or for a Conservative government, but the fact was that under such a government Summerhill School, the most radical in the land, was relatively safe from closure. Summerhill had always been under greater threat from Labour governments, with their blanket hostility to fee-paying schools, than from Conservatives in power. Neill, to his great and lasting embarrassment, was protected, under Tory rule, by the umbrella of Eton and Harrow. Under Labour administrations, inspection followed upon suspicious inspection. His old friend Bertrand Russell helped him out of some small difficulties with Ramsay MacDonald's first government. After Attlee came to power in 1945 a couple of His Majesty's Government inspectors spent two days in Suffolk. As it happened, they were entranced by the place and reported back to their ministry that 'a piece of fascinating and valuable educational research is going on here which it would do all educationalists good to see'. Neill concluded: 'We were lucky to have the two of them.'

But by 1967, with Summerhill's popular profile reaching new heights, it seemed that the luck might be running out. An inspection in that year, which was guided by the Wilson government's laudable intentions to root out the Dotheboys Halls from the public school circuit, and to issue a warning to Eton that not all monuments were sacred, insisted that 'all public schools must come up to [the Ministry's] standards in five years or be shut up.' These standards were not likely to tolerate Summerhill's pupils' voluntary attendance at (or absence from) lessons, or their disused railway carriages as dormitories. Neill was told by an inspector that Summerhill would die with him, and by educational journalists that Labour had Summerhill on its list of prospective closures, and he began to hear the ominous beating of wings.

In the event, the five years never elapsed. Edward Heath was elected as prime minister in 1970, Margaret Thatcher took charge of education, and fee-paying schools across the land, including of necessity that eccentric little outfit in Suffolk, were dignified once more as offering freedom of choice to parents. Neill recognised the fraudulence of that 'freedom of choice', and he characteristically took the opportunity of reprieve to go on the offensive. Summerhill had been denied by education departments of all governments the 'official recognition' which would have enabled local authorities throughout the land to grant-aid students who wished to attend the school. In a letter to *The Times* (which was far from being his favourite forum) Neill appealed to Margaret Thatcher for state recognition. This would, he wrote, 'mean nothing to me personally, but if I had it poor parents could send their children to Summerhill . . . I have to continue being ashamed that I have to take middle-class pupils only.'

The effort failed, as he had known that it would. No sooner had *The Times* letter appeared than he was confiding in a friend: 'I hear that Mrs Thatcher voted to keep hanging, so I doubt if she is a Neill fan. Still, Summerhill is safe under the Tories, for as long as they keep Eton and Harrow I am safe.'

These were the harsh realities, and they appeared to illustrate the contradictions of the times. Some styles of life and some ways of thinking had no orthodox political home, and had apparently little future even within a liberal western democracy. The right detested Neill and his 'piece of fascinating and valuable educational research', as much as they disliked their restive young, and for many of the same reasons: they knew instinctive opposition when they saw it. Summerhill's quiet, resilient existence from one decade to the next reproached the shrill arguments of the contributors to the 'Black Papers' on education, those freelance pedants of the Tory right who incidentally scattered the seeds of the Conservative Party's educational 'revolution' of 20 years later. But one substantial part of their dogma offered Summerhill protection. From the official political left A. S. Neill, the outstanding radical educationalist of the century, was offered—at best—no protection at all.

'He never discussed politics at home,' recalled his daughter, Zoe. 'I can never remember it. But I remember the first time I could vote going along with him to the polling station and saying to him: "You know, you really ought to vote bloody Conservative, you keep saying that Labour would close the school down, you ought to vote Conservative." He kept saying: "Yes, I know." I don't think he did, though!'

The joke, made to Bertrand Russell in 1931, 'I think I'll vote Tory next time', was too tired to be repeated four decades later. In the meantime Neill had, however, perfected the knack of standing quite still and assured amid the swirling whims and fashions of the rest of the world. Whether Neill was born both stubborn and iconoclastic, whether it was part of his late-Victorian upbringing in the Scottish lowlands, or whether he developed it as part of life's necessary armour, it served him and his school well. When Dartington Hall compromised, he did not; when Beacon Hill collapsed, Summerhill lived; when the British and American 'free schools' of the 1960s upon which, as his biographer Jonathan Croall says, he was a 'seminal influence', crumbled, Neill's little institution—fortified by clarity of thought and intensity of purpose—continued. It was to indicate the uncomfortable difference between fashion and a singular great idea: for unlike most of the readership of Oz and International Times and unlike the majority of those half a million people who attended the third Isle of Wight festival and, as it turned out, unlike most of the golden hordes who descended upon Max Yasgur's farm for the happening called Woodstock, A. S. Neill actually was moved by a passion to change society beyond recognition. To have fun was, to him, the undeniable right of children, but it was not a freedom to be confused with licence and it was not, above all else, it was not an end in itself.

Neill's messages appeared to be tailor-made for the times. 'That society is sick no one can deny,' this man had written while in his eighties; 'that society does not want to lose its sickness is also undeniable. It fights every humane effort to better itself. It fought votes for women, abolition of capital punishment; it fought against the reform of our cruel divorce laws, our cruel laws against homosexuals . . . Fight world sickness, not with drugs like moral teachings and punishments but with natural means—approval, tenderness, tolerance . . . I hesitate to use the word love, for it has become almost a dirty word like so many honest and clean Anglo-Saxon four-letter words.'

Those sentiments filled the school with the long-haired children of affluent Americans in the later years of the 1960s—ten-year-olds whose fondness of boasting to visitors that they had smoked cannabis filled Neill with foreboding, not because he held any strong opinion about the use of legal or illegal drugs, but because such rashness could close down his school and, unlike the organisers of a rock festival, his school had nowhere else to go. Twenty years after the end of the 1960s there were just two Americans on Summerhill's roll of 70 pupils. The yuppie generation had deserted the place. 'Summerhill is a bit too close to the bone for them,' suggested Neill's daughter, Zoe Readhead, who had succeeded him as head, 'a bit too nitty-gritty. But we have 20 Japanese, which got us a mention in the Financial Times for bringing in the yen.' She considered this peculiarity. 'We just guess that Japan is going through its hippy phase at the moment,' she ventured doubtfully. 'They do come from very laid-back parents.'

Sheltered under the patrician umbrella of Eton and Harrow, and jealously guarded by the gravitas of its founder, Summerhill School was never a victim of the police and the agitated office of Public Prosecutions as the 1960s turned into the 1970s. Other considerations aside, it was difficult to arraign a school under the Obscene Publications Act. *The Little Red Schoolbook*, which was as Neillian a tract as it would be possible to find, had no such luck.

The Little Red Schoolbook was the English translation of a Danish original. Simply, it was a guide to children's rights under the law, a radical view of the education system, and a matter-of-fact information tract on the variable hazards of drugs and sex. It advised children that the system of examinations was wrong and could be changed by getting 'a bit of discussion going between teachers and pupils', and it told them that school councils were a good thing which could be democratically achieved. It reflected that society was built on economic power, and released the fact that 'just five per cent of Britain's population owns 75 per cent of its wealth'. Small enough to fit into any pocket, like Chairman Mao's original, but at 30p well beyond the desirable spending limit of the average British schoolchild, *The Little Red Schoolbook* appeared to be little more than a stocking-filler for the liberal bourgeoisie, a worthy gift from a Hampstead parent. But *The Little Red Schoolbook* contained sections on dope and love, at a time when the two were increasingly confused in the minds both of the constabulary and of the libertarian left, and those sections sunk it.

'The usual word,' it told its readers, 'for a boy's sexual organ is cock or prick. The usual word for a girl's sexual organ is pussy or cunt. Many grown-ups don't like these words because they say they're "rude". They prefer words like penis and vagina ... If a boy and girl fuck, they may have children. To avoid this, contraceptives are used ... The Consumer Association's magazine *Which?* publishes a very useful survey of every sort of contraceptive ... People use the word "abnormal" to mean many things. They may mean something which doesn't fit in with their particular standards (for example regarding school or religion). They may mean something which goes against the traditional view of what is right and wrong. They may simply mean something of which they themselves are afraid.'

Drugs, this Baedeker to adolescence told its teenaged targets, 'are poisons which can have a pleasant effect'. All drugs could be damaging. Alcohol, heroin, tobacco, cocaine and amphetamines could be both addictive and life-threatening. Cannabis and marijuana should be taken with caution, not least because they were illegal. LSD, particularly when manufactured by underground chemists, was often literally poisonous, and always a gamble. 'Social habits', it concluded, 'are not harmful in themselves, but they can be indirectly harmful if the particular habit has bad effects.'

The kind of advice which would within ten years be commonplace in mainstream teenage magazines was itself judged to be seditious by an establishment which, having watched aghast as one generation appeared to go spectacularly off the rails, was determined that they should not take with them their younger brothers and sisters. The Obscene Publications Squad, happy as ever to take a break from sitting astride the humming hive of exploitative pornography which was growing fat and happy in the desolate streets of Soho, strode purposefully down to Gray's Inn Gardens, seized all available copies of *The Little Red Schoolbook*, and slapped a writ for obscenity on its publisher Richard Handyside. In July 1971 the presiding magistrate at Clerkenwell Crown Court found Handyside guilty of producing an obscene publication. He was fined only £50, with £110 costs, but the book was banned. His counsel, John Mortimer, reflected later: 'The blasphemy laws were used to imprison Chartists who sold the works of Tom Paine ... Among some much-needed advice on contraception, the [Little Red School-] book asked awkward questions about whether a capitalist society does not deliberately keep the majority of its citizens under-educated in order that they may be obedient and content with menial tasks. The question may have been naïve, but the fact that it challenged our brand of democracy may have had something to do with its prosecution.'

Following the disappointing—and portentous—verdict at Clerkenwell, John Mortimer hastened back to the Old Bailey on that July day in 1971, for there, in an arena which echoed with accusations of generational warfare, he was leading the defence of Jim Anderson and Felix Dennis on charges not only of publishing a magazine, namely the 'Schoolkids' issue of *Oz*, which offended against the Obscene Publications Act, but also of conspiracy with Richard Neville and others to 'corrupt the morals of young children and other young persons' and to 'arouse and implant in the minds of these young people lustful and perverted desires'.

The maximum sentence available to a judge under Roy Jenkins's poor, abused Obscene Publications Act was three years' imprisonment. The maximum under the first, conspiracy, charge was a lifetime in jail.

CHAPTER NINE

SEX

Almost all pornography gives a false idea of reality. It describes men who are able to make love for hours on end and have several orgasms within a short period. There are also stories about girls who want to make love all the time and in all kinds of different ways. Porn is a harmless pleasure if it isn't taken seriously and believed to be real life. Anybody who mistakes it for reality will be greatly disappointed.

The Little Red Schoolbook

Oz number 28, 'Schoolkids' *Oz*, had hardly appeared on the streets in June 1970, before Detective-Inspector Frederick Luff of the Obscene Publications Squad saw and took his chance. The police obtained a warrant and were able to pursue their case on the basis of a complaint which they claimed to have received from a member of the public. Luff had visited the *Oz* offices on more than half a dozen occasions during his first year in the Squad, which he had joined in June, 1969, delivering dark warnings about the invisible line which the magazine was in danger of crossing, and suggesting to female members of staff that they might be more safely employed in the typing pool of the Metropolitan Police. 'We knew that something was seriously different this time,' remembered Felix Dennis of the raid in June 1970, 'when he started to take away the filing cabinets'. Filing cabinets, artwork, private letters, business documents, pictures hanging on the wall: they were all removed by Luff and his men, who shuffled for what seemed like hours up the steps from the studio cellar and squeezed—laden down with newsprint—through the narrow doorway into Princedale Road. Neville telephoned from home while the raid was taking place, and was quickly disconnected. Dennis scrawled the message: 'Oz— buisness (*sic*) as usual' on a placard and posed outside for friendly photographers. Colleagues from other underground newspapers arrived to witness the sport, and nobody took it too seriously, this latest cock-crow from the law.

Nobody took it too seriously because it was broadly assumed that the sexual revolution, while it may not have triumphed, was at least holding the breach. From their earliest days *Oz* and most of the rest of the underground press had identified as a monstrous enemy the sexual repression which they perceived as endemic throughout western society. They were not alone in making this identification. D. H. Lawrence had arrived in the same corner, as had Wilhelm Reich, and as, indeed, had A. S. Neill. Remove the constraints from sex, constraints which it was assumed had been placed upon the subject by a muddled blend of protestantism, Victoriana and—even in those unreconstructed days, it was accepted—patriarchy, untie those fetters and what a happy, loving, tolerant and unwarlike humankind would surely emerge! Lawrence attempted this release through the power of the written word, Reich through psychology and the mystique of the orgone, Neill through suffering little children to be free, and *Oz* through vivid visual images. *Oz* considered that, broadly speaking, pictures of naked men and women did not constitute any form of pornography. The pictures in *Oz* were not the step-by-step come-hithers of corner-shop pornography, they were rarely titillating (and if they had been, so what?), and they were placed in the magazine by virtue either of their genuine artistic merit, or because of their humour, or because of some weird shock value. Thus, one *Oz* featured photographs of a naked woman cuddling an equally naked pig (no penetration was apparent). Another included competent artistic representations of erect penises. Germaine Greer posed for the magazine naked, with her knees held up to her shoulders, so that nobody might reprint the shot without displaying her cunt . . . whatever it was, and however open to denigration by a later and better educated age, it was not the coy and soulless tits'n'ass of the glossy pornographer. It was, at the very least, *fun* . . . 'Contrary to our contemporary image, *Oz* has never been solely sexual', wrote Richard Neville between the bust and the trial. 'In this respect it is like you or me. Sometimes it fucks, sometimes it's stoned, sometimes it dances to the sound of its own record reviews; but most of all it reflects a lively, diverse, informed concern for the far-flung issues of social, cultural and political evolution. Maybe it stems from its Australian origins, but whenever *Oz* does flash its sexuality, it does so with a vulgarity, ostentation and relish that happens to be the undistorted style of those involved with the production of the magazine. Few girls remember the *face* of the man who exposes himself on a train, likewise, out of a 48-page *Oz* our more repressed readers will recall *only* the two titillating pages of illustrated small ads.'

By 1970 the difference between the sexuality of the underground press and the exploitative titillation of the masturbatory porn that had become widespread in Britain was so *marked* to the gentle artisans of Princedale Road and of the offices of *International Times* that, while they were never so naïve as to suppose that the police would just decide to ignore them, they assumed that no prosecution would get very far, and that no police officer would pursue it to the very point of failure. The one offence that males on the underground press were beginning, slowly and often reluctantly, to feel themselves guilty of was the offence of displaying naked women with a greater and more obvious degree of salaciousness: the offence, in other words, of sexism. But sexism was an in-house argument. The law was not agitated by sexism.

And so Detective-Inspector Luff's raid immediately after the publication of 'Schoolkids' *Oz* was taken, despite the removal of the filing cabinets, in good heart, as just another clumsy lunge rather than as the investment of a steady and determined siege. That good heart missed a beat on the Friday before Christmas, 1970.

Richard Neville was in the shower at his Notting Hill flat when Luff burst through the bathroom door. 'After a strained exchange of courtesies' Neville hurried to the bedroom to dress, and discovered six plain-clothes police officers with sniffer dogs working their way through his wardrobe. Luff's warrant had been issued under the Obscene Publications Act, but the sniffer dogs belonged to Drugs Squad detectives who, he explained, 'happened to be passing by'. The police removed a roneod pirate edition of Philip Roth's novel *Portnoy's Complaint*, a complete set of Australian *Oz*, an old hookah, and a small amount of cannabis. Neville and his partner Louise Ferrier were then taken to Notting Hill police station, where Neville spent the night reading Evelyn Waugh's *Decline and Fall*.

He appeared before West London Magistrates' Court on the following morning, charged with the possession of dangerous drugs. Neville's friends had already prepared bail guarantees of up to a quarter of a million pounds, but the magistrate refused bail.

Such applications, he said, would have to be made to a judge in chambers. Christmas is upon us, protested Neville's solicitor. 'It is indeed,' replied the magistrate. Neville had scribbled some notes in the blank endpages of *Decline and Fall*, and as the police approached him to take him down to cells he asked for permission to make a statement. There was no answer from the bench, and the police began to remove the founder-editor of British *Oz*. 'This case has nothing to do with drugs,' he shouted as he was manhandled out of the dock and pandemonium erupted in the well of the court. 'I am in this dock because of the personal vendetta of one man against *Oz*.' He was then taken to Brixton prison.

Neville's notes, quickly scrawled into that Waugh novel and never heard in the West London Magistrates' Court, read in part:

'This is primarily a political occasion. In a broad sense, most cannabis charges are political to the extent that they represent a repression of a new culture by the old. I am in this dock this morning not because of any criminal activity . . . but because I am involved in publishing *Oz* magazine, one of the most articulate, informed and crazy-passionate voices of our generation . . . people such as Detective-Inspector Luff are determined to silence it . . . I look forward to the case even more than Mr Luff because it will enable me to establish that there is a real conspiracy to stifle dissent in this country, that the freedom of the press—the freedom of *our* press—is being forcibly stifled by policemen who have taken it upon themselves to enforce, not the law, but their own dismal and hypocritical standards of morality.' Heard or unheard, the statement was good practice. Richard Neville would be obliged to make several more statements from the dock before 1971 had run its course.

Neville spent Saturday night in Brixton prison, chatting to cell-mates about sawn-off shotguns and learning how to break into supermarkets, before being released on bail by a judge who had been roused from chambers on Sunday afternoon. He learned then that as the police dogs had been nosing through his belongings on Friday afternoon, simultaneous but unsuccessful raids had taken place at the flats of Jim Anderson and Felix Dennis and, again, at the Princedale Road offices of *Oz*. It seemed, finally, time to take things seriously. On 18 June 1970, in the middle of the same maelstrom month that had seen *Oz* so comprehensively raided by Luff, Edward Heath's Conservative Party had overthrown in a General Election the Labour Government of Harold Wilson which had presided over the better part of the 1960s, which had invited the Beatles to Downing Street and awarded them with medals, which had wooed the young by lowering the voting age to 18 and antagonised them by crushing pirate radio stations, which had adopted scorned equivocal positions on the wars in Vietnam and in Biafra; the government which had played nervous footsie with its scions was suddenly and unexpectedly out of office—and equally suddenly the editors of underground publications were being treated like Soviet dissidents. 'There may be just an inch of difference between the Labour and the Conservative Parties,' Richard Neville reflected to a passing journalist, 'but it is the inch in which we live.'

'Following my extraction from Brixton,' he considered later, 'I learned that the police had been watching all our houses for some time, that they virtually admitted to tapping our phones and they had even dossiered trivial, little known facts of our personal lives. So while the fearful significance of the *Oz* persecution became, has become, belatedly apparent to ourselves, many people are still more amused than amazed . . .'

A defence was clearly necessary, a defence which would combine all of the orgiastic vim of the alternative society with the clarity and wit of the traditional British libertarian left: a circus, with philosophers in the ring. 'It has finally dawned upon us,' the 50,000 buyers of *Oz* number 32 were told in January 1971, 'that the authorities in this country take our publishing venture more seriously than we do . . . so for God's sake all you out there—don't let the bastards grind *Oz* down—or it will cost you dearly. You'll be stuck with an eternity of colour supplements.' The defence of *Oz* Publications Ltd against charges of conspiring to 'produce a magazine containing divers obscene, lewd, indecent and sexually perverted articles, cartoons, drawings and illustrations with intent thereby to debauch and corrupt the morals of children and young persons within the Realm' readied itself to do battle. That meant, initially, taking a first good look at the magazine in question.

The editors of *Oz* had been as good as their word when they promised invited youngsters a free hand to produce their own publication, and thus armed with cow gum, an uncensorious typesetter and an impressive array of grievances, the schoolkids ran riot. There were 19 of them, 14 boys and five girls. Two were

15 years old, six were 16, three were 17, and the remainder were 18 or, like juvenile First World War volunteers in reverse, slightly older and lying about it. All but two, who arrived together from Bradford, were from the south-east of England. Released from the confines of the school magazine and the bike shed walls, and given the licence to reach out to up to a quarter of a million readers, they did what A. S. Neill could have advised the regular editors of *Oz* they would do: they vilified their schools, their parents' generation, and the magazine itself ('*Oz* sucks!'), and they revelled in scatology.

The magazine began with a survey of eight secondary schools ('During the last school year, after a Molotov cocktail had burnt a hole in the wall of the head's study; Pledger, the head, decided to ban boots from the school ...'). A section which followed on 'School Atrocities' told of a master 'who liked to wander around the juniors' showers "cleaning his glasses" as he looked at the kids' balls', and was accompanied by a large line drawing of an ageing teacher masturbating while tickling a schoolboy's bum, and by the smaller depiction of a triangle of teachers each caning his neighbour. There were regrets expressed about the lack of sexual freedom extended to teenagers, and a condemnation of examinations ('a primitive method of recording a tiny, often irrelevant, section of the behaviour of an individual under bizarre conditions'). There was a musical review by the fledgling rock critic Charles Shaar Murray (then aged 18 and a believer in 'the brotherhood of man and the dawning of the age of Aquarius'). There were letters and there was Dr Hipocrates, there were advertisements for sexual aids, and there was a review by Robert Hughes of Theodore Roszak's book *Making of a Counter Culture*—a review which had been first commissioned by *The Spectator* but then rejected by that magazine's editor, Nigel Lawson, on the grounds that 'it consisted of nothing but mindless ranting'. 'For the first time in modern history,' Hughes had written in his review, 'youth experiences itself *as a class*.' There were record reviews and a routine newsletter for any hippies who may have been fogged by the generational leap of the remainder of the magazine.

And there were three pieces of artwork which would raise the temperature of the Old Bailey during the following summer. A cartoon by the veteran American comic-strip artist Gilbert Shelton, which featured his favourite characters 'The Fabulous

Furry Freak Brothers' attempting to purchase marijuana in a violent inner-city recreational area named Ripoff Park, was run around the border of page 16. The cover, which was chosen at the very last, in what Felix Dennis was to describe as 'ten minutes which changed my entire life', was a duotone print from the collection *Desseins Erotiques* by the Parisian artist Bertrand. It showed eight identical black women making love to each other. One was teasing herself with a dildo, and another had a rodential tail emerging unquestionably from her vagina. A third was enjoying cunnilungus with a fourth, but that precise image was judged to be too near the knuckle for the front cover of *Oz* and a small head-and-shoulders photograph of one of the schoolboy editors was superimposed over it. And on pages 14 and 15 there was an inventive collage, by the young Viv Berger, of a cartoon by another American underground artist, Robert Crumb, and the old British classic Rupert the Bear. By the judicious impositions of Rupert captions and Rupert's unmistakable head upon one of Crumb's more lubricious scenes, the innocent young hero of the *Daily Express* was seen to be having sex with a virgin grandmother (?). That, and not much more, was *Oz* 28, 'Schoolkids' *Oz*. The making of it was possibly more enjoyable than the product—'we all had a fantastic month, milling around weekend after weekend in true communal style, gradually getting all the copy together, the drawings, the photographs, the freak-outs.' 'The first meeting with the schoolkids was a very confused situation,' remembered Felix Dennis. 'A lot of them came along just to have fun, they didn't realise that they were going to have to produce something. So we suggested to them that we wanted everything in the magazine, apart from the advertisements, either done by them or selected by them. And by the time of the second meeting they wanted to change the look of *Oz* as well as its contents.'

This lively combination of shrill adolescent militancy, new leftist intellectualism (or 'mindless ranting', as Nigel Lawson would have it) and soft-edged hippy erotica was always going to be difficult to explain away to such an unfamiliar section of the adult population as an Old Bailey jury. To the regular readers of *Oz* the issue had been pretty standard fare, if overly devoted to the uplifting news that the younger generation was turning out well. To a collection of ratepayers it would be . . . well, *what* would it be? Incomprehensible? A weapon of generational warfare? Cheap smut? Pederastic pornography? A bit of harmless fun?

In the days of not taking it seriously the editorial trio had followed their instincts and wandered down the well-worn path to harlequinade, adopting the old and honoured counter-cultural principle that if the law was laughed at long enough and hard enough, it would eventually go away. The three had turned up at their committal hearing at Marylebone Magistrates' Court on 1 October 1970 dressed in short schoolboy trousers, neat white socks, school blazers and caps and with satchels slung over their shoulders. 'The audience of *Oz* supporters who packed the public gallery,' reported *The Guardian*, 'some of whom had to be evicted from the press gallery on the magistrates' orders—found this amusing. The defendants' dress was otherwise studiously ignored.' That court heard Detective-Inspector Luff say that Felix Dennis had told him: 'Look, we're a reasonably happy bunch of guys— just a bunch of longhairs trying to bring out a magazine. I think it both necessary and desirable. Clearly you think otherwise.' The Marylebone magistrates, before committing Oz Publications Ink, Richard Neville, Felix Dennis and Jim Anderson for trial at the Central Criminal Court, heard also that Mr Robert Richardson, headmaster of the William Penn School, considered *Oz* to be 'wholly deplorable and an incitement to depravity'.

After the traumas of Christmas 1970, the tendency towards carnival became better organised. A group known as Friends of *Oz* was established, not so much to prepare a defence case, raise funds or gather witnesses, as to pursue relentlessly the cause of getting *Oz* and its impending trial recognised in the established media as a bizarre event. Publicity photographs were taken of the three defendants dressed as policemen, dressed as schoolgirls, dressed as stockbrokers, their long hair flowing incongruously out from underneath straw boaters, helmets and bowler hats. David Hockney was persuaded to make line drawings of the *Oz* three, who posed naked apart from spectacles, wristwatches and—in the case of Dennis—a fetching neckerchief. Friends of *Oz* issued a press brochure which contained all of this visual matter and invited journalists to: 'See . . . the Drama of the Courts, with revelations of conspiracy and debauchery never before made public. See . . . A ritual clash of cultures—a generation's lifestyle on trial! See . . . free speech fighting for survival . . .' A parade was planned to precede the opening of the Old Bailey trial, which was going to include elephants and howdahs, dancing bears, hired clowns and a gaily costumed mob, until the animals proved unavailable and local government was unprepared to permit such a spectacle upon its streets. The Robert Crumb cartoon creation Honeybunch Kaminskey, his mocking pastiche of the straight world's concept of an innocent hippy runaway, was adopted as the emblem of the *Oz* defence. An enormous papier-mâché model of Honeybunch was made, garishly coloured, and carried from one supportive event to the other like a sacrament. And a rally was arranged to take place in Hyde Park right in the middle of the *Oz* trial, an 'Independence Day Carnival' which would feature 'the massed choirs of the Underground ... Release, BIT, Agit-prop, Gay Liberation Front, Advise, Street Aid, Dwarves, UPS and other community groups to support the defendants in the *Oz* Obscenity Trial.' John Lennon released a fund-raising single titled 'God Save Oz'.

If British society had not been polarised before the trial of *Oz*, it was certainly the intention of the defence to force people into one commitment or another during that trial. *Time Out* described the magazine as 'the best and truest underground paper in the world', and the *Sunday Express* as 'crude, nasty, erotic and debasing'. The lines, it appeared, were clearly drawn, and the scene was set for the first Old Bailey trial in memory with the threat of life sentences hanging over the defence, whose accused considered the whole affair to be a cause of celebration and a reason for having *fun*, while not entering pleas of insanity.

There was fun, of course, in the environment of Friends of *Oz*, in the company of such sharp and talkative movers of the underground as Stan Demidjuk who, clad in leather and with straight brown hair hanging down to the small of his back, flew from one idea and one meeting to another like a genial leprechaun; there was laughter and wisecracking and a sense, as the hazy summer of 1971 drew closer, that the streets of west London actually were the centre of something larger and more important than the defence of the rights of a few southern schoolchildren to offend their teachers in the pages of a magazine. But beneath the chortling public front there was tension, there was even fear, and there were real contradictions to be faced.

It was no longer in doubt that the police and the public prosecution service, whether or not they were newly motivated by the arrival in office of a Conservative government, had determined to test the mettle of the underground press. *International Times*, which was still reeling from the £2,000 fines and suspended jail sentences which had been imposed on its directors in 1970 for running gay contact advertisements, was raided again on the very day before the *Oz* trial was due to begin, and later charged under the Obscene Publications Act for producing an ancillary comic book, a small collection of British and American cartoons called *Nasty Tales*. All across Britain policemen had taken to paying visits to the printers of small, regional alternative publications and advising them that, under Jenkins's Act, they also were liable to prosecution. The editors of *Oz*, who had taken pains to put themselves at the very forefront of this young counter-culture, who had advertised themselves as the fall guys for a generation, could not avoid the conclusion that if an Old Bailey jury and an Old Bailey judge took them at their word, they might be sent to prison for a very long time.

The legal world had made it clear at an early stage that even its more receptive members were unhappy with the publicity machine of Friends of *Oz*.

Richard Neville had decided to defend himself; the publishing company would be defended by a barrister named Keith McHale, and if a stylish performer could be found to speak for Dennis and Anderson, that would give the defence three voices against the prosecution's one. The Labour member of parliament, Tom Williams QC, had agreed in April to act as Dennis's and Anderson's counsel, but 11 days before the trial was due to commence, while posters supporting *Oz* appeared all over London, while Mary Whitehouse, Lady Birdwood, Lord Longford and other forces of moral rearmament prepared their counter-assault on the media, and while journalists flew in from all over the world to cover this racy story, Williams suddenly withdrew from the case, pleading that the pressure of other work was too much for him. With five days before the trial's opening, another barrister with liberal credentials, Basil Wigoder QC, seemed prepared to take on the job, but he too backed off within 24 hours, asserting that he could not be sure that the defendants would not treat the Old Bailey as a circus. The gentle, diffident figure of John Mortimer, who was already committed to his attempt to help *The Little Red Schoolbook* to escape the full wrath of Clerkenwell Crown Court, finally agreed to accept the *Oz* brief as well.

And beneath it all, itching like a sore behind the masquerade,

157

was the unpalatable truth that the *Oz* defendants were bracing themselves to defend an idea whose time had already gone. When they spoke of the prosecution being not of a single magazine, but rather of an entirely new happy-go-lucky ethic, of a fresh way of living and of relating to others, they knew that idea to be out of date. They knew it to have been, if not disproven, then certainly battered and flawed. Nobody who had stood in the mud and the rain of Ryde at the Isle of Wight festival in the previous summer, as Richard Neville had, could possibly have seen in that degradation and among those bedraggled children, in turn both docile and petulant, nobody could have witnessed there, and embodied in them, the embryo of a new and more satisfactory society. The spirit of the decade had, it appeared, followed the calendar with unnerving fidelity, and had died with the fading months of 1969.

Neville had written as much in 'End of An Era *Oz*', in the autumn of 1970. 'One of the premises of the new lifestyle,' he had said, 'was the abolition of false criteria for judging human beings. Today hip symbols and fashionable rituals count for more than ever. Dishonestly doubling travellers' cheques earns the required A-levels, familiarity with a supergroup's pedigree outmatches Alan Brien's literary snobbery, and a replay of last week's bad trip is flaunted like a duelling scar. Even the legitimate new freedoms are being bankrupted through criminal selfishness . . . The atmosphere created by most of these superhip freeloaders manages to be simultaneously hostile, slovenly, and as exclusive as White's Club. Membership to the inner sanctum revolves around facility with drugs . . . We blithely declare World War III on our parents and yet have already forgotten how to smile at our friends.'

Nine months later that same writer was to be obliged to justify those 'bankrupt freedoms' in a debate which would penalise its loser by removing his ordinary liberty. Neville and his friends were incapable of such contortions, and so the testimony supplied to the Old Bailey during the trial of *Oz* in the summer of 1971 was more of a swan song to a happier age than its prognostication. The *Oz* trial was a hugely expensive obituary notice. That was its fascination and its enduring value, as the generation of the 1960s handed over to the special interest groups of the 1970s, as the women's movement gathered its separate momentum and as *Gay News* started to outsell *International Times*, as the bombs of the Angry Brigade replaced the placards in Grosvenor Square, and as working class militancy, in the shape of the National Union of

Mineworkers, accomplished what no amount of rock'n'roll had been able to achieve: the destruction of a Tory government. By 1971 everybody who had wished to take LSD had done so and the effects were wearing thin. Powders as light and white as talcum insinuated themselves upon that responsive illicit marketplace which had been founded by Mods in another time; more profitable burdens than blocks of hashish were being carried back from the hill stations of the hippy trail.

There was something endearing in the sight of those three longhaired men, no longer young themselves (Anderson was 34, Neville 30 and Dennis 24), rehearsing and declaring the principles which had informed the misspent youth of an entire generation, which may be how *Oz* in its finest hour did what only the atrocious war in Vietnam had previously succeeded in doing: it united against a common enemy all of those bickering, divided factions of the young and of the left. The dreamy world in which dealers of hashish rubbed shoulders with contributors to *Private Eye*, where Trotskyists ran with Maoists and the rock stars stood side by side at some imaginary barricade with the most forlorn itinerant from the hippy tepees of Snowdonia; the world which Robert Hughes had identified as youth as a homogenous social class, was as close to being real as it would ever be during the six-week prosecution of *Oz* at the Old Bailey in 1971. And then it vanished, in a puff of sweet-smelling smoke. All too late, and all too little; the wheels of fashion had taken another turn and *Oz* magazine, despite its brief fling with international fame and the resultant shortlived circulation boom, would soon be seen, even by those who had fought for its life in the Central Criminal Courts, as a cheerless anachronism.

Those realisations may have been of assistance to the *Oz* defence only in so far as they tempered what could otherwise have been a piping, accusatory plea. His admission that his generation had proved itself to be far from perfect added an eloquent gracenote to Richard Neville's considered and beautifully written speeches which, combined with the patient sincerity of the three men and with John Mortimer's benign assessments of this strange legal case, won more sympathy—and, consequently, far more publicity when the trial reached its catastrophic end—than a thousand jokey press kits or carnivals in Hyde Park. *Oz* had not been resident in Britain at the beginning of the era, but it and its strangely attractive founder were destined to give the period a more dignified ending than it had, perhaps, deserved.

The judge appointed to preside over the trial was the 56-year-old Michael Victor Argyle, who had received the Military Cross in 1945 and had become a Queen's Counsel in 1961. In the General Elections of 1950 and 1955 he had unsuccessfully fought as a candidate for the Conservative Party. He looked at John Mortimer through half-moon spectacles as the barrister rose, at almost 3 p.m. in the afternoon of Wednesday, 23 June 1971, to tell the jury that 'this is a case about dissent'.

'It is a case about dissenters,' Mortimer continued, 'a case about those who are critical of the established values of our society, who ask us to reconsider what they believe to be complacent values and are anxious, on that basis, to build what they think (and what we may not think) is a better world. Members of the jury, we are all of us totally entitled to disagree with their views; but this is a case about whether or not they are also entitled to disagree with us ... When you hear the word "dissenter", you may think of those who in past times used to thunder their denunciations in dark clothes and rolling phrases from the pulpits of small chapels. Now, the dissenters wear long hair and colourful clothes and dream their dreams of another world in small bed-sitting rooms in Notting Hill Gate. In place of sermons with their lurid phrases about damnation, we have magazines reflecting a totally different society from that in which we live.

'You will probably hear a lot about sex in this case and you may hear something about drugs. We would also like you to hear something about the basic beliefs which the people who edited that magazine share, basic beliefs with which few of us would quarrel. A genuine, and generally held, belief that peace is preferable to war, for example. A genuine and generally held belief that racial tolerance is preferable to intolerance. That love between people is preferable to hatred. That freedom of expression is at all times preferable to censorship. An impatience, which may at times have been expressed childishly, with what they regard as the hypocrisies of conventional attitudes. The right to speak freely, without inhibition, about whatever matters there are that deeply concern them and their lives. A refusal to recognise that there should be taboos which would prevent our free debate about every single matter which concerns us as human beings. And it is in the pursuit of those beliefs that this prosecution and this trial originate.'

The prosecuting attorney, Brian Leary, a pleasantly spoken man with a fondness for his herb garden in Kent and his holidays in Acapulco, wasted little time in dangling the offensive *Oz 28* before the jury. 'It deals with homosexuality,' he said, 'it deals with lesbianism—on the front cover! It deals with sadism; it deals with perverted sexual practices; and finally it deals with drug taking.' Leary paused to regard the jury with a confident eye. 'You will, having read the magazine through,' he said, 'ask yourself: "Does such a magazine in fact tend to corrupt and deprave persons in whom those sort of practices are latent?" And I mean, members of the jury, those persons—and there are a lot of them about—who are anxious to experiment with drugs: children, teenagers, youngsters, call them whatever you will, into whose hands this magazine was clearly likely to fall.

'Some things, of course, may be indecent without being necessarily obscene. Let me give you an example. If a man strips off on a crowded beach and lies there naked for all to see, you might reach the conclusion that that was indecent. If that same man lying there started to masturbate himself, members of the jury, you must reach the conclusion that that was obscene . . .'

Richard Neville stood nervously to make his opening address, clothed, as John Mortimer had warned the jury, in a bright velvet jacket and a yellow Honeybunch Kaminskey T-shirt. 'I have no wish to hide behind the gowns and wigs of the legal profession,' he said. 'I believe I should try and talk to you direct and tell how and why we all publish *Oz* magazine, and what we hope to achieve.

'Every day there are new examples of erosions of our liberties. Erosions which are all connected with the current economic, moral and political climate. Some of them are minor, others are more significant . . . Members of the jury, none of these threats to freedom may yet apply to you personally. But those of us in the dock are aware of them all the time. The Misuse of Drugs Bill, for example, has given the police even more power to search and interfere with the rights of young people like us. Underground magazines and newspapers have been persistently harassed by authorities. Three days ago, police raided yet again the offices of our friendly rival, *International Times*. Thus, it comes as no surprise to us that the National Council for Civil

Liberties should have accused the police of political censorship in their efforts to suppress magazines like ours. We should be on guard against those who seek to close down political discussion under the guise of its so-called "obscenity" . . .

'Remember, if you convict us at the end of this trial, you are in reality convicting schoolchildren. And if you convict school-children, then you yourselves must accept some responsibility for their guilt. So far from debauching and corrupting the morals of children and young persons within the realm, our evidence will show that *Oz* is part of a communications network which intends the very opposite. It sets out to enlighten and to elevate public morals.'

Prosecuting counsel Leary smiled at this, and made notes. Upon rising to cross-examine Neville he suggested that the material in *Oz* might be particularly accessible to schoolchildren who 'could not get up to Soho in term-time'. Neville answered that such schoolchildren would find greater sustenance from freely available magazines such as *Penthouse* and *Playboy*.

'Have you ever seen a *Penthouse* cover,' drawled Leary, 'with a girl wearing an artificial male penis? A "dildoll", as it's called?'

Justice Argyle sighed wearily. 'Let's call it an imitation male penis,' he suggested.

Neville nodded. 'The word "male" is actually unnecessary, my lord,' he added. The busy public gallery, which had previously been warned of the consequences of unnecessary hilarity, stifled its laughter, and the sophistical exchanges continued.

The Earls Court area of London, in which one issue of *Oz* had been cryptically announced to be selling well, was famous 'for male perverts', opined Brian Leary.

'It's famous for Australians,' corrected Neville. 'I always thought that homosexuals were mainly settled around Piccadilly . . .'

'Isn't it Piccadilly for drugs? Earls Court for queers?' insisted Leary.

'You've been in London longer than I have, Mr Leary,' conceded Neville, 'so I'm sure you know what you're saying.'

The prosecution had called no expert witnesses, but the defence—following doggedly in the footsteps of the Chatterley defence of ten years previously—had called a mule train of them, and for day after day they rolled through Court Number Two of the Old Bailey like a Fabian convention.

The critic, jazz musician and author of the book *Revolt Into Style*, George Melly, attested that if he had a daughter he would be happy for her to marry a man like Neville. Each generation, he said, had its moment of revolt which in turn was packaged and sold back to them as style. Forcing his attention back to the item of packaging in question, Mr Leary asked if Melly saw anything wrong with an article in *Oz* 28 which dealt with cunnilingus.

Justice Argyle looked perplexed. 'For those of us who do not have the benefit of a classical education,' he asked Melly, 'what do you mean by this word . . . *cunnilinctus*?'

The amiable witness raised his eyebrows and looked help-lessly around the silent court. 'Perhaps I'm a little inhibited by the architecture,' he pleaded, and then ventured: 'Sucking—or blow-ing, your Lordship. Going down. Gobbling, is another one—oh, and an expression I remember from my naval days is "yodelling in the canyon".'

Caroline Coon of Release told the court that the principled and educated stand of the underground press in general and *Oz* magazine in particular may have thus far helped to prevent a heroin epidemic in Britain. The psychologist Dr Lionel Haward said that the rude words in 'Schoolkids' *Oz* were 'very commonly written on the walls of school lavatories . . . nothing surprising.' Michael Schofield, a social psychologist, fielded a range of ques-tions about the deleterious effects of the use of cannabis before having his attention drawn to the Rupert Bear collage. Briefly, he lost his temper. 'Your treatment of this magazine is absurd,' he cried at Leary. 'People do not read a magazine like this as if it were a legal document. They read it, it has some minor effect and then they forget it. To go through it inch by inch, line by line, makes no sense . . . The cartoon is intended to be humorous. It is a joke. It may not be a very good joke, but I maintain that even the funniest joke in the world would, after you, Mr Leary, had finished with it, not be very funny . . .'

'What sort of *age* would you think Rupert is?' inquired Brian Leary.

Schofield looked stunned. 'I'm very sorry,' he said. 'I'm not up to date with bears.'

'He's a young bear, isn't he? He goes to school, that's right, isn't it?'

'I don't know whether he goes to school or not,' answered

Schofield patiently. 'I'm sorry, but I'm obviously not as well informed as you are about little bears.'

And still they came on, the expert witnesses testifying to the artistic merits, the social worth, the literary quality and the wit of that rushed and ramshackle publication. The director of Goldsmith's College, Josephine Klein, said that the cartoon of three schoolmasters caning each other was an expression of children's fears. Edward de Bono of Cambridge University argued that *Oz* was a harmless, egocentric platform for sounding off, not unlike a soap box in Hyde Park. De Bono also found himself ensnared by Brian Leary in a debate on the respective readerships of an average toilet wall and an issue of an underground magazine. 'The turnover of a normal lavatory wall would, I expect,' he offered, 'be in excess of 30,000.'

'One lavatory?' exclaimed Leary, sceptically.

'If you stop to calculate it,' insisted the professor, 'I expect so.'

The educationalist Leila Berg told the jury that 'When children can discuss, and are free to discuss, all kinds of things with their teachers, this results in what I would call true education.' The disc jockey John Peel said that sex had been an important part of music since the early days of dance. The comedian Marty Feldman alarmed the defence which had enlisted him by falling out with Judge Argyle and, as he left the well of the court, calling that august figure a 'boring old fart'. The American Professor of Jurisprudence from Oxford University, Ronald Dworkin, agreed with Richard Neville that such a prosecution as the trial of *Oz* would be unconstitutional in the United States by virtue of the First Amendment. And the artist Feliks Topolski, having testified that *Oz* was 'an inventive paper which has introduced a completely new graphic approach', was taken by Brian Leary on a walk with the Fabulous Furry Freak Brothers through Ripoff Park . . . 'Art or not?' demanded Leary.

'Strip cartoon art,' replied Topolski. '. . . any visual performance if executed in earnest, is a branch of artistic creation.'

The forensic skills of Brian Leary were tested by this formidable range of academics and media personnel, but would be proven only in his handling of the two remaining defendants, Jim Anderson and Felix Dennis. His treatment of Anderson in particular was the cause of some tension in the camp of the defence. For Jim Anderson was gay, and he was quite unprepared to deny the fact if it was put directly to him. It was considered, in 1971, that the release of such information would lead a jury which had previously considered itself to be dealing only with the production of a magazine of doubtful probity, to be swayed by wilder fantasies about what had occurred in that Princedale Road cellar during the early summer of 1970. In short, the defence feared that Brian Leary might resort to homophobia.

And he almost did so. Anderson's examination started convincingly and well, as that tall, thoughtful man described to Brian Leary how he had come to desert a career at the bar in Sydney, Australia because of his discontent with the adversarial system and his growing belief that such courts of law were not the way to uncover any worthwhile truths. Then Leary came to his point.

'Some of the advertisements in this magazine are for sexual perverts,' he suggested.

'I would not agree with the word "pervert",' replied Anderson.

'Oh? Why?'

'I prefer the words "erotic minorities, sexual minorities".'

'Abnormal?' probed Leary.

'It depends on your definition,' said Anderson.

Turning again to the front cover, Leary teased the unspoken issue. 'You see the girl wearing a male penis? A penis strapped to her?'

'Yes.'

'Nice?'

'That's just a dildo.'

'Of course it is, but is it *nice*?'

Anderson looked exasperated. 'Well, it's beautifully drawn.'

'Do you find the erect male organ nice?' pounced Leary. 'Would you agree it's clearly indecent?'

'No, not indecent in the least.'

'*What?*'

'I don't find it indecent in the least.'

'Do you,' asked Brian Leary, 'find *anything* indecent?'

Torn between the tensions of having coyly to deny his sexuality, or run the risk of helping to send his friends to prison, Jim Anderson stumbled through the remainder of his cross-examination, while Mortimer and Neville looked on with real concern and Felix Dennis determined, as he said that evening, that he must tame Brian Leary. And Dennis, when it came to the bit, was as good as his word.

Having answered several questions about the business of *Oz* Publications Ink, Dennis was asked by Leary if *Oz* 28 was now quite valuable.

'Indeed,' he affirmed, 'there was a gentleman the other day who offered me £5 for a single copy.'

'Did you hold out for more?' laughed Michael Argyle, and the courtroom chuckled obediently.

Dennis looked gravely at the judge. 'I told the client,' he said, 'that if I gave him a copy and accepted his money, I might be in very serious trouble.'

Brian Leary switched the subject to that of illegal drugs, and was informed by Dennis that *Oz* had campaigned actively against the use of amphetamines, heroin and other hard narcotics. Of an advertisement in *Oz* 28 for a gay magazine, Leary put it to the youngest of the three defendants that it was 'there to pander to the lusts of homosexuals'.

'Mr Leary,' said Dennis, 'I find that phrase repulsive. Would you please rephrase your question.'

'Certainly not,' replied Leary.

'Just answer the question,' interposed Argyle.

'In my opinion,' said Dennis, enunciating with distaste, 'it is not pandering to the lusts of homosexuals.'

That particular page, suggested Brian Leary, contained a service 'whereby perverts were introduced to one another'.

Dennis held his ground. 'Is that a question, Mr Leary? If it is, I would have to say that I can't accept your phrase "perverts".'

This time, Leary received no help from a judge who was clearly unaccustomed to such fastidious use of language. 'Did you or did you not,' he asked the stonewalling former street-seller of a speech which Dennis had given to the Independence Day Carnival on the previous Saturday, 'deal with the idea that *Oz* had relentlessly promoted some elements of the new culture: dope, rock'n'roll and fucking in the streets?'

'No sir,' said Dennis, sensing Leary's frustration. 'I did not deal with that at all.'

Leary looked at Dennis for several seconds. 'Because,' he said finally, 'that's just about the size of it, isn't it?'

'Sorry?' said Dennis.

'Just about,' barked Leary, sitting down and shaking his head, 'the size of it, isn't it?'

'The size of what, Mr Leary?' asked the puzzled defendant.

'Members of the jury,' said Brian Leary in his final address. 'Oz 28 is nothing more or less than propaganda. It's not a proper vehicle for the assessment of ideas. Surely, on that first reading it left you with an ugly taste in your mouth. Let me seek to analyse what that taste was. It's the very epitome, is it not, of the so-called permissive society? The idea that experimenting with drugs is alright and that the law is a silly one and shouldn't be complied with; that a man whose job it is to act as police officer is always aptly called a "pig"; that sexual freedom is to be encouraged; that everyone should sleep with everyone else as soon as they are able to understand what it is all about; that sexual activity is to be admired for itself; voyeurism, homosexuality, flagellation, necrophilia—making love to a dead person—that's all fun and to be encouraged . . .'

'Mr Leary began his closing speech by painting a cheap stereotype,' said Richard Neville in his own final plea before the verdict would be given. 'Lazy, good-for-nothing hippies, who worship sex for its own sake when they are not lying around in some drug-induced stupor . . . It seems to me that the question to ask is not: "Why does Oz include references to police as 'pigs'?" but: "What sort of pressures make a 15-year-old girl refer to those who are paid to protect her, the lovable British bobby, as pigs?" The reason is that her friends are being jailed for smoking a drug not sanctioned by her parents . . . Those who grew up in the early 1950s were known as the "Silent Generation" because they seemed to accept that the most important goal in life was to get rich as quickly and ruthlessly as possible, while ignoring those who were poor, homeless and discriminated against. Old gentlemen with cigars and curly moustaches could push buttons which might blow up the whole world. So young people came onto the streets with their duffle coats and guitars to protest. They discovered they had a collective identity, a fellowship, a brotherhood. Sometimes these people merely rejoiced in the discovery of their own identity. They sprouted bright plumage to distinguish themselves from their predecessors and gathered in large numbers to hear their particular style of music. As they searched for new values and experiences, they stumbled upon an old drug, cannabis, which would also help distinguish them from their parents' generation.

Each generation has a duty to develop a new culture and new values. It faces a different world from its parents, with fresh excitements and novel dangers. Bob Dylan sang nearly ten years ago:

> Come mothers and fathers throughout the land
> Don't criticise what you can't understand
> Your sons and your daughters are beyond your command
> Your old road is rapidly aging.
> Please get out of the new one if you can't lend a hand
> For the times they are a-changing.

Neville looked anxiously at the attentive rows of jurors. 'Will you lend a hand?' he asked. '. . . Let it be a verdict which will confirm the values of tolerance, reason, freedom and compassion. Let it be a verdict which helps to remove the barriers between us all.'

Justice Michael Argyle's summation to the jury of the six-week long trial which was behind them all was later judged to be the reason why he never again was given the bench in an obscenity prosecution. Having defined 'obscenity' with one hand resting accusingly upon a copy of *Oz* 28 as 'loathsome, repulsive, filthy, lewd', he went on to summarise the testimony of the expert witnesses who had been called by the defence. 'You may think,' offered Judge Argyle, 'that most of these so-called experts either had to admit the magazine was obscene or else tell lies.'

Miss Caroline Coon, said the judge, had 'sounded like an old-fashioned English imperialist . . . Miss Coon said that hash and pot may have destroyed other countries but that's not relevant to us at all . . . We had Dr Schofield—do you believe Dr Schofield, ladies and gentlemen? Do you? . . . We had Mr De Bono, a gentleman from Malta. The only thing he didn't lack was self-confidence. He said *Oz* was a window into the hippy culture. Well, ladies and gentlemen, sometimes that window needs cleaning . . . and Professor Dworkin: he gave us a lecture on morals which I am sure was of great benefit to anyone who listened to it . . .'

On Wednesday, 28 July 1971, the eleven jurors (a pregnant woman had been excused from service by Judge Argyle halfway through the hearings) retired to consider their verdict. They were out for three and three-quarter hours, returning to the court at ten minutes to five in the afternoon, by which time the *Oz* trial had become the longest-running and most expensive obscenity trial in British history (as well as, incidentally, provoking more letters to the correspondence columns of *The Times* than had the Suez affair).

Their foreman announced that the defendants had been found not guilty of conspiracy to debauch and corrupt young persons. A sigh went around the Court Number Two. There would be no life sentences. On all three of the other charges, however, the charges which had been brought under the Obscene Publications Act, 1959, the three men were found guilty by a majority of ten to one.*

Justice Michael Argyle promptly asked if a deportation order had been served on Richard Neville. He was told that it had been. The judge then announced, to outcry from Neville, Mortimer, and people in the public gallery, that he would be withholding sentencing until full medical and psychiatric reports had been compiled on the three defendants. Until that time they would be held in custody. Argyle was apparently, it has been suggested, under the impression that the three young men before him might be drug addicts.

Eight days later, on Thursday, 5 August, Neville, Anderson and Dennis were taken from Wandsworth Prison back to the Old Bailey. While in remand awaiting a probation report, their hair had been coarsely shorn—a routine which caused great outcry, seeming as it did to represent a kind of cruel and petty emasculation by the authorities. Such compulsory barbering was, said the *New Law Journal*, a 'monstrous violation of an individual's integrity', and Home Secretary Reginald Maudling immediately announced that the rule would be amended at an early date.

Hundreds of demonstrators chanting 'Freedom, freedom' had gathered outside the Old Bailey to protest the anticipated finale, and Michael Argyle did not disappoint them. Having in his hand a report which confirmed the physical and mental health of the three, and which stressed that they were 'proud of *Oz* and say that they will do their best to see it continue as a platform for reformative views', Argyle listened to the mitigating pleas. He heard John Mortimer argue that a custodial sentence would 'create

---

* The importance of the divided verdict was lost to most lay observers in the mayhem which followed, but not to the defence team. 'I am convinced,' said Geoffrey Robertson, Mortimer's assistant, 20 years later, 'that if they had been found guilty on the conspiracy charge, the defendants would have been sent to prison for 10 or 12 years.'

terror in the hearts of those who in this day and age are trying to deal with the spoken and written word . . . Let us return to a sense of proportion.'

As the chanting from outside the Old Bailey echoed through its marble corridors, the courtroom heard Felix Dennis say: 'We are no martyred angels. We have our share of original sin. But . . . in your summing up you flagrantly misrepresented our case through lack of sympathy between your lifestyle and our lifestyle.' Richard Neville told Argyle that 'If you jail us you will do damage, [and] the damage you will do—and it is yours alone whether or not you are acting for God or Christianity—is to the concept of tolerance . . . You will show to the world that your generation, which appears to be listening with every courtesy, is in fact deaf.'

In the traffic-free streets outside the Old Bailey more demonstrators were arriving and scuffles broke out with the police. Inside, Argyle surveyed the defendants. 'This obscene little magazine,' he said contemptuously. Neville, Anderson and Dennis were, he said, 'comparatively poor men so a fine is inappropriate. It follows therefore that the sentence of the court must be a custodial one.' Their period of custody would be, in the case of Richard Neville, 15 months followed by deportation, of Anderson, 12 months, and of Dennis, nine months. *Oz* Publications Ink was fined £1,000 and ordered to pay costs up to the value of £1,250. 'Jailer, take them down,' ordered Judge Argyle. 'That was predictable,' said Richard Neville as the officers led him away. Out on the street effigies of a Crown Court judge were burnt and scattered about the cobbled street, smoke bombs were thrown, and Nazi salutes were offered to arresting policemen. Eleven demonstrators were removed in Black Marias. The National Council for Civil Liberties declared itself to be 'appalled and disgusted'. Dr Jonathon Miller said he was 'revolted', Michael Foot MP was 'shocked', and the Labour MP for Woolwich, William Hamling, told the *Evening Standard*: 'I was disturbed at the humiliations inflicted on these three young men when they were on remand, but I can only say that the severe sentences on top of all this passes my comprehension.'

'I am glad these sentences have been passed,' said Mrs Mary Whitehouse. 'It is high time that the line was drawn.'

The three *Oz* defendants served just four days and nights of their sentences in Wormwood Scrubs Prison. On the Thursday and the Friday of that week Prime Minister Edward Heath found it difficult to enter the House of Commons without Michael Foot or Tony Benn springing to their feet and wanting to know if he had imprisoned any more young people, lately, for writing on lavatory walls. A motion was put down in the House which considered that terms of imprisonment 'are wholly unjustified and constitute a punishment for political and social attitudes rather than for criminal offences.'

And on the night of Sunday, 8 August, Neville, Dennis and Anderson were taken in handcuffs and prison clothes from their cells and put into separate Black Marias. They were driven through the darkening streets of London to a building unknown to any of them. A butler ushered them indoors, 'and there', remembered Felix Dennis, 'is an old geezer with a smoking cap on, sitting in front of this fire, writing away.'

Lord Chief Justice Widgery, according to Dennis's Apocrypha, ordered the police to remove their handcuffs and offered the three men sherry. He then told them that their appeal was almost certain to be a success and that they would be released from prison on bail on the following day, if he could be given a guarantee that they would no longer work on *Oz* magazine. It was given. 'Now get out,' said Widgery, 'and leave those sherry glasses behind you.'

They were granted bail on the following morning, and left Wormwood Scrubs that afternoon. Three months later the Appeal Court quashed their conviction and nullified the deportation order on Richard Neville. The Appeal judges criticised Justice Michael Argyle for misdirecting the jury and for denigrating the defence witnesses. Neville, Anderson and Dennis never again worked together on an issue of *Oz*, and in the winter of 1973 that magazine published its last issue. Sue Miles, who had worked on Friends of *Oz* with Stan Demidjuk throughout the trial, said many years later: 'Then it was goodbye, thank you very much, enough. It was the end, and I wanted it to be the end.'

It was not quite the end. In January, 1973, four directors of the company which had, two years earlier, published *International Times*, also arrived at the Old Bailey to face charges of publishing an obscene article—the comic book *Nasty Tales*, which the police had seized during their raid on *IT*'s offices at the start of the *Oz* trial. After a shorter trial before a judge who was no more friendly towards the underground press than had been Michael Argyle, the jury found them Not Guilty by a majority verdict.

Germaine Greer gave evidence for the defence at the trial of *Nasty Tales*. Speaking of a character devised and drawn by the cartoonist Robert Crumb, she said: '[He] is one of the many people who is disenfranchised by our society, in this case sexually. The only people admitted to the permissive society are the good-looking, young and relatively well-to-do ... [There is] a seminal notion that the underground entertained for a long time, the "group-grope" concept. It was of course absurd. It is impossible to behave as if a sexual revolution had occurred before it has occurred ... [Crumb] satirises the underground for its servility, lack of democracy, complacency, inability to see what the political explanations were for the manifestations that surrounded it.'

In 1976 the Obscene Publications Squad was uprooted and reformed following the series of corruption trials which revealed that, ever since its inception 16 years earlier, the squad had operated a massive bribery racket, collecting dues of up to £1,000 a month from traders in hard-core pornography in return for protection from, or warning of, raids. The squad had also, Justice Mars Jones said in the Old Bailey, 'sold back into the trade' much of the pornography which they had seized. 'The long-term effects of the way bribes had been demanded from pornography traders is not yet known,' declared Justice Jones, adding that he was glad that the unit known as the 'dirt squad' no longer existed.

And in 1980, two decades after Chatterley and nine years after *Oz*, a Home Office committee on obscenity decided that there was little point, in future, in prosecuting the written word for such an offence. 'The trials of the underground press,' wrote Geoffrey Robertson, the Queen's Counsel who as a young and enthusiastic man had sat at John Mortimer's side throughout the *Oz* trial, 'damaged respect for the obscenity laws among a younger generation who began to appear on juries after 1972, when property qualifications were abolished.'

That was the end. And hardly anybody under the age of 30 noticed a thing.

CHAPTER TEN

RELICS

*A breeze had come up and begun to move the leaves of their tree.
'Frenesi, do you think that love can save anybody? You do, don't
you?' At the time he hadn't learned yet what a stupid question it
was.*

THOMAS PYNCHON, *Vineland*

Twenty years and five months after that bonfire of inanities
outside the Central Criminal Courts in August, 1971, I found
myself walking down a rutted, sodden track 600 miles to the north
of the Old Bailey. The track formed a kind of main street between
rows of parked trucks and rattletrap caravans, and halfway along
it I was approached by a young woman wearing thick, unlaced
hod-carriers' boots, jeans and a couple of sweaters, and hair which
hung down in rough, uneven hanks of light brown dreadlock. She
had been battling the northern weather to accomplish some basic
household chore and there was a large smudge on her left
cheekbone.

'Reporter?' she asked. 'Are you for us or against us?'

'Has it come to that? Taking sides?'

'Yes,' she replied. 'Yes, as far as I'm concerned it has come to
that.'

'I'm part of the problem or I'm part of the solution?'

She looked at me quizzically. 'What?' she said.

The young woman and her 30 friends had trundled into the
north-west Highlands of Scotland in the early winter of 1991.
They travelled through Ballachulish, Invergarry and Glen Moris-
ton, rolled along the wind-whipped banks of Loch Cluanie, and at
the head of Glen Shiel, three miles from the nearest steading and
20 miles from Kyle of Lochalsh, the nearest settlement of any size,
they found what they had been looking for. Just a few yards below
the December snowline, the new road deserted the old to skirt an

acre or more of flat land, where the River Shiel rushes under a disused 200-year-old bridge on its way down past the Five Sisters of Kintail into Loch Duich. In summer it can be an idyllic spot. In winter, when gales and horizontal sleet funnel through the steep and frosted walls of the glen, there can be few places in Britain which are more inhospitable, more hostile, more *uninhabitable*.

But this caravan of young southerners recognised firstly the worth of a broad, flat and lonely parking place beside running water, and they pulled up their vehicles and set up camp at the head of Glen Shiel. Having roamed through the wilder parts of Wales and England, disputing with angry landowners, congregating at summer music festivals and being ritually roughed up by policemen during the summer solstice at Stonehenge, the New Age Gypsies had discovered the Scottish Highlands. I had last spent any time with them (or, to be more accurate, their forebears) at the 1975 Windsor Free Festival. I was a reporter then, as well, and stood aghast while the rain teemed down and a self-appointed high priest, a former Communist Party member named Sid Rawle, stripped naked and conducted in the downpour the marriage of an equally naked hippy couple. The photographer Byron Newman said something at my side about terrible mistakes and some people being beyond redemption, and we took the dual carriageway back to London.

Sixteen years after that, some vestiges of Rawle's itinerant fantasy had constructed a hamlet in the Highlands. Letters appeared in the local newspaper, under the heading 'Hippies Can Damage Your Health', which suggested that the inhabitants of that bleak plain at the head of Glen Shiel should be barred from shops in Kyle of Lochalsh. 'These filthy people in their evil-smelling clothes,' wrote one woman, 'can be seen frequently in the shops poking and prodding amongst uncovered food, vegetables and fruit (even the children's sweets)'. A councillor for the area said: 'They're living in squalor, offending local people by the fact that they are so frightening. They are bringing the whole fabric of life there crashing down round our ears.' They were 'bums, deadbeats and parasites,' he continued. 'I am very worried that people get more frustrated than they are at the moment. We've had shots fired. There's been a couple of shots fired at an encampment. If people get frustrated, somebody has a dram one night and you've got problems.'

A meeting was held in a community hall and the chief

executive of the district council was angrily asked to justify the placing of two of these travellers—a young woman and her infant son—upon the hard-pressed housing list. Flushed out of neutrality by the hostile inquisition, the official curtly replied that the two were on the housing list 'because they are human beings'. Faint echoes of earlier exchanges jostled my memory, and *The Scotsman* newspaper sent me to the head of Glen Shiel.

Some 20 vehicles and caravans were arranged along the grid accidentally formed by the old Wade highway, the bridge and a parallel track. The trucks had been narrowly saved from the breaker's yard, the sheet aluminium roofs of the caravans flapped in the breeze, and most of the windows were patched up with insulating tape. On the green surrounded by the rolling stock, chained dogs yapped at the entrance to their polythene kennels, ducks and hens foraged, and goats tended to their young. A double-decker bus, half-heartedly painted with swirling patterns, stood where the town hall might be, and on the grassy flood-shelf by the river, below the bridge, four 'benders' had been erected— small dome-shaped constructions of pliable wood and plastic sheeting, each with the chimney of a stove poking out of its ceiling. My photographer on this occasion, a man from the island of South Uist, said gloomily: 'They'll never get planning permission for this lot.' Flying from the cabin of a truck, in jokey confirmation of the worst fears of the owner-occupying bourgeoisie, was possibly the last red flag in Europe still bearing its white hammer and sickle.

In his sparse and leaking caravan, Phil was not amused by talk of local frustration leading to gunfire. He had been in a site which had been fired upon once before, during the previous winter in Northumberland. 'It was dark and I heard a shot,' he said. 'I looked outside. A car was there, just sitting there. Then it quickly drove away. Nobody was hurt. But you get people talking about guns and things like that and, well, it puts ideas into some people's heads.' Phil was 30 years old and he had been on the road for just 18 months. He left school in Birmingham with nine 'O' levels, took an OND course at technical college, and then found himself delivering takeaway pizzas in Milton Keynes. 'The housing in towns for young people on a low income is pretty impossible,' he said. 'I sometimes wonder if that is properly understood. It is very pricey for very low quality, and there's no council houses.'

He tossed back his long hair and glanced anxiously out of the caravan's broken windows at the gathering storm. He looked briefly affronted and angry. 'How dare councillors and politicians complain about travellers,' he said, 'when there's people living in cardboard boxes in the cities.'

It was the Sunday before Christmas, and the population of the settlement at the head of Glen Shiel had been reduced slightly by some of its members visiting family and friends for the seasonal festivities. Phil and a score of others remained to tie down the caravans with guy ropes against the winter winds, to collect fuel for the essential stoves and to go shopping in Kyle of Lochalsh . . . 'I've wanted to winter in Scotland,' said Phil without apparent irony, 'because the good thing about Scotland is that you can get away from people who don't want you there.' I mentioned their reception in Kyle, and he shrugged reisgnedly, as much as to say: 'We're used to it.' 'It didn't surprise me, although they did seem to go over the top. It's usually just a vociferous minority wherever you go, there's always a high proportion of quiet people.'

Phil collected a fortnightly dole of £39 from the post office, which happened to be near his parked caravan. It was enough, he said, for food. 'In the future, I don't know what I'm going to do. I wouldn't mind working, actually.' He looked at me squarely, as if expecting the statement to engender disbelief. That's one big difference, I noted silently. You wouldn't have caught your forerunners protesting their will to labour. Not down on Maggie's farm, no more. 'But not cooped up in some town,' added Phil, 'in some low-paid job, paying an enormous rent. There's freedom for me at present.' He indicated the caravan swaying in the wind and the fire dying in the stove. 'There's enough to keep you busy in this life,' he said, 'working on the vehicle and the van, collecting fuel, just surviving. Time doesn't drag.'

People from the remainder of the encampment gathered in the upper deck of the bus. There was much rolling of tobacco, but little else on £19.50 a week. Indie music danced out of the cassette player and much of the vocabulary was instantly recognisable. They did not refer to themselves as hippies or as freaks, but the rest of society was certainly identifiable as straight. There was none of the arrogance and deceit which Richard Neville had castigated at the end of his decade, but rather a vaguely sad desire to be accepted and appreciated. 'It's good that you actually came to see us,' said Becky through long blonde dreadlocks. 'One newspaper sent a photographer a few weeks ago. He parked in the lay-by and got out and took a few shots from a distance. Then, when someone walked over to say hello, he turned and ran, full-pelt, back to his car, dived in and drove away.' My friend from South Uist preened himself. 'There are nasty travellers, of course,' continued Becky as though describing the facts of life to children, 'but there are nasty straight people as well.' The coal man stopped, they told us, and the winkle collector paid for the results of their occasional efforts upon the sea shore. Following the unrequested publicity which they had been given in the local press, two women appeared carrying food parcels and expressing regret for the intemperate statements of their neighbours and representatives. These small deeds were recalled, in the upper deck of that rusted, draughty bus, as affectionately as any civic reception.

Was there a heaven for these children? 'There was one place,' replied Becky instantly and quite without sentiment. 'It was on a pheasant farm near Hungerford. We were in woods, surrounded by beds of bluebells, bluebells as far as you could see. We had a birthday party there and the farmer came to join us for a drink in the bluebell woods.'

A fondness for bluebells notwithstanding, they were not flower children. Apart from anything else, they were far too approachable. They were children of the 1960s only in the most literal sense: they were born in that decade. In the excruciatingly common metaphorical use of the term, the chief executive who defended their right to housing because they were human beings was the child of the 1960s. They were products of the 1980s, a travelling subsidiary of the 156,000 young people who were without homes in Britain at the end of Margaret Thatcher's decade. It was difficult to imagine a naked wedding being conducted, at any time of the year, in that camp at the head of Glen Shiel.

They had some things in common with the *wunderkind* of 25 years before, mannerisms and habits which had survived the decades in slightly corrupted archaisms, like the English which is spoken in abandoned South Sea islands, but they were of a wiser and more cynical generation. They did not perceive themselves to be the missionaries of a new social order. They did not believe that everybody could or should live as they lived. The pride that they expressed in the hardiness and the adaptability of their lifestyle was merely making a virtue out of necessity. Occasionally I sensed an inchoate, itching suspicion that I may have come like a time-warped visitor, from that golden age when people of their type were threatened with shotguns because they were feared as the harbingers of dramatic change, rather than because they were seen as common vagrants, but it passed, there was nothing to it, and, had they brought the matter up, I must have told them that there was not and never had been much of a difference between young people who let their hair grow and hit the road, unless it was in their own illusions about themselves.

I left that camp at the end of a year of archaeology. Three months earlier a lavish ball had been held on the Roof Gardens in Kensington High Street, to celebrate the twentieth anniversary of the Oz conspiracy trial. It was entirely financed by Felix Dennis from his international publishing fortune. The £20 entry fee paid by over 350 invited guests was equally divided between three charities nominated by the three Oz defendants: The National Library for the Blind (Dennis); Amnesty International (Neville); and the Terrence Higgins Trust (Anderson). In the warm late summer evening, high above west London, scores of waiters allowed no champagne glass to become empty and sufficient food was left uneaten to feed a dozen hippy encampments for the winter—but nobody was gauche enough to suggest that if it had not been consumed on the Roof Gardens that night, it would somehow have found its way to the head of Glen Shiel.

Immediately after entering the building I was introduced to a dapper, portly little man of about 55 years, wearing a tuxedo and a bow tie. He pressed his card into my hand. It read: Dr Eugene Schoenfeld. Dr Hipocrates no longer. 'I think somebody should go over to him,' reflected a friend, 'and say how much they had been looking forward to this moment, on the grounds that in 1969 he advised them that it would be alright, in their search for the perpetual orgasm, to puncture their scrotum with a knife and blow it up like a balloon, so long as the knife was disinfected.' Jim Anderson and Richard Neville, both novelists by now and living respectively in northern California and in the Blue Mountains of New South Wales, circulated with ageless charm among the seal-sleek barristers and New Age socialities, the Trotskyite general practitioners and journalists now attached to *The Independent* and *The Guardian* and, even still, *Time Out*. Mick Farren, with distinguished flecks of white in his undiminished hair, had flown in from Los Angeles, and the young man who, with a flower in his hair, had helped Yoko Ono to prepare her early, bizarre exhibitions in the communal basements where she had first met

John Lennon, Chris Rowley, had left behind his science fiction manuscripts in upper New York State. A single Hell's Angel in faded colours tramped the dance floor like something from the Mesozoic era, still a touching minority, almost endearingly immutable among all of those reconstructed Mods. The former *Time Out* journalist Neil Lyndon was to write later in *The Times* that not one of his friends had become a member of parliament or a spy, they were too untrustworthy; and he may have had a point. Regretfully, I do not think that a single MP or servant of MI5 was on the Roof Gardens on 4 September 1991.

The second and the third memorable political speeches of the 1960s—Harold Wilson's 1963 promise to deliver to Britain the 'white heat of the technological revolution', and Enoch Powell's suggestion in 1968 that if coloured immigration was to continue, 'like the Romans, I seem to see the River Tiber flowing with much blood', had, for different reasons, largely left these people cold. There were professional environmentalists, though, and health food moguls, and campaigners for most sorts of animal and human rights, and there were one or two who had risen from their time to compose the agenda of debates which changed the way in which many in the western world regarded themselves. I doubt if any of that large gathering had slipped to themselves, as 25 years earlier they certainly would, a fortuitous tab of LSD before getting into the taxi, but some were on Ecstasy and others on heroin and many, certainly, were enjoying the recreational use of cannabis, alcohol, cocaine and tobacco.

And surprisingly few people had died.

The resurrection of the *Oz* conspiracy came to its climax a few weeks later, when BBC2 broadcast a dramatisation of the trial which was followed by a discussion between some of the participants and one forlorn Aunt Sally, the Conservative MP Ivan Lawrence, whose irksome presence on the programme gave Germaine Greer, Caroline Coon and the three former trialists the opportunity to bury many of their own little local differences and to round, once again, upon an identifiable common enemy. Together once more under the spotlight, they presented a pleasingly liberal case.

Shortly before the *Oz* reunion party I received from an old acquaintance, Michael Horovitz, a copy of an article by Geoffrey Wheatcroft which had recently appeared in the *Daily Telegraph*, and Horovitz's reply to it. Wheatcroft had been moved to write a

diatribe against the whole decade by Oliver Stone's film of the life
and death of Jim Morrison, *The Doors*—a film which recreated as
accurately as I would have considered possible the world of
American rock'n'roll in the later years of the 1960s, and which
presented that strange blend of costume, money, noise and hedon-
ism almost without prejudice.

In those days, considered Wheatcroft, there were not giants,
but pygmies photographed from below. Morrison 'embodied the
Sixties creed of sex and drugs and rock'n'roll. The second of these,
along with booze, seems to have incapacitated him for the first,
and even the last, before killing him.' The 1960s, intoned Wheatcroft, had elevated artless monsters like Morrison while promoting
a divorce rate and a drugs epidemic which the middle classes could
handle but which devastated the poor. Such 'social disintegration'
was accompanied by an 'artistic emptiness'. No worthwhile novels
had been written in the 1960s.

Horovitz had sprung to the defence of the period. A man
who is in his fourth (or fifth?) decade of restless creative endea-
vour, he has a personal distaste for being himself bottled in the
formaldehyde of 20 or 30 years previously, but Wheatcroft had
touched a nerve. 'Wheatcroft declares the multi-racial civil rights,
CND, anti-war, women's and green movements, "hollow in the
outcome",' said Michael. 'How so? Only one Chernobyl, no more
Hiroshimas, the continuing reluctance of hitherto supermanic state
powers to engage nuclear arms in the Gulf and elsewhere, and
their token concern to give the female principle its due ...
Wheatcroft brands the songs of Berry, Dylan, Lennon and
McCartney, the art of Peter Blake, Hamilton, Hockney and Kitaj,
and the poetry of Ferlinghetti and Ginsberg "a catalogue of fake,
a compendium of kitsch" ... the best work of these and hundreds
of others active 20 to 30 years ago has survived and will go on
doing so exactly because they are committed to the creative
continuum of art, not reductive clichés of decadology.'

The 1960s had become, as Horovitz hinted, a handy catch-
phrase, a whipping-boy for the use of bad grammar and the spread
of sexually-transmitted diseases, the source of contemporary hooli-
ganism, extra-marital families and a dulling of the entrepeneurial
flair of the British people. The only consolations that an apologist
could take lay in the fact that while the 1960s were in progress,
Geoffrey Wheatcroft's equivalents blamed the icons of the era for
all of those things and more; and that in the succeeding decades

critics of his type have, in such reiterated assaults, effectively conceded a kind of victory to the libertarian propagandists of that time. I personally know more people who would happily share the credit for helping to dismantle the nuclear family, as it was glibly called, than would admit to a fondness of the music of Jim Morrison and the Doors.

When I received Michael Horovitz's letter I had just returned from visiting Jeff Nuttall on the twentieth anniversary of our first meeting. That had been in the spring of 1971. I was editing an alternative magazine in South Yorkshire, and he was teaching art at Leeds Polytechnic. We knew of him, everybody knew *of* him, he was a figure in our neophyte history. He had marched from Aldermaston, playing 'Didn't He Ramble' with Dave Aspinwall and Mick Wright at the door of a café in the pissing rain as 100,000 duffle-coated banner carriers, beatniks and bishops trooped towards Trafalgar. He was friends with Trocchi and Laing, and he knew William Burroughs. He had launched *My Own Mag*, a prototype cut'n'cow-gummed piece of print media, and introduced the 'People Show' to the basement of Better Books. He dressed in blue paint and an Aztec costume fashioned from books at the Albert Hall poetry reading in 1965 ('the summer was out of control'). With Bruce Lacey, Criton Tomazos and John Latham he prepared the sTigma standing exhibition, a rotting nightmare, a maze of pornography, atrocity, blood and shit, an insectivorous plant, a Venus fly-trap from which there was apparently no escape until the voyeur had reached its stinking heart of hair, two-month-old cod's roe, and spluttering detergent bubbles. He was the first cartoonist on the first British underground paper, *International Times*, in 1966. He called the hero of his strip Clifton de Berry, until it was pointed out to him that one or two of his memory banks had shorted; there actually *was* a Clifton de Berry; he was black, American, old, and a venerated member of the International Workers of the World—or Wobblies, as they were affectionately known. Nuttall changed his cartoon hero's name, safely, to Seedy Bee. Five years later, in 1971, he resumed cartooning for my magazine in Yorkshire. He was dreadful about deadlines, but we humoured him.

In 1966 Jeff Nuttall wrote what was then, and remains today, the best book about his times and his generation. *Bomb Culture* was the work of a happy artist. In the preface to *Bomb Culture* he was able to say: '. . . the plain and obvious fact is that between the

[time] when I completed this manuscript, and the [time] when I am writing this preface, young people, under various pretexts, made war on their elders, and their elders made war on them. The war continues.'

In 1971 he barnstormed into my office in south Yorkshire, big and brash and booming 'Horovitz, you old bastard' at the visiting poet in the back room. We acolytes watched approvingly, happy to be there. He lit endless cigarettes but refused a joint, and I wondered about that.

Twenty years later, the first meeting was still my main memory. Its successors had faded. I took the tube from Ladbroke Grove to Hammersmith. I strained, unsuccessfully, to catch sight from the high line of the quiet street between Avondale and Holland Park where the offices of *Oz* magazine had been raided by the police in the months before my first meeting with Nuttall. I caught a bus from Hammersmith Broadway into the rainforest of suburban south-west London. In a kitchen behind a bric-a-brac shop on a street of expensive houses, Nuttall was making coffee and lighting cigarettes. Avuncular, I thought. Large, lined and avuncular . . .

'Have you read Nigel Fountain's book on the underground press?' I asked.

'No.'

I shoved it across the breakfast bar.

'Okay?'

'It's okay. He calls me an *ingénue*. He was an International Socialist.'

Nuttall guffawed. 'I don't mind IS. It's the health freaks I can't stand. You know, well people are *better* than ill people.'

We carried the coffee through a sunlit yard into his studio. A rusted old sit-up-and-beg bicycle lay on the paving stones. Nuttall indicated it approvingly. 'That's what I'd call a bike,' he said.

'Not me. I prefer ten speeds and drop handlebars. They're easier.'

'Not when you're 18 stones, they're not.'

We sat on old wooden furniture among drapes and statuettes and pottery, a low table between us and an ashtray apiece. Nuttall picked up, and recommended to me, Thomas Pynchon's *Vineland* and Eric Mottram's *Blood On The Nash Ambassador*. I thought, I never knew how he lived before. He lived like this. So, still, do some of my friends.

'The 1960s,' he said. 'Have you banked the advance?'

'Yes. I wanted to write a travel book, and this one feels like a travel book. Describing a foreign place. The difference between what you hoped for and what you get.'

'There was a lot of hope. There certainly was a lot of hope.'

'What did you hope was happening?'

He drew a breath and began, like a swimmer of long distances, or a man who talks for his living.

'I suppose I hoped that in the 1960s the criteria which had been present in most art movements since the 1890s might begin to be fused into some kind of purpose, and militate against the dehumanising element of the industrial revolution. Ever since the industrial revolution art had been saying: "This is a vulgarisation". Ever since the acceleration of science and technology, art had been trying desperately to say, well, the Church has thrown the initiative away, and somehow naked individual inspiration has to regain that initiative and keep things magic.'

Nuttall looked at me, apparently for a sign of recognition.

'There has to be some defence of magic. Not naïvely, because we like it, like Peter Pan, but because it is a special area of knowledge which science so far does not have access to and which it rather despises—the necessity for vision and the necessity for the intuitive evaluation of knowledge which has always been the only access of the poet. I've always worked in art, you know, not as a social commentator, and my belief always was that art is a special kind of information and at that time I believe it is *better* than other information. And the world is dying of a negation of that kind of information. The world is dying because it pretends not to need it anymore.'

'How does that translate . . . practically?'

'Practically, right from the start my whole concern was to obviate nuclear war. That was my initial terror. I'm in late middle age now, possibly old age, so I find it difficult to get a nerve grip on that terror any more, because it hasn't happened, and I doubt whether I'd give a tuppenny shit whether it happens or not. But at that time I did very much love existence, and I loved humanity, which I saw as being involved in a programme of progress and movement towards greater joy; and I saw the bomb as something that was going to end that. I saw the bomb as being the instrument of a mistaken rationalism. And I saw that the main weapon against the bomb was artistic and creative vision. And I think that, given levels of repression, we will build up levels of energy within us that will ultimately be murderous and destructive. I have always believed—at least, I used to believe, certainly in the so-called Sixties I believed—that that was the cause of war. War was the accumulated violent outcome of mountainous Judeo-Christian repression. If you sit on it for hundreds and hundreds of years it will explode, and it will be terrible when it does. The world has forgotten Freud, and Freud was germinal to the movement that I belonged to in 1964 and 1965. Now the world doesn't want to know about Freud very much. He's notoriously fallible, but Freud can't have been all wrong. The *notion* of the subconscious, and the *notion* of the obviation of individual responsibility in the onrush of libido, cannot be blown away. Any more than Marx can be blown away because Eastern Europe has decided to go capitalist. The theory is still there, the theory is still valid, and the theory will come back, I hope, in a more sophisticated and viable form. Those two figures, Freud and Marx, set the twentieth century spinning before the twentieth century had begun. And now we seem, *fin de siècle*, to be at the close of a century which has denied itself.'

'Did it ever look like resolving itself?'

'Oh yes. I thought we'd won. From 1967 through to about 1973.'

That was where I sat up.

'You thought we'd *won*? What . . . why . . .?'

'I thought that something incorruptible within young people had nailed what was wrong with the way society was going. Young people like you, at the time I met you. And that young people were proceeding to do something about it, were intolerant of what had gone wrong. That you would no longer tolerate anything which was going to impede sexual joy, which was going to impede human equality, or which was going to impede our disregard for national boundaries. Also, I thought that it was too late to make war. I used to look around me and think, try and impose a call-up on *these* bastards. You will find that it won't work. I really thought that it was just a matter of time before the insurrection would happen from within, that a certain cultural ethos had been spread so powerfully and so thoroughly that war and all of these general social repressions were going to just drop off and die.'

It had been two decades since I had heard this kind of talk. I could think of nothing to say. I looked at him and nodded.

Nuttall chuckled. 'I believed in Woodstock Nation,' he said. 'I believed very much that it was a primitive model of what could be done on a global level.'

'Tell me.'

'One of the reasons I conducted myself so . . . bombastically, when I was working at Leeds, at the time I first met you, was because I felt: Don't these people know we've *won*. Why don't they shut up and get out of the fucking way. When the curator of Leeds City Arts Gallery tried to censor a student's exhibition I thought: Doesn't he know that he *can't do that any more*? And all the students withdrew their work. I always got the whiff from the people I was teaching. When I wrote *Bomb Culture* I was working in a big secondary modern school in East Finchley, around the corner from a rock club in Barnet, and I listened to the sounds that were coming out, and I heard the reverberations through the kids in the school, and suddenly the kids were terribly responsive to what I'd been saying for the past ten years, all of a sudden they were eating out of my hand—'

'And you thought, that was it, the battle was resolved?'

'I thought we were going on through.'

'After writing in *Bomb Culture* of an engagement of hostilities, you had more than half a decade of triumphalism when you thought the engagement had been successful?'

'More successful than I'd ever dreamed it could be.'

That's why people require travel books on the 1960s, I thought. They want to go there. They want to feel that sun on their backs.

'What brought you,' I asked, 'to that frame of mind?'

Nuttall was about to get truly avuncular.

'How old were you in 1963?'

'Fourteen.' I nervously rolled a cigarette.

'Cast your mind back, my friend. Look at the difference between Tony Hancock and Frank Zappa. Compare Zappa with the ultimately suicidal pessimism of Hancock, and think what Hancock meant to the many millions of people who laughed with him . . . the notion was in the late Fifties and early Sixties that the nuclear holocaust was right on the bloody doorstep. You were convinced that the fucking planet was going to be *fired*—'

'But the bomb was still around after 1967. There were no

signs that it was going to be done away with. Where were all the governments going to go? What were John Major, and Margaret Thatcher, and all of *their* friends going to do? Disappear?'

'What was Major doing then?'

'He was a young Conservative, I think. Working towards being a councillor in Lambeth.'

'And Margaret Thatcher was a Conservative MP for Finchley, and very silly she looked.'

'But they weren't about to fall into a hole in the ground, those people, don't you see? This is what I wonder—'

'I thought they would simply go to the wall, like primitive Baptists.'

'And what would replace them? What would have happened to the Palace of Westminster?'

Nuttall deliberated for about half a minute. 'I just thought that ultimately,' he said, 'if people had ceased, almost biologically, to be possessive and competitive, then the Palace of Westminster would become a little bit like Bradford Wool Exchange—still there, but nobody in it.' He chuckled. 'Still with the wool prices posted up every day, but who the fuck is interested? I suppose I thought that such a vast number of people would start to drift around the planet without passports that people would gradually begin to feel a bit silly about nationhood anyway—ah, now, you can laugh—'

'No, I'm—'

'But it came near, it came near—'

'I wouldn't laugh. I was drifting about the planet a bit myself, I was smiling fondly at the memories. I was drifting around *with* a passport, mind. You had to have a passport. They swapped it for money at distant embassies and posted you home—'

'And I thought that the sheer weight of young people, whose numbers were increasing, and who seemed to be at that time of a similar, benevolent and humanitarian mood, massing in a global culture, would stop taking any notice of all those people telling them that they're market-competitive by nature, and should buckle down to the fact of hard work. Something very important happened in education in the Sixties as well, in this country anyway. Education was actually *working*. It produced thousands of young people who were able to think articulately for themselves and were able to dissent, and were able to live their lives critically of society and say, no, I want an alternative.'

There was a lengthy silence, which Nuttall ended with a Falstaffian laugh.

'The great naïvety,' he said, 'was that we didn't know about economics. We didn't know about *money*. Money is what we didn't know about. We said money doesn't matter any more, who cares about money, we'll give money away. We were very, very naïve about the forces of the market, and none of our Marxist brothers at the time were sufficiently sophisticated to be able to warn us exactly how the market was outdistancing us even as we reacted—'

'They were along for the ride too, with a different set of delusions, hedging their bets.'

'We tried to demonstrate that if you were kind enough to one another you didn't need money. One of the main features of arts festivals was that you'd have a bowl of money and you'd say to people: Got too much money? Put some in here. Anyone doesn't have any money? Take this away! We were trying to demonstrate that it was possible, if you were kind enough to one another, that scarcity would disappear. Obviously it was tremendously naïve, but it wasn't *so* naïve. It wasn't so naïve because the *counter*-naïvety is that it is never possible to behave towards money in such a way, whereas *only* our naïvety, *only* that is what is necessary. That is the *only* solution.'

'Because it just takes one or two people to collar the whole bowl and you're buggered.'

'Yes, indeed. It wasn't invented in the 1960s, it was anarchism, as laid down and described in detail by Jean Jacques Rousseau and Proudhon and William Blake. But the anarchist communities of the alternative society in the 1960s didn't work. You could see they didn't work because—' Nuttall lowered his large, amiable, battlefield face towards me and giggled '—the *stairs* were always dirty. Everybody kept their own little rooms in the squat nice and clean, and kept their own bed linen and bed roll clean—' (the last two did not square with my experience, but I let it pass) '—and above all defended their own sound systems, and *above even that* defended their stash of *dope*, but the stairs were filthy and any food left in the kitchen was immediately nicked ... and I could see that the members of the alternative society were congenital thieves—' I thought uneasily of sequestered tins of food and of money borrowed but never returned. He had a point. '—and were not just ripping off the system as Abbie Hoffman recommended they should, but were quickly ripping off one another, because they were drug addicted—'

Hold up. 'Drug addicted to . . .?'

'Drug addiction is a quick way of making somebody steal off anybody, of destroying any kind of mutual trust or mutual caring amongst any group of people. If you're addicted to a drug you're as callous towards other people as somebody who's in love.'

'Not everybody was addicted to drugs.'

'Vast numbers were.'

'But the key drug of the period was non-addictive.'

'Marijuana?'

'Yes.'

'I began to believe that it was the most addictive of them all.'

'Habitual . . . but not like heroin, alcohol, nicotine . . .'

'Not with the same urgency, but with the same effect. It clouds the rationale, and it clouds the collective issue, and it clouds any attempt at organisation. Stoned people are great postponers, aren't they? You buy the milk, I'll get it tomorrow. Why is there no food? It was your turn to get the food . . . by the end, the awful vagueness and floundering incompetence of that kind of thinking was everywhere, and I was quite anxious to get out of it.'

I had stopped rolling my own cigarettes and was smoking Nuttall's. Such a burden of optimism, I thought, to leave behind. Where do you hide?

'In the Fine Art Department at Leeds, in the early Seventies, I began to sense recoil, and cynicism, and scepticism among students. I tried to locate this and it was traceable to rock and to fashion. I taught Astrahal Stroheim Garheid, who became Green of the rock band Scritti Politti, and my relationship with that student was maybe significant, in my realisation that things were going badly adrift. He was a kid that did nothing, and yet regarded inactivity as being more significant than the brilliance of certain very good students. Creativity had become uncool. He had an elegant girlfriend at the time, and she would come in wearing Burton suits and a short back and sides, and he'd be in makeup and jewellery, and their point was that cross-dressing is more important than being able to paint a fucking picture or write a poem or *imagine* anything. And this would have been *okay* had it been an audacious gesture in 1964, because then it would have been tremendously audacious. But in the early Seventies it was . . . just style. It reflected Bowie, mostly, and what Bowie got from the real artistry of Lindsay Kemp, who fed those fuckers style like some people dish out smarties. A whole androgynous docket came out of Lindsay! But Stroheim Garheid, with his colossal half-baked contempt for people who'd try to tell him things that he didn't know . . .'

'You began to think, well, maybe they *will* be able to impose a call-up on these bastards?'

'I thought, it's gone wrong. I thought, they no longer really care about society, they don't want to change society, they want to go along with the new trends in society, and above all they want to be *successful* in society, they want to be—' he hissed the sibilants furiously '—*ssstars* . . . And this leads me to the person who I think was the main flaw, and possibly the person who wrecked my Sixties revolution, our revolution, more than anybody else, and that was Warhol. Warhol was the snide capitalist who crept into the nerve centre. He didn't do it militantly, he was no passionate crusader for capitalism like Thatcher, but Warhol was the John the Baptist of Thatcherism. In the western world, he made the way for her. The effect of Warhol's peddling of style, his manipulation of imagery, his realisation of the potency of the urge for stardom, of the possibility of stardom without talent or intelligence or achievement—in fact, the *desirability* of such stardom. It stemmed from round about 1966, when the market began to see that rebellion was a saleable quality.' Nuttall laughed loudly. 'And the market thought, we'd better get some rebels and slap as much hype around them as possible, and sell this whole thing—this thing which was intended to be a redirection of history, but ended up reinforcing the nineteenth-century direction of history as marketing . . . marketing, and Andy Warhol's stars.'

'The desirability of stardom was implicit in what Warhol suggested, never actually stated—'

'That's right—'

'So when he said everyone can be famous for 15 minutes, he was working on the unspoken assumption that that would be a good thing.'

Nuttall shook his head sadly. 'It seemed so democratic, that aphorism. It seemed to chime in with Lautrement's statement of 70 years previously that in the future poetry will be written by everyone. But it didn't mean that at all. What it meant, curiously, was an aristocracy of anonymous figures, which is what we are.'

'The upshot is that if stardom, if celebrity is your only aim, then *anything* goes. You can be a celebrity *soldier*.'

'Oh, for *sure*—'

'Norman Schwarzkopf.'

'That's right. The week after the SAS captured those beleaguered IRA men in a London flat and leapt in, and instead of a long siege it was bang bang bang, Tony Wilson of Granada Television said to me: "You can't get away from it, the SAS are *stars*." This was about 1973. I thought, well, *shit* . . .'

'It's only capitalism.'

'It's only capitalism. It's insidious. It's like trying to fight cancer, you never know where it's going to come up next. You identify the sarcoma, and lance it, and heal it over, and WHOOPS! it's back, you're surrounded by them, suddenly cancer is selling the surgeon.'

'How much of what we see and fear now has some sort of twisted root in the notions of the Sixties? What debts did Thatcher owe? Where did yuppies come from?'

'Who were the yuppies? Just a vowel away from yippies . . .? Yuppies were hip conservatives. They were conservatives whose culture was not Mantovani and Bournemouth and golf courses in the south of France. Their culture was still that of music with a strong beat. They got into jazz, actually, they virtually created the new fashion in bop, the new young lions of bop owe a lot to the yuppies. And they were drug-using. They were cocaine using and dope smoking. They were hip, and they were very fashion conscious. It all rings bells . . . they had a totally different lifestyle from that of the old Macmillan conservative class. They certainly didn't belong to the culture *against* which the Sixties counter-culture was rebelling.'

'And they flaunted it.'

'And they flaunted it. Now Thatcher, Thatcher's ascendency certainly had some roots in the Sixties alternative society—'

'Jesus. You're happy with that, are you?'

'Mm.'

'It all sounds a bit easy. You mean in the *laissez-faire*, get-government-off-my-back idea, let me get on with doing my own thing?'

'I mean that Thatcher was beyond the class war. She was not concerned with class domination at all. She loved Freddie Laker much more than she loved Edward Heath. And the working-class, as we understand it, has now virtually disappeared. I was quite bewildered when it started to evaporate, but Margaret Thatcher was not. I was doing a radio broadcast with David Widgery in about 1987, and I had to say, well, I'm a bit baffled about life because I used to believe in something called the working class and all of a sudden it seems not to be there. And Widgery nodded, yeah, it doesn't seem to be there, where's it *gone*?'

'But how, precisely, was Thatcher's rise assisted by what happened in the Sixties? If it was she's a terribly ungrateful beneficiary. She goes out of her way to say how much she hates the period.'

'She sure does.'

'Can we resolve this?'

'No. It can't be resolved.'

'She doesn't understand the debt? Nor do I—what was the debt, anyway?'

'Well, I don't think it was in bourgeois individualism.'

'Right.'

'She was assisted in her task by the fact that common to her aggressive market ethic and the aggressive self-realisation of the talentless who wish to be stars and regard themselves as having a right to stardom, there was a freezing of compassion . . .'

Nuttall thought in silence for quite a long time. He absently put the wrong end of a cigarette in his mouth and I, anxious not to break his concentration, let him almost light the filter before yelping 'Wrong end!'. He jumped, thanked me, and continued.

'There was a point, a period of a year, or perhaps six months, in which people changed. People who would have been organising the dwellers of cardboard cities, or the single-parent junkies who are begging on the underground, people who would have assisted them and wanted to do something about them 20 or 30 years ago . . .' Nuttall was speaking slowly and, for the first time, not looking at me, not preparing to chuckle, '. . . those same people seemed suddenly to say, Fuck you, you can't make it, can you? Well, that's your own problem. It was almost the EST ethic: if you are not prepared to be a god, you get pissed on. And somehow, in the business of aggressive self-celebration and the rediscovery of the work ethic, something which those two things had in common, something very powerful and potent, fused. And it became a direction.'

'A direction out of the Sixties?'

'Yes. Because the Sixties in, I suppose, its weak element,

wanted to kick *dullness* out of the way. It wanted to get rid of drabness. In the beginning we considered that dullness and drabness were part of oppression. And later on, when the whole business became streamlined and capitalised on by—initially—the drug and the rock industries, and then by the media generally; at that point people no longer wanted to help the drab and the helpless and the underprivileged, but regarded them suddenly as an embarrassment. You might call it *lookism*. I'm on the 'phone to the literary editor of *Time Out*, and she says, "You're not going to vote *Labour*, are you? Who votes for *Kinnock*? He's so *naff*." And Major, somehow, isn't . . .? I noticed it very vividly when I went back to the "People Show" as an actor in 1988. They conducted themselves quite differently from when I was first with them, in the Sixties. Various people were regarded as an embarrassment. It struck me thunderously, actually. We were at Brighton, in Sussex University, doing a gig, and some girl stoned out of her head wandered into the dressing room and invited us to a party. I say, yeah, yeah, good, good—and I get a kick in the back. It was Mark Long, my old friend of the Sixties. And he says, We don't want her, man. I said, Wassamatter? He says, Well, look at her. I said, What do you mean, look at her? She's a fucking mess, man. We don't want her. I thought, What's happening? He said, And by the way, get some new shirts.'

'Did you go to the party?'

'I went over to the hotel and got drunk.'

'Did you get some new shirts?'

'No. I left.'

'I think that Thatcher dislikes the Sixties so much because most of that generation—not all, but most, certainly all of *my* friends—have always been fairly frank about *their* detestation of *her*. When her lieutenants used to lambast the middle-aged programme-makers at the BBC, and elsewhere in the media, for anti-Thatcher bias, they were pretty much on target. It may have been shrill and hysterical and a gross interference with the freedom of the broadcasters . . . but they were *right*. They'd identified their—her—enemy. I know those people. Twenty years ago they were throwing eggs at her and calling her a milk snatcher. She was spotted *very* early on. She was hated by my generation.'

'And she still is, much hated by them.'

'It's wonderful to see what's happened to her.'

'Oh, it gives me great joy.'

And then, I thought, it became suddenly fashionable to dislike Margaret Thatcher, and she fell. Discord and fashion make a formidable coupling.

'This new line in fashionable dissent in American universities, PC, or Political Correctness,' said Nuttall, 'that comes straight out of the old Sixties underground.'

'Warped by age.'

'Oh yes. One of the elements of Political Correctness is lookism. Not appearance or fashion, but *lookism*. Politically Correct people applaud lookism because what you're wearing is a better cypher of what you stand for than what you say. Well, that's a revamping of Hip, but on the other hand it's narrower, because what is being worn now is not self-invented as it was in Harlem, or as it was even in Carnaby Street, but is massively marketed. And a generation which is Politically Correct is in fact weirdly and contradictorily . . . *sceptical* towards anything which is outside of market motivations. Somehow you have a kind of protest movement which is in defence of women and in defence of blacks, beyond that they are very, very naïve and strange about their favourite hobbyhorse of ethnic issues. They frown upon a category of past achievers called Dead White European Males. And Dead White European Males, of course, cannot possibly include Giotto and Velasquez, because they are Latins and Hispanics—' Nuttall laughed loudly '—you know! And there is a whole bunch of them! You may not be able ethnically to discard the whole fucking Italian Renaissance, because they were a bunch of greasers! And they hadn't thought of that. They try to say, ah, yeah, but they were sufficiently aligned with the establishment culture to be defined as Dead White Males—but NO! Already the theory is exploded . . . Political Correctness is impervious to quality of mind, impervious to intelligence. I don't give a shit what colour intelligence is, or whether moles or bats generate it, as long as it is generated. Intelligence and imagination are the high activation of the human mind, and the only possible salvation of humanity unless you're going to leave it all to evolution in which case nothing matters anyway. If we are evolutionarily *done*, then we'd better just accommodate ourselves to the notion of our decline and live with it as comfortably as possible. But if we are going to struggle, then the only thing we have to struggle with is the human mind, and that can *not* have any kind of a racial or ethnic bias, it simply has to do with what can be reasoned and what is convincing, and what makes the goose-pimples stand up on the back of your neck. These people, Politically Correct people, are insensitive in that area because they are thoroughly numbed and dulled by media. As numbed and dulled by media-degraded aesthetics as the old-fashioned working class was dulled by overwork and exploitation. There seems to be a vociferous body of people in society who are speaking, all the time, and in all sincerity, from an under-informed point of view.'

'And the lineage of PC goes back to the old underground?' I could see that it did, I heard the echoes of brash certainties.

'I'm sure that it very largely comes out of the old underground. The Sixties underground took on an enormous body-swerve when it took feminism on board, and feminism took a number of bodyswerves as well.'

I knew of Jeff Nuttall's line here, and I flinched. I thought of the woman in whose house I would be staying that night and decided not to tell her of this part of the conversation.

'Feminism,' he continued cheerfully, 'deserted whole areas of main underground concern. Since William Blake and since Rousseau and de Sade and the Romantic movement of the early nineteenth century, eroticism and the claim for free realisation of erotic joy has been a main cutting edge of any kind of reasonable revolutionary movement. Feminism suddenly had elements in it which turned against that, which said: No, we're prudes. We actually are prudes. Stop all that. Sex has to be *evaluated*. Sex is not valid in its own right. *Joy* is not valid in its own right. Only *some* joy is valid. What about the joy of the Yorkshire Ripper? What about Peter Sutcliffe's joy? Sadism said, we have to take on board the joy of such people because they are the neurotics of centuries of repression. But feminism was not willing to do that, and this was a naïvety, because in order to crash the repression of centuries there was going to be some blood, and not just female blood . . . the quick, easy thing was to say that all men are beasts, all men have a latent sexual motor inside them.'

'What about punk?' Quickly.

'Oh . . . the inept street dope-heads like Lydon and Sid Vicious struggling against the sophisticated manipulation of McLaren, who had read the writing on the wall, who had understood Warhol completely, but who was still presenting himself as a Situationist and a Marxist . . . punk celebrated its patheticness, although it got rather scary when you had people wearing their aborted foetuses as jewellery—like the early "People Shows" . . . and that bloody film of Jarman's, what's it called . . .?'

'*Jubilee?*'

'*Jubilee*. A most disturbing film. I hated punk, really hated it, but I wanted to know what was happening, and I still don't know what was happening.'

'I went to see Oliver Stone's film *The Doors*. Warhol's in that. He doesn't come across well.'

'Good, good.'

'He's made out to be an evil little man.'

'Morrison was a genuine artist.'

'He was a curiosity.'

'A marvellous man. The real thing. I think he was genuinely inspirational. As were Dylan and Hendrix.'

I made the first signs of departure: pocketing my tobacco box, sitting upright, and looking absently about the room.

'Good luck,' said Nuttall. 'Something happened then.'

'Which won't happen again.'

'No. But on the other hand . . . Tories, capitalists are very fond of quoting human nature, the basically self-seeking drift of human nature, as being the elixir against such thinking as Marxism. Capitalists are always saying, Why don't you bastards grow up, don't you know everybody wants a buck? Everybody wants to be rich and famous, and everybody wants to control everybody else—don't you know that? That's human nature. I would counter that by saying, Don't *you* know that human nature is endlessly intelligent, don't you know that human nature is endlessly inventive? Don't you know that throughout the millenia of human life, changes of direction have *not* been made by changes in the markets, but because some awkward bastard has always come up with ideas that nobody had before, and stuck by them. And this is going to go on. Many of the ideas which you think you can put in a box called the Sixties, put on a shelf and forget about, are in fact part of the ongoing business of human intelligence, and they are not going to go away. You can turn the universities into market training units, but you will not stop human thought by that. Just as human thought invaded universities which were controlled by the Church, so will human intelligence invade universities which are controlled by the market. You will find that progressive thought, even in *marketing*, is based on free thought in psychology, philosophy and creativity, and you will find that it's going awfully stagnant unless you allow those things to take place. It is all to do with art . . . art is not just a phenomenon of the past. You can't stop art. You really *can not* stop it, it is the high end of eroticism.

'Quote human nature back at them again. Say that the voracious need to extend and improve and explore further—joy is something that they have not taken into account, and that any stabilised market will, ultimately, be *boring*. That's all I have to say, really.'

We wandered towards the door, and the rusted bike in the shabby yard. He lit another cigarette and leaned on the jamb, his blue eyes watching me steadily.

'I'm almost 60 now,' he said, 'and I'm glad that I shall die within the next ten years, because I really do not want to see what's going to happen. And I shall never know such optimism again.'

We looked from the doorstep into priceless Barnes. Whatever substance was to come, what blurred prospectuses of alternatives to society, what troops of western youth meandering between Goa and Glastonbury, it began with nothing more than style in places like this. It began with the clean clash of major chords in basement clubs in the west end of London, in the performance lounges of pubs in Ealing and Richmond, in the still surrounds of Barnes. It began with Italianate style, greaser style, Levis, Fred Perry T-shirts, Madras jackets, Zigoni shoes, and young men wearing mascara. In its end was its beginning, the drone of a thousand two-stroke engines, sweeping towards Clacton.

'This is a leafy area, Jeff. Select.'

'It'll do. It's good enough.'

ACKNOWLEDGMENTS AND BIBLIOGRAPHY

My main thanks must go to the people who launched and sustained the British underground press between 1966 and 1974, and especially those with whom I worked on *Styng*, *Oz*, and *International Times*. I owe a particular debt to Felix Dennis for inviting me to play around with four-colour overlays in the glamorous surroundings of Great Newport Street, and for later giving me my first opportunity to write books; to Ed Barker for the laughs; to Brian Montague for consistency; to Jonathon Green for his book and generous help; and to Caroline MacKechnie for, among one or two other things, a view of Brighton during the Easter Bank Holiday of 1965. Thanks also for help offered then and now to Richard Adams, Duncan Campbell, Houston Brown, Pete and Cath Kyle, Mick Farren, Chris Rowley, Jill Nicholls, Dave Goodman, Jim Haynes, Mike Horovitz, Judy Moir, Bill Campbell and Peter MacKenzie. The library of former BBC press clippings at Edinburgh University was invaluable.

The following books were a great help: *Vineland*, Thomas Pynchon (1990); *The Trial of Lady Chatterley*, edited by C. H. Rolph (1961); *On The Bus*, Paul Perry (1990); *Bomb Culture*, Jeff Nuttall (1968); *Days In The Life*, Jonathon Green (1988); *Buttons*, Jamie Mandelkau (1981); *Summerhill*, A. S. Neill (1962); *Street Fighting Years*, Tariq Ali (1987); *Watch Out Kids*, Mick Farren (1972); *Folk Devils and Moral Panics*, Stanley Cohen (1972); *Underground*, Nigel Fountain (1988); *Too Much*, Robert Hewison (1986); *The Little Red Schoolbook*, Soren Hansen and Jesper Jensen (1971); *The Private Eye Story*, Patrick Marnham (1982); and *The Rolling Stone Story*, Robert Draper (1990).

INDEX